CLINICAL AND SOCIAL JUDGMENT:

The Discrimination of Behavioral Information

CLINICAL and SOCIAL JUDGMENT:

The Discrimination of Behavioral Information

James Bieri

Alvin L. Atkins

Scott Briar

Robin Lobeck Leaman

Henry Miller

Tony Tripodi

John Wiley & Sons, Inc. New York London Sydney

Library of Congress Catalog Card Number: 66-13525
Printed in the United States of America

AUTHORS' AFFILIATIONS

James Bieri
Department of Psychology
University of Texas

Alvin L. Atkins
Department of Psychology
Yeshiva University

Scott Briar
School of Social Welfare
University of California, Berkeley

Robin Lobeck Leaman
Formerly Research Associate
Brooklyn College of the City University of New York

Henry Miller
School of Social Welfare
University of California, Berkeley

Tony Tripodi
School of Social Welfare
University of California, Berkeley

PREFACE

The inquiry into the nature of judgment is germane to so many aspects of human behavior and personality that it is necessary at the outset of this book for us to present the scope and depth of our subject matter. Our title indicates that we will focus primarily on judgments of *behavior* as distinct from judgments of inanimate objects. In particular, we will be concerned with judgments of the kinds of behavior that are most relevant to the student of clinical phenomena and the student of social attitudes. However, throughout these pages we will bring the reader into contact with research and theory stemming from judgments of physical stimuli, for several reasons. Foremost, the psychology of judgment is rooted in the long history of psychophysical research, and we believe that concepts and methods stemming from this history provide a necessary backdrop for much that we have to say. Indeed, our indebtedness to this more classical field of inquiry will become evident. Like many others, we believe that an active attempt to extend the experimental tradition into realms of personality and social behavior is a basic requirement for the development of systematic knowledge of clinical and social cognition. Our presentation, therefore, is geared to theory and research which certainly should promote a two-way commerce between those who are primarily interested in research in judgment as an experimental enterprise leading to more adequate theories of judgment and those who seek to understand the nature of judgment in "everyday" social behavior, including clinical practice.

The subtitle of the book indicates a further delimitation on our part of the field of judgment. That is, from the many psychological part-processes that may contribute to form a judgment, we have been concerned primarily with the process of discrimination. We are not seeking answers to such questions concerning the outcome or product of judgment as, How valid are clinical judgments? or How veridical are our social judgments of others? Perhaps the fundamental question underlying our approach to judgment is *What factors in the judgment situation lead to differences among judges in their ability to discriminate among the behavioral information available to them?* In our quest for the answer to this problem, we shall present the reader with concepts and methods from such seemingly disparate fields as information theory, anchoring, cognitive personality theory, and the social psychology of attitudes. Although we make no presumption that we have welded a unified conceptual structure to present to the reader, we hope that our efforts have indicated fruitful avenues for the future development of theory and research in this area.

This book is the product of a truly collaborative effort. All the authors have been associated with the thinking, research, and writing that have created it. Our original locus was the Columbia University School of Social Work, and we wish to acknowledge the contribution of its Research Center to our endeavors. Subsequently, we have branched out in many directions, including Brooklyn College of the City University of New York, The University of California at Berkeley, Yeshiva University, and The University of Texas. We acknowledge the stimulation and contributions of a number of our colleagues whose assistance has been invaluable. In particular, we should like to express our indebtedness to Dr. Ben Avis Orcutt, whose productive efforts as a stimulating coworker and generous spirit contributed so much to our work. In addition, we thank Dr. Harold Plotnick, Joan Rigney Hornsby, Janet W. Bieri, Bruce Meyers, Kay Kujala, and Eugene Shinn for their contributions to our work. We also want to acknowledge the assistance of the National Institute of Mental Health, U.S. Public Health Service, for grants M-3611 and MH-08334, the National Science Foundation for grant GS-842, and the Institute of Social Science, University of California, Berkeley, for grant 362, all of which supported our research efforts.

We are grateful to a number of publishers for permission to use material in this book: The American Psychological Association, publishers of the *Journal of Abnormal and Social Psychology,* the *American Psychologist,* and the *Psychological Review;* the American Psychiatric Association, publishers of the *American Journal of Psychiatry;* Duke University Press, publishers of the *Journal of Personality;* the *Journal of Counseling Psychology;* Yale University Press, publishers of *Social Judgment* by Sherif and Hovland; W. W. Norton and Company, publishers of *The Psychology of Personal Constructs* by G. A. Kelly; McGraw-Hill Book Company, publishers of *Psychology: A Study of a Science;* and Holt, Rinehart, and Winston, publishers of *New Directions in Psychology*.

Finally, we wish to express our special feeling of appreciation to Dr. William J. McGill, whose intellectual stimulation and scientific originality provided a continuing spark for our endeavors.

J. B.
A. L. A.
S. B.
R. L. L.
H. M.
T. T.

Austin, Texas
August, 1965

CONTENTS

CLINICAL AND SOCIAL JUDGMENT:

The Discrimination of Behavioral Information

chapter 1 INTRODUCTION

HISTORICAL BACKGROUND OF CLINICAL JUDGMENT

It is informative to consider the history of the field of clinical judgment in order to understand the purpose of the present book. Considering the fact that many of the major theories of personality in contemporary psychology are founded upon the judgments of clinicians in their professional endeavors, there have been remarkably little systematic analysis and theoretical development of this cognitive activity. Indeed, taking the fundamental work of Freud as a starting point in this historical analysis, psychologists and other critics of his clinical formulations have been more concerned with the adequacy of the sampling on which his judgments were based (middle-class, Victorian, Jewish patients) than on the processes by which these judgments were evolved. Generally, when these analyses of the clinician's formulations have been attempted (often by a clinician as an expert observer of himself) the results have not been particularly helpful in terms of elucidating the cognitive processes involved. For example, Erikson (1959) has recently attempted to unravel the processes behind some of his own clinical interpretations. In so doing he has perhaps indicated more about how his formulations of case material fit into a psychoanalytic framework than how his formulations were generated. The kind of introspective analysis about one's own thought processes in dealing with clinical material which was given so much impetus by Freud probably is capable of bearing more fruit than has been true to date. As Freud's own theory indicates, however, and as empirical study demonstrates (e.g., Cutler,

1958), observing oneself is fraught with possibilities for distortion, denial, and other mechanisms. As an exclusive approach to the understanding of the nature of clinical judgment, then, we must question the reliance upon introspective analysis by the clinician.

A second phase in the analysis of clinical judgment we may call the reliability-validity phase, which roughly parallels the development of the diagnostic art in clinical psychology. A major factor in this phase was the increasing concern with the adequacy of projective techniques as diagnostic tools. The plethora of studies dealing with the validity and reliability of projective techniques written during the decade or so following the Second World War may be considered to be studies of the clinical judgment process. After the sampling of patient behavior was obtained from a projective test or battery, questions were asked as to the reliability and validity of the clinical judgments based on these protocols. Toward this end empirical methods such as blind analysis and matching techniques were developed. The residue from this feverish activity of the forties and fifties is difficult to evaluate, yet it seems likely that because this research centered on the validity of the projective methods, we have learned more about the methods themselves than about the nature of the clinical judgments upon which these methods ultimately rest. While every clinician realizes that the adequacy of a psychological interpretation of test behavior rests upon the adequacy of the clinician making the judgments, we know relatively little about the nature of the differences between the cognitive processes of more gifted and less gifted practitioners. It is possible that the yet untapped value of projective methods will be of use in studying the cognitive operations of clinicians.

A third phase in this chronology may be dated from the appearance of Meehl's book on clinical versus statistical prediction (Meehl, 1954). In a sense this work represented a continuation of the validity phase of clinical judgments begun in the projective era. In this important landmark in clinical judgment Meehl was primarily concerned with a comparison of the relative adequacy of so-called statistical methods of clinical prediction, presumably based upon some mathematical regularity such as actuarial tables or multiple regression equations, and of clinical methods, based upon the judgments of clinicians. Aside from the impetus this book gave to the study of clinical judgment, several aspects of this work are worthy of comment. First, it served to crystallize interest in a more statistical approach to the clinical judgment process, a direction initiated by Sarbin (1942) some years earlier.* Next, it brought out vividly to the reader the relative paucity of conceptualization concerning the nature of clinical judgment. This point seems to have been over-

* For a detailed history of the clinical-statistical judgment issue, the reader may consult Gough (1963).

looked in the heat of the controversy generated by Meehl's book as to whether a frequency table can predict more accurately than a living, breathing clinician. Except for extended comments about the nature of intuition and of the clinical judgment process as a "creative" act fitting into the "context of discovery," Meehl is relatively silent about the nature of cognitive processes in clinical judgment. However, he has emphasized the possibility that the configural weighting of cues may prove to be an important aspect of the cognitive activity of the clinician (Meehl, 1959).

The fourth phase in the history of clinical judgment is the contemporary one with which the present book is concerned, a phase which appears to be directed toward the development of theoretical models of the clinical judgment process. A very important aspect of this phase is that these developments in clinical judgment theory are taking place within the broader context of general psychological theory. That is, clinical judgment is viewed as representative of the larger general psychological field of judgment, and approaches from this larger field are used for the theoretical bases of clinical cognition. To date, three major general psychological bases have been evident in current concern with clinical judgment. One of these bases is the increasing interest in personality and social psychology in the development of theories of judgment, clinical inference, social perception, and predictive processes. The book by Sarbin, Taft, and Bailey (1960) is an example of an attempt to develop a theoretical approach to clinical judgment within the broader context of cognitive theory, especially as it relates to problems of social perception. While primarily concerned with the development of a theory of personality emphasizing the cognitive aspects of construing and predicting behavior, G. A. Kelly's psychology of personal constructs (Kelly, 1955) considers in some detail the relation between his more general approach to cognition and the nature of clinical judgment. The work of Kelly and of Sarbin et al. reflects this growing tendency to place clinical judgment within the wider context of social perception and personality, and we view our work as consonant with this trend. A second basis for contemporary work in clinical judgment has been the theories of judgment developed in general psychology, especially in the field of psychophysics. In particular, concern with phenomena related to absolute judgments, such as anchoring or context effects, has been reflected in the clinical judgment research of Hunt (Hunt and Jones, 1962) and the social judgment research of Sherif and Hovland (1961). Our approach in this book has been markedly influenced by this psychophysical tradition in the psychology of judgment. We shall devote considerable space to an evaluation of the importance of this tradition to the field of clinical judgment. The third basis for current work in clinical judgment has been the attempt to apply various mathematical models to the understanding of judgment processes. One aspect of this endeavor is the continuing effort to fit mathematical formulation to the judgment processes of clinicians or other judges. This work carries on the influence of the third phase of clinical judgment noted previously, namely the comparison of the clinician with statistical models of judgment. The work of Hammond and his associates (Hammond, Hursch, and Todd, 1964), set within the framework of Brunswik's lens model, exemplifies the use of multiple correlation methods in analyzing aspects of clinical inference. However, another aspect of this fourth phase has been the application of formal mathematical models in studying the judgment process. In this book we exemplify this trend by our use of concepts and methods from information theory which we will elaborate in subsequent chapters. Another example of this increasing attention to mathematical models in judgment is the work of Restle (1961), who uses formulations from set theory as they relate to the judgment process.

The present book, then, represents the influence of each of these three aspects of the contemporary phase of clinical judgment theory and research. First, our approach emphasizes the essential unity of the psychological processes involved in clinical judgment and in social judgment. Second, we will underscore the utility of formulations stemming from psychophysics, especially as they relate to absolute judgments. Third, we will elaborate the particular values we see in applying formulations from information theory to analyses of clinical and social judgment. We believe these three areas of psychological inquiry are germane to the concerns of those who would study clinical judgment, and one purpose of this book is to discuss each in some detail. However, our major purpose is more ambitious and reflects our belief that these several areas of thinking about judgment have convergent conceptual properties. We have attempted a formulation about judgment processes which we think moves in the direction of integrating these points of view. Thus from the outset we disclaim any notions as to either developing totally new conceptual approaches to the problems of judgment or to developing a systematically complete framework within which judgment may be construed. We are concerned rather with determining just how far the formulations we have used may be stretched in dealing with the multifold aspects of clinical and social judgment.

THE NATURE OF JUDGMENT

Ever since the formulations of Weber and Fechner concerning the relationship between the physical magnitude of stimuli and their perceived magnitude, the ensuing several generations of psychologists have been in quest of a greater understanding of the judgment process. Judgment may be said to occur when an individual assigns one of a set of stimuli to one of two or more response categories. These response categories are usually well defined for the judge and bear a more or less direct relation to the stimuli being judged in that the task requires a fairly immediate perceptual discrimination. When the assignment of a stimulus to a category involves a consideration by the judge of the value, preference, or outcome of each response alternative, the judgment task assumes more of the characteristics of decision-making. As we shall see, such distinctions are by no means easy to maintain in the analysis of judgment processes. It is apparent today that, whatever else it may be, the cognitive behavior which we call judgment, even in the controlled setting of the psychophysical experiment, is an intricate amalgam of cognitive processes which may include perception, concept formation, thinking, memory, discrimination, decision-making, and creative imagination. Is it possible that a theory of judgment can be evolved which can encompass such a diversity of psychological processes? Our answer is "probably not" at the present stage of development of each of these aspects of cognitive behavior. The student in this field must concentrate on selected aspects of the judgment process, and the present work exemplifies this selectivity. In this book we will focus primarily upon the *discriminability* aspect of judgment and only indirectly upon what some may consider the more "involved" types of clinical judgment. As the reader will come to appreciate, the problem of discriminability in clinical judgment is relatively complex and worthy of our systematic efforts.

However, such a concentration on certain aspects of judgment does delimit the range of possible types of clinical judgments with which we will be concerned. For example, we will present empirical studies in which the judge must select a response from among a small pool of available alternatives. In its simplest form such a judgment may involve a decision as to the presence or absence of schizophrenia. In contrast, consider the type of clinical judgment which represents a detailed diagnostic formulation concerning the psychodynamics of the client. In what sense is it reasonable to assume that similar cognitive processes may underlie these two types of clinical judgment? It would seem that when a clear-cut decision of a binary sort is required, like the presence or absence of schizophrenia, one type of judgment process is involved, whereas when a more complicated formulation is called for, another type of judgment process will ensue. While we believe our formulations have an applicability across varying types of judgment situations, the possibility must be faced that the researcher or the clinician will tend to formulate his theories of judgment in relation to the type of judgment most congenial to his theoretical predilections.

Several observations can be made about our position in this regard.

We do not assume that our approach is a "basic" one in the sense that it applies to all clinical judgments. It is more important, in our view, to attempt to delimit the range of convenience of our approach in terms of the types of judgments to which it might apply. In addition, we should point out that while some clinicians may demean the value of "simple" nosological judgments, for example, in contrast to "deeper" psychodynamic formulations, it is possible that the former type makes up the bulk of the important judgments made about clients in clinical settings. In terms of their ultimate impact on the future life of the client, decisions such as presence or absence of psychosis, suitability or nonsuitability of potential adoptive parents, or likelihood of suicide certainly form an important segment of clinical concern. Finally, we must recognize that the distinction between the more involved, inferential judgment of the psychodynamics of the client and the more simple judgment of the clinical diagnostic category (for example), is at best a relative distinction. For example, some dynamic interpretations may be little more that aggregates of categorical judgments, resulting in the so-called "Barnum effect" (Meehl, 1956) or the "Aunt Fanny" judgment (Tallent, 1958); or, having formed a more detailed, comprehensive statement of the dynamics of the client, the clinician may next make some sort of summary judgment upon which some definitive clinical action can proceed.

The importance of the action-aspect of judgment appears to be especially relevant in relation to clinical judgment. That is, we must be concerned ultimately in a comprehensive theory of judgment with the influence of the *effects* of having made the judgment, effects which can involve either the person being judged or the judge himself. These postdecision effects can be variously construed and may be thought of in terms of the relative utility or *value* attached to each judgment alternative by the judge, the perceived *cost* involved for the client or the judge, or the relative *payoff* value of each possible alternative. Thus, to present a rather gross but not entirely unlikely example, if a clinician anticipates that a particular judgment of "schizophrenic" will result in institutional placement which both he and the client abhor, then a more moderate judgment, e.g., "schizoid personality," may result. That is, it is entirely possible that a retrospective process occurs based upon the relative value attached to the possible alternatives, which under certain circumstances would lead to a different judgment if the cost or payoff values of the judgment alternatives were altered. In this respect certain aspects of the clinical judgment process resemble the decisions which are reached in a court of law. At times the clinician in his judgmental behavior is like the juror or judge who must decide if the defendent is guilty or innocent. Knowledge of the consequences of either decision, and an evaluation of the relative cost to the defendent of each, may be a potential source of influence in the choice of a verdict. Similarly, the prosecuting and defense attorneys, each valuing diametrically opposed judgments as to guilt and innocence, garner and interpret those facts from the available pool of information which fit into their prearranged judgment. Cowan (1963) has presented an analysis of such problems in relation to decision theory in law.

It is apparent that when we concern ourselves with the relative value attached to judgment alternatives we move into a more complex realm of judgment processes and confront problems associated with decision theory and choice behavior. Because social and clinical judgments involve alternatives in which value, utility, and preference are operative, it is inevitable that the analysis of judgment will merge with the analysis of decision-making. In the present work we will focus on empirical studies in which this evaluational component of clinical judgment is relatively slight. To the extent that it is difficult in the experimental situation to replicate the conditions of utility that may influence judgment, our understanding of the judgment process will be incomplete. However, we will deal with the evaluational aspect of judgment in our discussion of *situational* variables which impinge upon the judgment process (Chapter 8) and return to the relation of judgment and decision processes.

WHAT MUST A THEORY OF JUDGMENT INCLUDE?

We have suggested that both the *kind* of variables included in one's approach to judgment and *how* these variables are conceptualized will be influenced by the particular aspect of judgment one wishes to emphasize. As we indicated in the preceding section, the *discriminability* aspect of judgment is given major emphasis in this book, and our selection of variables is partially determined by this emphasis. The reader will find that one of the main questions we are asking is, "How many unique discriminations can a judge make?" Or, more exactly, "What conditions affect the number of unique discriminations a clinician can make?" If a clinician must make differential diagnoses among 20 patients, into how many categories can he reliably assign these patients? Analogously, if our judge were asked to judge the brightness of a series of 20 lights, say on a scale from 1 to 20, how many unique matchings will he make between brightness and number? Furthermore, at times we will be interested in determining if there is a relationship between the judge's ability to discriminate among the patients and his ability to discriminate among the lights. Answers to these questions can be obtained only insofar as we specify what variables might be expected to affect discriminability.

We may introduce our theoretical construction of the judgment situation by marking off for ourselves four main areas of the situation in which variables relevant to discriminability of judgment may be present. These include (1) stimulus variables, or the nature of the *input,* (2) *output* or response variables, including the nature of the judgment task, (3) characteristics of the judge, who must function as a *transmitter* of the information, and (4) *situational* variables, which include the kinds of restraints imposed upon the setting within which the judgment occurs, as well as the expected outcome or consequence of the judgment.

Stimuli or Input

Defining the stimulus in a judgment task is not an easy matter. What is involved is both a *denotative* definition (what is the stimulus?) and a *conceptual* definition (how do we develop a language to compare stimuli systematically?). The denotative stimuli in clinical judgment may be relatively easy to specify, and include forms (acts, verbalizations, or gestures) of interpersonal behavior such as affection, aggression, or dependency, life conditions such as family structure, social class, or religious affiliation, or more private behavior such as fantasy, imagination, or dreams. It is evident that such a potentially complicated array of stimuli imposes a major task on both the judge and the experimenter. This input complexity creates problems in definition for both the denotative and the conceptual realms, but since the first may be less involved, let us turn to that initially.

It is a well-known problem in psychological research that what the experimenter denotes as the stimulus may not be what the subject defines as the stimulus. In the classical psychophysical situation this is not likely to be a major problem. For one thing, the stimulus is usually relatively unidimensional, representing an intensity, e.g., along some sensory continuum. Furthermore, the stimulus is usually physical (i.e., inanimate) in nature, leading to a greater degree of consensus about "what" it is. Even in subthreshold studies, the judge is often told what stimulus class to expect, e.g., a word or a length of line. Denoting a social stimulus is a much more complicated proposition. Not only are social stimuli unlikely to be unidimensional, but they may be so multidimensional that we as experimenters cannot be sure as to those aspects of the stimulus complex to which the judge is responding. In this regard it is probably no accident that so many of the empirical studies of social perception have used trait adjectives as stimuli. Even if such inputs do not necessarily represent the input "stuff" out of which most of our real-life social and clinical judgments are formed, they at least have the virtue of relative simplicity. This denotative problem, then, is a major one in the clinical judgment realm. To be sure, it can be solved by using as inputs such relatively simple stimuli as IQ scores, Rorschach indices, and MMPI profiles. Our preference in the work to be reported in this book is to try to retain as stimuli those descriptions of *social behavior* which can be specified in certain ways. Such stimuli have the virtue of being applicable to differing professional groups of clinicians, as well as retaining a certain "lifelike" face validity for the judge who may be less content with an array of test scores or trait names.

Once this type of stimulus is decided upon it next becomes necessary to define conceptually the nature of the input used in the judgment situation. Here the researcher or theoretician meets a major hurdle, i.e., how can we compare systematically two sets of stimulus input so as to be able to make differential predictions concerning how each is likely to be judged? A major portion of this book is devoted to this problem. In general, we have attempted to characterize the nature of inputs in clinical and social judgment in a form which renders comparison with psychophysical judgments possible and at the same time permits combinations of stimulus elements which "make sense" to the clinician judge. Our approach to the systematic definition of stimuli can be labeled a "dimensional" approach and will be spelled out in detail in subsequent chapters. However, several characteristics of this approach can be mentioned at this point.

We assume that each social stimulus can be defined in terms of the selected dimensional characteristics which it possesses. In particular, we identify two such characteristics of dimensions as *differentiation* and *articulation.* Differentiation refers to the number of independent dimensions which we can identify in a given stimulus. Such a notion enables us to compare the relative dimensionality of two or more inputs, which may range from unidimensionality to multidimensionality. Since most of the stimuli upon which clinical judgments are based are likely to be multidimensional, some of our efforts have been directed toward understanding the effects of varying degrees of input dimensionality upon discriminability. Articulation, as we use it in reference to the nature of dimensions, refers to the number of intervals which can be discriminated along any given dimension. Such a notion concerning the property of stimuli implies that some estimation of the strength or *magnitude* of a stimulus dimension can be obtained. Thus, if we consider Bill Jones to be a "fairly dependent" person, we are assigning him both to the dimension of dependency and to an interval along that dimension which falls somewhere between "no dependency" (or "very little dependency") and "extreme dependency." That is, we assume that the attributes or properties of most stimuli can be defined not only in terms of a number of relatively independent dimensions but also in terms of points or intervals along each of the dimensions identified. Thus both Bill Jones and Bob Smith may have the attributes of dependency and aggression, but Bill may be fairly dependent and extremely aggressive, whereas Bob may be extremely dependent and moderately aggressive. Exactly how many discriminations of magnitude one can articulate along a social dimension is an interesting problem, and one to which we will devote some attention in subsequent chapters.

Responses or Output

In certain respects, the problems of defining the nature of the responses with which we will be concerned in clinical judgment are parallel to those involved in defining the stimulus. That is, judgment tasks may be seen to differ from one another in terms of whether the subject is asked primarily for discriminations along a single attribute dimension or for differentiations among dimensions. In psychophysical judgment tasks, discriminations along a single stimulus dimension are often of major interest, although stimuli may be varied in degree of multidimensionality to determine the effect of differentiation upon discrimination. In standard concept attainment tasks, on the other hand, there is usually no problem for the judge in discriminating among the two or possibly the three values of stimuli along the several dimensions or attributes involved. For example, the judge may receive white objects and black objects, tall objects and short objects, and light objects and heavy objects. His task is essentially one of determining which combination of values along the several dimensions defines the relevant concept. It would seem that clinical and social judgments involve aspects of both psychophysical discrimination and concept attainment, as we shall note in Chapter 7. The clinician must know not only what dimensions are *relevant* in identifying a patient as psychotic, for example, but also what *degree* of value along any relevant dimension (e.g., reality-testing) may distinguish the psychotic from the nonpsychotic.

In part, this particular concern with discriminability results from the need to circumscribe the response alternatives available to the judge. As we have noted before, this poses a potential source of difference between the research setting and the actual clinical setting in studying judgment. However, in either setting the *range* of possible response alternatives which the judge must consider is an important parameter of the judgment task. The clinician who in an interview poses for himself the problem of determining what the client is like has a much broader array of response alternatives potentially open to him than does the clinician who must decide if the client is schizophrenic. Of course, as we have noted, the more diverse responses to the first problem may be subsumed by the clinician in reaching a judgment concerning the second problem. In the research situation, in order to achieve comparability of conditions across judges, it is often necessary to confine all judges to the same set of response alternatives even though any given judge may feel that this is an irrelevant domain or not the most important one for this particular client.

In specifying the domain of alternative responses in a clinical judgment task, we run into a major difficulty in that such response domains are relatively underdeveloped. Except perhaps for the standard nosological categories and estimates of levels of intelligence, clear-cut response alternatives are difficult to find in clinical work. Frequently the response alternatives with which a clinician must deal are quite specific to the setting in which the judge is working. These are likely to be the binary type of choices that include decisions to place or not to place, to provide a type of treatment or not, or to discharge a client or not. It would seem likely, then, that one important factor in the judgment situation is the number of response alternatives available to the judge. Furthermore, it is necessary to consider how distinctly these alternatives are separated from one another. It may be easier to decide if a patient is to be judged schizophrenic or not than to determine if he should be labeled one of several different types of schizophrenic.

In general, we might expect that if the alternatives are nominal in character, i.e., represent relatively independent dimensions, judgments might be less difficult than if ordinal discriminations along a response dimension are called for. Although we will consider in subsequent chapters the relation between nominal and ordinal judgment processes in detail, it should be noted here that within the general task of discriminating the values along some given attribute dimension, judgments will be affected not only by the fineness of the discrimination which must be made but also by the kind of ordinal judgment which is required. Thus the clinician may be asked which of two cases appears to be more pathological, or he may be asked to select a case which falls exactly halfway between two extreme cases of high and low pathology, or he may be asked to judge the degree of pathology of a single case.

Characteristics of the Judge

Professional education in clinical psychology, social work, and psychiatry is based upon the assumption that it is possible to develop within the clinician capacities to render judgments which are both accurate and therapeutic. For example, accuracy in rendering a diagnostic judgment concerning a client is presumed to be important in clinical work in planning therapeutic strategy. Similarly, arriving at a timely and opportune interpretation during a therapeutic interview is considered a desirable judgmental activity for the neophyte practitioner to learn. What characteristics of the judge are pertinent to differences in judgments elicited among clinicians? Here again, the relative lack of systematic conceptualization in approaching answers to this question is a problem the researcher must face. In the clinical judgment field it has become commonplace to consider such asystematic variables as professional affiliation, theoretical commitment, level of experience, or even "intuitive" sense to be sources of individual differences in the ability to judge others. Needless to say, the empirical evidence relative to the influence of these variables is both spotty and inconsistent. Although it is fashionable to criticize some studies of clinical judgment because relatively untrained judges are used, reliable evidence concerning systematic differences between untrained and trained clinicians in making judgments is difficult to find. As an alternative, one may turn to the research literature in social perception dealing with the characteristics of a "good" judge (Taft, 1956; Allport, 1961). Unfortunately, familiarity with this research literature is not particularly conducive to definitive statements about those variables which are most relevant to individual differences in judgment.

Our approach is to conceptualize individual differences in judges in terms of variables which can be related systematically to the analysis of the judgment task confronting the judge. We assume that it is not fruitful to attempt to define a "good" judge or a "bad" judge in the absolute. Rather, if characteristics of the judge can be systematically related to characteristics of the judgment situation, predictions may be made about the effect of differences between judges on the outcome of the judgment.

Our approach in this regard is to conceptualize the judge in terms of certain attributes he has relative to his ability to process information concerning his social environment. Primarily, we will be concerned with those characteristics of the judge which can be subsumed under the rubric of *cognitive structure*. The concept of cognitive structure has been posited by a number of theorists and investigators in personality to account for relatively enduring patterns of organization in the person's representation of the social and physical environment. Presumably, if we know something about how the individual judge characteristically organizes social inputs in his interpersonal behavior, we are in a position to make predictions concerning his ability to deal with varying types of input-output relations. This essentially is the assumption underlying our concern with studying the cognitive structure of judges in order to understand the judgment process. In our approach, we will build upon an analysis of personality formulated by G. A. Kelly, which he calls the psychology of personal constructs (Kelly, 1955). In particular, we will deal most extensively with the concept of *cognitive complexity-simplicity,* which is concerned with the relative degree of *differentiation* of the person's construct system (Bieri, 1955, 1961).

Kelly's position, like that of Osgood (1952), Sarbin et al. (1960), and others, stresses the *dimensional* nature of cognitive structure. The individual is assumed to possess a finite number of bipolar dimensions along which he discriminates aspects of his social environment. The representation of these structures is usually in terms of a hyperspace containing a finite number of dimensions, the latter being called *personal constructs* by Kelly and *modules* by Sarbin. Although our approach to this problem will be spelled out in detail in Chapter 7, it should be stated here that in common with our earlier analyses of the nature of inputs and outputs, we conceive of the dimensional nature of the judge's personal construct system as having two major components. One of these, as we have said, is the matter of differentiation among dimensions, which we called cognitive complexity-simplicity. Presumably, the more complex judge has available a greater repertory of construct dimensions along which to construe others than does the less complex judge. However, we are also concerned with the second aspect of the judge's dimensional structure, namely his ability to *discriminate* along each construct dimension. This aspect of discriminability centers on the judge's versatility in making reliable discriminations among the categories or intervals of each dimension, and generally it has been overlooked as a systematic variable in dealing with cognitive structures. However, as we shall see, devoting more systematic attention to discriminability differences may be fruitful both in terms of analyzing the judge as a transmitter of information (Miller and Bieri, 1963) and in terms of understanding such classical judgmental phenomena as anchoring and context effects (Chapters 5 and 6).

It is in dealing with the characteristics of the judge in relation to judgment that we believe systematic analysis of the judgment process can contribute to general personality theory. It is no secret that present theoretical formulations and empirical analyses of the problems of cognitive structure are both vague and at times contradictory. But as we shall see, the concept of cognitive structure presents us with basic issues in psychological theory, including the nature of perceptual learning (Gibson and Gibson, 1955; Bruner, 1957) and the relation of association and cognitive theories of learning (Mandler, 1962). In Chapter 2 we will analyze some of these problems in more detail.

Situational Factors

Having its ancestry as it does in the studies based on controlled laboratory experimentation in psychophysics, it is no wonder that judgment theory has underplayed the role of situational factors in judgment. A major exception in this regard would be the development of adaptation-level theory by Helson (1947), an approach that continues to provide a meaningful context within which to construe the influence of certain situational variables in judgment. As Galanter (1962) has pointed out, it is only in relatively recent years that a broadening of the psychophysical situation has occurred to permit analysis of motivational, situational, and other "extraneous" sources of influence in the judgment task. Actually, when one speaks of *situational* factors which are relevant to the judgment process, it is apparent that one could include a great variety of possibly disparate phenomena. Furthermore, in terms of ultimate systematic parsimony, one could perhaps just as well discuss these phenomena under the three categories of input, output, and judge characteristics presented above. However, it is our belief that situational factors in judgment deserve to be treated separately as part of an analysis of the judgment process because of their pervasive influence, particularly in the realms of social and clinical judgment with which we are concerned. As we noted earlier in mentioning the parallel between legal and clinical judgment, when one human being is called upon to judge another the possibilities for various external constraints to influence the judgment are apparent. In the perception of physical objects, as aspects of the setting or situation undergo change, we can observe perceptual constancies operating, "resisting," as it were, the changes in situational factors that surround and embed the object. Whether in fact such constancies occur in the realm of social perception is a matter of conjecture. The view of human personality which emphasizes the essential stability and internal structure of behavior, as in trait psychology, would tend to underplay the importance of situational factors in social perception. On the other hand, the social psychologist who defines personality in terms of its interpersonal locus would certainly emphasize the potential importance of the situation to judgment.

Granting the role of situational factors, how are we to conceptualize them within our framework for the analysis of clinical judgment? We will consider two types of situational influences on judgment which we will denote as *setting* factors and *interpersonal* factors. The former relates particularly to the social structure within which the judgment occurs, and can usually be identified with the specific agency or institution within which the clinician is functioning. We will emphasize in particular two types of *constraint* which the setting may exert on the judgment situation, i.e., constraint upon the input and constraint upon the output.

If we consider the clients available to the clinician within the context of a particular clinical setting as stimuli, it is apparent that any given setting will have associated with it a *range* of clients or stimuli which may influence the context within which a specific client will be judged. For example, if the clinician operates in a hospital for chronic schizophrenics, his range of background stimuli is likely to be markedly different from that of the clinician who conducts treatment in an outpatient clinic. The constraints imposed by the previous range of stimuli experienced, associated as they are with the setting, form a major variable in the judgment situation, one to which we will return in a number of chapters throughout this book. Related to this range problem is a further constraint imposed by the setting, that of the *typical* or characteristic cases experienced previously by the clinician. Particularly in the case of a setting which attracts a relatively restricted range of clients, such typical or frequent cases may influence the judgment process by operating as *anchors* or comparative stimuli in the judgment process.

Output constraints associated with the setting would appear to operate primarily in two ways. The first of these we may term constraints upon the *availability* of response alternatives. That is, each clinical setting has a function or set of functions, and the nature of these functions tends to constrain the type of response alternatives available to the judge in making a decision. In a foster care agency the potential range of alternatives for the clinician's ultimate judgment may resolve simply into whether or not to place a child in a foster home, whereas in a diagnostic center for juveniles a larger range of alternative judgments may be available, depending upon the resources characteristically employed by the setting. Knowing the range of alternative judgments available to him, the clinician is likely to be influenced in his decision-making by these available pathways. A second source of output constraint stemming from the setting has to do with the relative *evaluation* of the alternative judgments. As we noted earlier in this chapter, the relative value placed upon each judgment alternative can be defined in terms of the relative costs and rewards which each poses for the client and for the clinician. That is, from among the potentially available responses, those which are more highly valued in the setting will more likely be selected. Thus, if a clinician must judge whether a client should have electric convulsive treatments, drug therapy, or psychotherapy, his judgment may be influenced by the relative value attached to each within the setting.

The second type of situational influence, *interpersonal* factors, relates specifically to the nature of the *interaction* between client and clinician. The influence of these interpersonal factors in social judgment has been emphasized by Jones and Thibaut (1958) among others, and it can be thought of in terms of the impact of the level of *involvement* of the judge in the clinical situation upon his reactions to the client. In particular, we will focus on the potential influence of the clinician's involvement upon his set to react to the client in an *evaluative* manner and upon his set to react to the client in what we may call a *diagnostic* manner. The potential conflict between these two sets has been a traditional preoccupation of clinicians and has been variously conceptualized in terms of problems of "counter-transference" in judgment or in terms of the difficulties of the clinician in assuming the role of the "participant observer." It should be noted that such evaluative sets toward the client may be consonant or dissonant with the values placed upon response alternatives stemming from the setting factors briefly discussed above.

RECAPITULATION

In this chapter we have presented a brief historical overview of the field of clinical judgment and have emphasized that the approach to the problem represented in this book reflects three contemporary trends: (1) the essential unity of the psychological processes involved in clinical judgment and in social judgment; (2) the continuing impact of the field of psychophysics upon the analysis of judgment; and (3) the potential value of informational analysis in the study of judgment. It has been noted that the term judgment subsumes a variety of cognitive processes and that our primary emphasis in this book will be upon discriminability, i.e., the identification of stimuli. In this regard our approach probably has primary relevance to certain types of clinical judgments in which response alternatives are relatively "fixed," in contrast to more open-ended or "creative" hypothecation (although the distinction between these two is by no means clear-cut). Four major aspects of the judgment task must be incorporated in any complete theory of judgment, including input, output, judge, and situational variables. In introducing our approach to conceptualizing each of these kinds of variables, our emphasis has been upon the *dimensional* attributes of each. In particular we distinguish between the relative multidimensionality of an input, which we call *differentiation,* and the relative number of intervals along any given dimension, which we call *articulation.* Similarly, the judgments which a clinician must make involve distinctions between possible output dimensions as well as discriminations within dimensions. An important problem in this regard is the specification of output dimensions in clinical judgment. The major characteristic of the judge with which we shall be concerned is his relative *cognitive complexity,* a structural variable which reflects the versatility of the judge in differentiating among dimensions of social judgment. If we can systematically define the dimensional nature of the input and output in a given judgment task, we will expect that the relative cognitive complexity of the judge should influence his judgmental behavior. Finally, we underscore the neglected role of situational factors in judgment, and we will analyze in particular the influence of setting factors upon the range of stimuli previously experienced by the judge as well as upon the relative availability of response alternatives and the value attached to each. The interpersonal situation of client and clinician will be analyzed in terms of its impact upon alternative sets of evaluative or diagnostic responses.

In the next chapter we will turn to a more systematic consideration of two possible alternative processes of judgment which may be important to an understanding of the nature of clinical and social judgment. We have termed these the *categorical* approach and the *dimensional* appoach, and our effort will be directed toward elucidating the similarities and differences between each. While our approach to judgment starts from a dimensional base, we will analyze points of contact with categorical processes as our presentation unfolds.

chapter 2 CONCEPTUALIZING THE JUDGMENT PROCESS

THE NATURE OF THE PROBLEM

In the analysis of judgments of clinical materials specifically, or social stimuli more generally, a theory of judgment seeks to explicate the processes which intervene between a given stimulus array and the final judgment which is produced. Beginning with whatever "raw data" are available for him to work with, which we call the stimulus, the judge's task is to make sense of these cues symbolically within the cognitive system of meaning which he brings with him into the situation. We may have available a chaotic multiplicity of stimulation when we perceive a person, and we perceive many different people. Yet our minds are orderly enough so that we do not hopelessly confuse everyone with everyone else, nor do we necessarily react to each person as if he were uniquely strange or maddeningly complicated. We are able to consider the individual in this respect and that respect, and to place him in relation to likenesses and differences with other people whom we know. In short, our minds are organized in some way, which we will refer to as our *cognitive* structure. Our mental apparatus for construing others is apparently not as akin to a disordered attic as we sometimes experience it to be but is more in the nature of a reference room kept both orderly and flexible by some complex system of cross-filing. The question for us here is, how can we best represent the operation of this structure in a way that will aid our understanding of what occurs when we go about identifying to ourselves what sort of person another is?

TWO APPROACHES TO THE JUDGMENT PROCESS

It is possible to identify two types of approaches, differing in certain respects, which provide a basis for the study of judgment processes. For our present purposes, we shall call one of these a *categorical* model and the other approach a *dimensional* model. Presumably, each of these models posits differing intervening cognitive processes which mediate the attainment of a judgment. While a major focus in this book is on an examination of the usefulness of the dimensional model of judgment, in this chapter we wish to analyze in detail each of these approaches and determine points of contact between them. As Attneave (1962) has pointed out, although it is possible that each approach may be conceptualized in terms of the other, it is also possible that differing types of judgments demand differing frameworks of explanation. In general, our approach is consonant with this latter view, in that we wish to specify the range of convenience of the dimensional viewpoint.

The adequacy of one theoretical model or the other in representing the judgment process may depend on the specific nature of the task confronting the judge. That is, with judgments which may be analyzed from a categorical viewpoint, the stimuli to be judged are likely to differ from each other in what we intuitively call a *qualitative* manner, consisting of different objects (e.g., in object-sorting tasks, scissors, a toy car, or a whistle), and often particular attributes differ among the stimuli in a dichotomous fashion (e.g., in a concept formation task, some objects are black, others are white, and some are large and some small). Moreover, the response demanded of the judge appears to be a *nominal* discrimination, in terms of deciding if a stimulus has attributes which indicate that it belongs to one category or another. In judgments considered from a dimensional viewpoint the stimuli to be judged appear to differ from each other in what we would call a *quantitative* manner (e.g., consisting of tones of varying loudness). The response required of the judge is more likely to consist of attributive, *ordinal* discriminations, as in determining *where* between two endpoint standards a given stimulus lies. Such task differences would seem to settle the matter of distinguishing between categorical and dimensional approaches in a rather obvious fashion were it not that in certain clinical judgments, for example, it is not at all evident which kind of task we have! When a judge is presented with several case descriptions and must assign them, as he sees fit, to the alternative response categories of "schizophrenic," "schizoid," "psychopathic deviate," "neurotic," and "normal," shall we say that he is making quantitative discriminations among them, judging their relative severity along some dimension of pathology? Or shall we say that he is making qualitative discriminations among them, matching each case to the set of prototypic attributes it best fits? *

Examples of this categorical-dimensional distinction can be pointed out in the clinical literature. Speaking of the "Tentative Criteria of Malignancy in Schizophrenia," Harry Stack Sullivan (1928) criticized the prevailing categorical quality of thinking in relation to this disorder which stemmed from the Kraepelinian system:

> No diagnostic criteria have yet come to light the application of which would make possible a rigid classification of these people as victims of schizophrenia and of other disorders. A considerable number of the individuals concerned in the summary would ordinarily be regarded as "mixed" states, or psychoses associated with psychopathic personality, or eccentric alcoholic psychoses, and the like. From another viewpoint, a number of them would be considered as cases of malignant hysteria, extreme psychasthenic reactions, or "grave parapathias, unclassified." Continued experience with mentally disordered persons weakens the writer's hope of finding clear nosological entities. The more one learns of what is going on in his patient, the less faith he can retain in the alleged types of anomalous and perverted adjustive reactions. The field of mental disorders seems to be a continual gradation, in which little of discrete types is to be found. (p. 760)

Even granting Sullivan's strong tendency to find common ground among the so-called normal and abnormal behavior patterns, his dimensional bias does not seem misplaced today. If anything, the subcategories of schizophrenia which are currently finding increasing acceptance have a more dimensional bias than the older classifications of simple, hebephrenic, catatonic, and paranoid. In particular, one should note such dimensional distinctions as the process-reactive continuum (Herron, 1962) and adequacy of premorbid adjustment (Rodnick & Garmezy, 1957) which are used in contemporary research and theorizing about schizophrenia. Later in this chapter we shall return to a consideration of dimensional processes in clinical judgment. First, we must look more closely at both the categorical and the dimensional viewpoints, in order to determine (1) whether *any* judgment can be alternatively conceptualized in either categorical or dimensional terms, or, if not, (2) whether there are indeed two alternative kinds of cognitive processes involved in judgment and under what conditions the judge can be expected to engage in one or the other.

* The advantage of using an informational analysis, as we shall see, is that it allows us to assess the judge's ability to discriminate among a set of stimuli such as this apart from a consideration of which kind of discriminatory process may be involved.

The Categorical Approach in Psychology

In general, a categorical approach to perception and cognition is associated with the view that psychological processes are *discontinuous,* discrete phenomena, that an event can be designated or defined in *absolute* rather than relational terms, and that a correspondence between two events can be seen as a direct *matching* between the terms that define each of them. Events are seen to be matched according to either of two principles, (*a*) their spatial-temporal continuity or (*b*) their possession of the same property or properties in *kind,* or the same amount of a single property. Because the property or properties defining an event can be specified as categorically fixed, one can also specify the absolute degree of relationship between two events without invoking a third event as a further standard of reference. However, in estimating the empirical probability that two events will be matched, it is necessary in some manner to weigh the probability of one matching against the probabilities of *alternative* matchings. A given matching is then a *choice* among alternative possible matchings.

The categorical approach has most often been utilized in describing those mental processes which are seen to involve *memory*. The process to be explained will be understood in terms of a matching between what is currently perceived by the person and what he has already learned and retains in the cognitive system. This approach also provides a general model of processes involving *judgment,* insofar as the subject is seen to evaluate the matching between what is "already in his head" and what he currently observes. (This is, of course, how we usually conceptualize the scientific procedure engaged in by the psychologist himself when he matches observations to theoretical formulations, and then matches theoretically derived hypotheses to further observations, and finally evaluates the adequacy of these matchings according to agreed-upon scientific criteria.) As we shall see, the cognitive processes thus understood in terms of such memory and thinking models have included form recognition, instrumental, associative, and discrimination learning, problem-solving, concept formation, and stimulus identification. More recently the process of perception itself has been considered in these terms. For example, simple *recognition* of a pattern which has been seen before has been attributed to a matching between the present pattern of stimulation and a perceptual trace of the same pattern remaining from past stimulation on the basis of their formal similarity (Kohler, 1940).

The application of the categorical approach to problems of *perceptual learning* has been common in psychology and is often presented under the rubric of *schema* theories. Such theories of perceptual learning, seen in terms of schema, categorizing, or classification models, have been reviewed by E. J. Gibson (1963). In such approaches, perceptual learning can be seen to occur as traces of specific experience become integrated into a *perceptual* schema. This process is sometimes seen to account for our ability to perceive three-dimensional objects as such because we retain and integrate together partially similar perceptual patterns of the object as it is seen from various angles. It is also sometimes seen to account for our ability to notice increasing detail in a complex visual pattern which is seen repeatedly. Each time we see it, the aspects we notice enrich the existing trace a little more, and this trace in turn aids in our articulation of the present percept. *Stimulus identification,* in terms of being able to remember an object's proper *name,* can also be thought of as dependent on the formation of a perceptual schema. As the name is heard when the object is seen repeatedly, the two become associated into one complex perceptual schema on the basis of their temporal perceptual proximity. When the object is seen later, the pattern-matching process (recognition of the visual form) will result in recall of the schematically integrated name: "That's Bill." Perceptual schemata in general are seen to be memory integrations either of stimulation received in close temporal or spatial proximity, or else of stimulations formally similar in their patterns.

Stimulus identification, in terms of being able to identify an object conceptually, can be thought of as dependent on the formation of a *conceptual schema.* In contrast to a perceptual schema, a conceptual schema is more abstract, containing the distinctive *defining* properties associated with a *noun.* Quite dissimilar perceptual patterns, and ones not experienced together, may all be matched to a common, learned, conceptual schema, e.g., mammal, merely on the basis of a few *selected* mammal-defining attributes. One of the first psychologists to utilize the notion of the schema in understanding cognition was Bartlett (1932) in his classic studies of memory. Bartlett was able to show how, in attempting to *recall* a story one has heard, one will distort the tale in such a way that those parts of it which were strange to himself will be either forgotten altogether or else modified to conform to his more familiar ideas and existing experience, that is, to his cognitive schemata of the world. If we hear a story, for example, which describes "a feather, hurtling forward with the speed of light," because this description does not conform to our schema of what a feather is like we are more likely to remember the passage as "an arrow, hurtling forward with the speed of light" or perhaps "a feather, floating lightly." It is our existing knowledge which we bring to new experiences and to which we refer new experiences in order to comprehend them. The above example of the feather also illustrates that many of our schemata derive from both personal experience and abstract language comprehension.* Theorists such as Piaget and Vigotsky conceptualize mental development as in part a gradual separation of the two. As long as the child is able to understand or use a semantic definition only insofar as it refers to his actual experience, he is said to be using schemata that are preconceptual or primitive concepts. The criterion of a truly conceptual schema is that it can carry meaning for the individual in terms of its definition alone, quite apart from any reference to empirical reality; it allows us to conceive of hypothetically defined relationships among purely abstract symbols, and also to approach experienced entities "from above" (Duncker, 1945), examining them to see if they contain a property one has abstractly in mind.

Because only certain properties are selected from a given percept to match it with a given conceptual schema, the percept is *ambiguous conceptually*. By selecting successively different sets of its properties, one can match it with alternative schemata. A person one knows as Bill can be conceptualized alternatively as a mammal, a man, a worker, a father, a jolly good fellow, and so on. In these terms one can understand the difficulty involved in the processes of *concept formation* and *problem-solving*. In both these tasks, as well as that of stimulus identification on the conceptual level, ease or difficulty of the task will depend on such factors as complexity of the stimulus (its potential for alternative schematizing) and the range of conceptual alternatives available to the judge in matching percept to concept.

Interest in problems of stimulus identification was aroused particularly during World War II, which presented the task of training personnel to identify fast-moving enemy aircraft or ships seen at long distances or in the dark, to read radar patterns, and so on. The problem here is one not only of the conceptual ambiguity of these stimuli but of their *perceptual ambiguity* as well. In fact, while we can usually make rather clear distinctions between problems of perception, recognition, and conceptual identification, in these instances the distinctions become lost, to the judge himself as well as to the theorist. Under inadequate viewing conditions, the subject may be fairly sure what the object *is,* what conceptual category to place it in, although he may be quite unable to sketch what it *looks like* perceptually. In fact, what he is likely to sketch, or to recognize as the object seen when he is presented with various sketches, will more closely resemble the conceptual prototype than the pattern of stimulation he actually received (Bruner and Minturn, 1955). This sort of problem had the effect, so far as psychological the-

* The use of metaphorical dimensions in social judgment, e.g., "warm-cold," can be considered an example of how interpretations of behavior are assimilated into previously existing schemata concerning the physical world.

ory was concerned, of drawing *perceptual processes* within the realm of the categorical approach, i.e., perception was viewed as itself a function of memory and conceptualization. As Bruner stated succinctly (1957): "Perception involves an act of categorization." Because at least certain perceptions have been more often understood from a dimensional viewpoint, we shall discuss below in more detail Bruner's position in this matter.

While the categorical approach to cognitive processes has a long history, fairly recently the formulations of set theory in mathematics have provided this approach with an appropriate method of measurement. The application of set theory to a wide variety of psychological problems has been undertaken by Restle (1961), and because his concerns, too, overlap those of the dimensional approach, we wish to discuss his views.

The Approach of Bruner. We have noted above that Bruner defines perception as a categorical process. He states: "Put in terms of the antecedent and subsequent conditions from which we make inferences, we stimulate an organism with some appropriate input and he responds by referring the input to some class of things or events" (Bruner, 1957). Unfortunately, the specific sense in which Bruner is defining the term *category* is not clear. There appear to be two major ways in which we may use the concept "category." One meaning of the term is equivalent to class, or set, a usage which is common in concept formation when we speak of an *object* belonging to a particular class or category on the basis of specifiable defining attributes. Any other object possessing these "criterial" attributes may also be considered to belong to this category. The cognitive processes associated with this type of categorization are concerned with *identification* of an object, i.e., what is it? Categorization, as such, has a "noun-like" quality. Thus, in his discussion of categorization in perception Bruner uses as examples the perception of an orange, a goblet, *a* sound, *a* touch, and *a* pain. He then states:

> Categorization of an object or event—placing it or giving it identity—can be likened to what in set theory is the placement of an element from a universe in a subset of that universe of items on the basis of such *ordered dimensional pairs* [emphasis ours], triples, or *n*-tuples as man-woman, mesomorph-endomorph-ectomorph, or height to the nearest inch. In short, when one specifies something more than that an element or object belongs to a universe, and that it belongs in a subset of the universe, one has categorized the element or object. . . . So long as an operation assigns an input to a subset, it is an act of categorization. (p. 124)

A second meaning of the term category is *interval.* When we speak of categories of an ordered scale, we are using the term in this interval sense. In set theory terms, such intervals *may be* subsets of a larger set.

Although Bruner speaks of the "ordered dimensional" basis upon which an element may be placed in a subset, he implies an ordinality of scaling (e.g., height in inches) which may be difficult to reconcile with a set theoretical approach, as we shall see in the discussion of Restle which follows. Ordinarily, one may consider subsets in terms of *nominal* categories or intervals. When an object is classified as belonging to a set we identify as "fruit," it may be further specified in terms of the subset of "citrus fruit," and so on, perhaps, to such identification as "orange" and "navel orange." Again, the use of category as a subset may serve a purely identification purpose in this nominal sense, such that orange, lemon, and grapefruit are subsets of the larger set "citrus fruit."

To avoid confusion we prefer to speak of *intervals* when we are referring to *ordered* subsets. In his analysis of magnitude judgments Bruner (1957) refers to "category systems" and "category sets" as providing the basis for such ordinal discriminations. He states: "Ask the person to deal with one stimulus at a time, to array it in terms of some magnitude scale, and immediately one is back in the familiar territory of inferential categorizing." He goes on to note:

> In short, the category systems that are utilized in arraying magnitudes are also affected by the requirement of matching one's model of the world to the actual events that are occurring—even if the categories be no more complicated than "heavy," "medium," and "light." (p. 128)

Whether one is indeed back into the "familiar" world of categorizing, as Bruner uses the term, when one deals with magnitude judgments is a moot question. Rather, this distinction between judgments as identity-seeking processes and judgments as magnitude-estimation processes may be fundamental to the distinction between a categorical and a dimensional approach to cognition. Thus, we must ask, what does it mean to consider "heavy" or "medium" a category as Bruner defines "category"? What are the defining attributes of the model set we call "heavy"? If, as Bruner states, "by a category we mean a rule for classifying objects as equivalent," what rule can be invoked in the case of a magnitude judgment? Obviously such a rule must be *relational* in nature and deal with the comparison of one element with another. Such a notion would seem to place the categorical approach in a logical impasse in that one must consider as an attribute of a set or category its relation to attributes of another category which acts as the standard of comparison (implicitly or explicitly) in making the magnitude judgment.

Before considering in detail Restle's attempted resolution of this problem, we should sum up Bruner's general attitude toward the categorization-dimensional problem (Bruner, Goodnow, and Austin, 1956):

We have found that such a controversy is relatively fruitless. We have found it more meaningful to regard a concept as a network of sign-significate inferences by which one goes beyond a set of *observed* criterial properties exhibited by an object or event to the class identity of the object or event in question, and thence to additional inferences about other *unobserved* properties of the object or event. We see an object that is red, shiny, and roundish and infer that it is an apple; we are then enabled to infer further that "if it is an apple, it is also edible, juicy, will rot if unrefrigerated, etc." The working definition of a concept is the network of inferences that are or may be set into play by an act of categorization. (p. 244)

The Set Theory Approach of Restle. Perhaps the most detailed consideration of the categorical approach to judgment is contained in Restle's (1961) development of the set theoretic position. In his exposition, Restle, unlike Bruner, emphasizes some basic discontinuities between the categorical and dimensional points of view. He states:

It would be possible to use set-theoretic methods for some problems and the classical dimensional analysis for others. This is not a fundamentally clean solution to the issue, for the set-theoretic and dimensional models are logically incompatible and lead to entirely different approaches to theoretical problems. (p. 39)

Restle's approach relies heavily on the concept of *schema* in explaining how a particular judgment is attained. On the basis of prior experiences, ideal schemata are laid down in the brain and the perception of an object, say in terms of recognition, becomes a "random access" matching problem. That is, schemata are randomly matched to the available input until the best fit is attained. A best fit is defined in terms of that ideal schema which has the maximum number of elements in common with those found in the stimulus array. As in Bruner's approach, such a notion seems particularly well suited to explain perceptual phenomena related to recognition and identification but runs into difficulties when magnitude judgments of the "more than" or "less than" variety are made.

If two stimuli differ only in terms of a quantitative distinction, rather than in terms of qualitatively different attributes, a set-theoretic approach would appear to have two options in deciding if a third stimulus would be judged as more like one than the other. In either option it is assumed that a *linear array of sets* is formed such that the two extreme stimuli represent the ends of the linear array. Under one option, the third stimulus is matched against each extreme stimulus and is judged more like the one with which it shares the most elements. Note that these elements are "more of the same," that is, that the elements are identical and differ only in quantity. However, as Restle notes:

To say that a bright and dim light are exactly alike except for their brightness is to claim that the difference is solely quantitative—the brighter light is merely "more of the same." In the ordinary use of set theory this is not an admissible concept, though it seems to be sensible to psychology. . . . Set theory cannot express "more of the same" where same means "identical." However, psychological theory needs a concept of equivalence or indistinguishability of elements within a class so as to say that a bright light is "more of the equivalent" elements. (p. 142)

Restle then proceeds to the second option which could incorporate the notion of equivalence of elements by considering what he calls the "homogeneous classes of aspects." Unfortunately, as Restle frankly notes in advancing this intriguing notion, the conceptual and mathematical properties of homogeneous classes of aspects remain to be determined: "Being unable to frame an adequate definition he has written around the point in the hope of communicating the idea intended. . . ." Restle states further, "Despite the importance of the concept of homogeneity, it became clear that homogeneous elements are not identical in the usual sense." Should these problems be worked out, the difficulties noted above in Bruner's elaboration of the use of categories in magnitude judgments might be resolved. At this juncture, it seems reasonable to conclude that the set-theoretic approach to judgment operates best in the realm of the detection or recognition of qualitatively discrete stimuli.

The Dimensional Approach in Psychology

A contrasting framework for conceptualizing psychological processes has its roots in the fairly consistent tradition of modern science which represents events in terms of *continuous variables*. Along a given dimension of variation, a given event will be designated as a particular *value*. What this means is that the event must be designated in *relational* terms, as a matter of *degree,* and its value will be "defined" only in reference to some parameters of the given dimension, whatever one's "level of measurement." Two events can be matched only insofar as they represent corresponding "positions" in regard to some common third term of reference, whether this term is seen as a standard *magnitude* of comparison (ratio scaling) or as a common *system* of reference (equal-interval or more primitive ordinal scaling). The degree of correspondence between an event on one dimension and an event on another dimension can be specified only insofar as a series of values along the one dimension can be matched against a series of values along the other.

The academic psychologist himself has long tended to approach his subject matter in such a fashion. In psychophysical studies as well as in the study of discrimination learning, the *stimuli* presented to the subject are defined by the experimenter in a dimensional manner in terms of differing in value along some continuum such as brightness or loudness. In both psychophysical judgment and in discrimination learning, stimuli are usually presented to the subject two, or perhaps three, at a time. What may then be a series of either-or responses of the subject (e.g., "same" vs. "different," "more" vs. "less," respond vs. don't respond) can nevertheless be translated into dimensional terms by plotting the probability of one of the alternatives as a continuous function of variation along the stimulus dimension. In general, one can dimensionalize *responses* in terms of their probability, if not more obviously in terms of their frequency or intensity. Furthermore, we find that often the asymptotic value of a subject's overt response on a behavioral continuum is taken as the operational measure of his position regarding an *intervening* variable. For example, the probability, after sufficient training, of a subject making a particular response to a stimulus is taken as an indication of the *strength* of the habit for this subject. The "presence" of any personality trait is often inferred in a similar manner (Bieri, 1962). Actually, it is the degree of the trait's presence in the individual, e.g., how dependent a person is seen to be, or how anxious, which is inferred from the modal probability or frequency of his dependency or anxiety responses on some assessment procedure such as the TAT or a personality inventory.

Although it is quite common practice, in a variety of settings, for the *theorist* to view the response (or the trait behind the response) of a subject as a value on some dimension, not all these theorists would agree that the *subject* cognitively utilizes a dimension as reference in defining the value either of his response or of the stimulus to which he is responding. It is the dimensional approach as it has been applied as a model of the subject's own cognitive functioning which here concerns us. This model tended to evolve, not in settings where the subject's "response" is one of bar-pressing or other motor behaviors, but in situations more akin to what the theorist himself is doing in "responding," namely judging or identifying what he observes. Thus we first find the dimensional model of cognition applied to the subject in his sensory-perceptual reactions to physical continua, i.e., in the area of *psychophysics*.

Classically, the concern of psychophysics has been to determine as accurately as possible the functional relationship between an incoming intensity of physical energy and the organism's sensory reaction. Psychophysical theory is often a physiologically oriented theory. From such a viewpoint, if a given stimulus value (e.g., a weight of 3 grams) is assigned varying values by the subject one would seek ways of either eliminating, allowing for, or controlling such variability, in order to approach as closely as possible a reliable psychophysical relationship. On the other hand, some psychophysicists, and also psychologists approaching the field from external vantage points, have been interested in such response variability as a phenomenon in its own right. Briefly, there have been two trends away from the traditional psychophysical concerns. One may infer from this variability that the response to a particular intensity of physical energy is not simply a sensory reaction but *a more complex judgment;* or one may infer that the subject is not reacting to this particular stimulus energy alone, in a one-to-one matching fashion, but rather that the subject is responding to *a more complex stimulus situation.* In the first instance, one may view the subject here as being in the position of attempting to perform mathematical operations upon the input he receives, however nonconsciously, at however "low" a level of measurement, and with whatever unreliability the unassisted human mind is capable of in carrying on such operations. In the second instance, one may view the subject as reacting to a stimulus in terms of its position relative to the value of other stimuli he is receiving (along this attribute dimension), and perhaps also to the values of other stimuli he has received in the immediate or even more distant *past.*

Finally, as these two approaches to the psychophysical task become theoretically integrated into one dimensional viewpoint, we have the following hypothesis: Out of his experience with many different values of physical input, the subject will form in his mind some kind of implicit representation of a given stimulus dimension, and will judge or "measure" the value of further incoming stimuli in reference to the parameters of this (psychological) dimension. More specifically, it is suggested on the basis of subjects' responses that a psychological dimension is somewhat analogous to an equal-interval scale, for which the values defining either end of the dimension are more or less specified, so that an incoming stimulus will be judged particularly in terms of its value in relation to the values of these two endpoints.

Such a dimensional formulation, thus developed to deal with the judgment of sensory attributes, has also been applied to judgment of the "psychological" attributes of people, e.g., warmth, friendliness, and dominance. Outstanding examples of the use of this model of person perception are found in the work of G. A. Kelly (1955) and Charles Osgood (1957), and we shall return to a further consideration of these theorists.

Identification of a stimulus in terms of the ordinal value of one of its attributes is seen, in this dimensional analysis, to involve an interaction between the present sensory input and what the organism retains in the cognitive system as a dimensional ordering of past stimulation. This means that the dimensional approach has developed its own paradigm of *memory* processes and cognitive structure, an area previously considered the domain of the categorical approach.

Dimensionality and Personal Construct Theory. In the elaboration of his psychology of personal constructs, G. A. Kelly (1955) has provided one of the more explicit dimensional analyses of judgment in contemporary psychology. Although Kelly's primary concern is with the development of a theory of personality, his is a conception which stems from clinical concerns and is articulated in terms of the implications of the theory for clinical practice. At this juncture, however, we are most interested in the nature of his conceptions rather than their applicability. For it is an interesting fact that Kelly, like Bruner, begins his consideration of cognitive processes from the vantage point of concept formation. However, whereas Bruner follows a categorical analysis of this problem, Kelly is led to formulate a concept in terms of "personal constructs," which, as we shall see, have a dimensional quality. We can recognize this difference in the following statement: "A construct is a two-ended thing, not merely a category of likeness with no inferred difference in the offing" (1955, p. 133).

That is, Kelly makes a basic assumption about the use of concepts in the interpersonal realm that these *constructs* are dichotomous in nature. The nature of this bipolarity is one of likenesses and differences: "A construct is the way in which some things are construed as being alike and yet different from others" (1955, p. 105). Kelly is essentially saying that we cannot know the *similarities* that exist among a group of elements unless we simultaneously infer *differences* between these elements and another set of elements. This rather novel approach to the problem of similarity in behavior has been reiterated by Wallach (1958) and invites a closer analysis of what we mean by "similarity" when we use it in such psychological concepts as generalization, displacement, and concept formation. Let us quote Kelly more fully in this context:

> We have departed from conventional logic by assuming that the construct is just as pertinent to some of the things which are seen as different as it is to the things which are seen as alike. For example, suppose a person construes in terms of a *black vs. white* construct. His field comprises a number of things. Some of them, such as his shirt, his shoes, his house, the paper on which he writes, the skin of his neighbor, and so on, are amenable to the *black vs. white* construct. . . . Now conventional logic would say that *black* and *white* should be treated as separate concepts. Moreover, it would say that the opposite of *black* can only be stated as *not black,* and the opposite of *white* can only be stated as *not white.* . . . we have chosen for the time

being, to abandon the classical notion of concepts and to assume a somewhat different structure of thought. . . . From our point of view, each construct, as used by a person, has a limited range of convenience. Outside that range the person does not find it relevant, one way or the other, to the objects located there. For example, the time of day is an element most people would place outside the range of convenience of their personal construct of *black vs. white.* But within the range of convenience of the construct there is a relevant similarity and difference which together form the essence of the construct. (pp. 105 ff.)

The nature of this difference is basically the distinction between the categorical and dimensional approaches to judgment which we have been considering in this chapter. However, although Kelly has committed himself to a dimensional view of the conceptual process, his is perhaps a *transitional* view in that it tends to focus on the *two-interval* nature of dimensions. As we noted earlier, the categorical view of judgment *in practice* is quite similar to the two-interval dimensional approach. In the former, an element either belongs to the category or it does not. In the latter, the element either fits into one end of the construct dimension or the other or it falls outside "the range of convenience" of the dimension. The linking of two intervals into a common dimension, however, has obvious advantages for Kelly. For one thing, it indicates the *possible* direction of change in construing if a change were to occur. That is, if a person is not this, he may be its opposite; if I decide that Mr. Jones is not a liberal, it is possible I may consider him a reactionary. If Miss Smith is not domineering, she may be submissive. By linking the juxtaposed categories of domineering and submissive in a common construct dimension, Kelly has at the least suggested the direction in which changes in conceptualization are likely to occur.

It is one of the major assumptions of the viewpoint developed in the present book that it is fruitful to expand this two-interval dimensional view of conceptualization into an *n*-interval approach. That is, we believe that dimensions of judgment may differ in terms of their articulation, i.e., the degree to which *discriminations* can be made along the dimensions. We assume, furthermore, that judges may differ in terms of their ability to make discriminations along dimensions of judgment, a characteristic that can be assessed through the use of *n*-interval scales such as those used by Osgood in the semantic differential. The same view, actually, has been taken by Kelly, as we note in the following passage:

From time to time we have used the notion of a construct as if it were an axis or dimension. Since we have assumed that constructs are essentially dichotomous, it may appear that we have ruled out the possibility of scales or continua involving more than two steps. . . . Even though we envision the basic constructs out of which our systems are built as dichotomous, it is still possible to conceive of gradations . . . along a dimensional line. (p. 141)

As we have observed, a related view of the dimensional basis of judgment is contained in the work of Osgood (1957), even though he starts from a more associationistic and less perceptual base than does Kelly.

Osgood and Dimensional Analysis. In one sense the use of a dimensional approach to judgment by Osgood and his associates (1957) stems from less urgent theoretical dictates than is true in Kelly's work. That is, Osgood is rather frank in pointing out that his use of bipolar adjective dimensions on the semantic differential is less a reflection of his theoretical conviction about the nature of *meaning* (his primary interest) than it is a natural empirical continuation of an earlier use of bipolar scales in judgment in research involving synesthesia. In fact, Osgood discusses at some length whether there is any necessary link between the semantic differential and his conceptions of meaning, and he appears to resolve the matter largely on the basis of convenience in measurement. He tends to feel, for example, that a unidirectional scale might have advantages over a bipolar scale (e.g., it would circumvent the assumption with bipolar scales that the opposite adjectives defining the ends of the scales are equidistant from the midpoint) but that unidirectional scales might ignore the "natural" tendency for human observers to think in terms of opposites (a basic assumption for Kelly). Similarly, Osgood feels that the use of adjectives to anchor the ends of judgment scales is perhaps not necessary.

Despite possible differences in dimensional commitment Osgood and Kelly share two major assumptions about the perception of objects. First, both hold that people perceive objects in terms of a finite number of properties, which Kelly calls constructs and Osgood refers to as dimensions of meaning. Next, as we have seen, both assess a person's object perception in terms of where the object is judged to lie on a succession of bipolar dimensions defined in terms of an adjective and its opposite. Unlike Kelly, however, Osgood attempts a more refined assessment of the judgment along a dimension by using more *intervals* (usually seven) along the scale, thus allowing both direction and intensity to be measured. Furthermore, whereas Kelly takes a psychological approach and a definite theoretical stand that the meaning of one pole of the scale depends on what the subject uses to define the opposite pole, Osgood's approach is more semantic. That is, he relies upon a thesaurus for his opposites. This difference underscores the more *relational* view of judgment assumed by Kelly in contrast to the view of Osgood. For Kelly, the subject judges the object in terms of where it stands in relation to the extended dimensions, taking into account both poles at once (even though one pole may be more accessible or salient). In a sense, one might say that the meaning of the judgment lies in the relationship of the two words to each other. For Osgood, it would seem that the subject judges the object as to some degree of warmth (e.g., on a warm-cold scale) if he rates it anywhere from the midpoint of the scale toward the warm end, no matter what word is at the opposite end of the scale. The judge makes only one rating on the dimension because he has to make a choice between which trait better characterizes the object. The mutually exclusive traits at either end of the scale simply give the judge a clearer choice to make. In this sense, Osgood is more categorical because the judge matches the two polar schemata against the object in arriving at his judgment, whereas for Kelly such nonrelational matching of end-points is ruled out.*

Finally, it might be noted that Osgood goes to some length to make the distinction that he is primarily concerned with what he calls *connotative* meaning and points out that one cannot infer on the basis of judgments made on the semantic differential what object is being *denoted.* Such an analysis is diametrically opposed to that of Bruner, who argues that the properties of the stimulus discriminated by a judge form the basis of its identification as an object.

RELATION OF CATEGORICAL TO DIMENSIONAL FORMULATIONS

Having presented and discussed some of the underlying issues in the categorical and dimensional approaches to judgment, we shall consider briefly some similarities and differences in the two formulations. A succinct statement and an analysis relating these two approaches have been put forward recently by Attneave (1962). He states:

> The question of whether this analytical process may better be conceived in terms of psychophysical dimensions or in terms of discrete classes or elements is difficult, important, and unresolved. Both continuous and discrete variables seem to exist subjectively; in certain contexts, one formulation seems the more appropriate; in other contexts, the other. It would appear that either is potentially reducible to the other. (p. 638)

Attneave points out that with a dimensional approach classes of objects may be considered regions within a multidimensional space. Because each region may define a given complex object rather completely,

* A further consideration of the relation of both Kelly's and Osgood's viewpoints to the role of cognitive structure in judgment is presented in Chapter 7.

we experience the objects as relatively "discrete" in spite of the dimensional basis of perception. If, however, we consider class distinctions to be basic to judgment, Attneave enumerates the following possibilities for conceiving of dimensions:

> . . . (1) a series of partially overlapping classes, (2) a series of classes, each of which includes all the elements of the preceding class, (3) a series of classes that vary in relative communality with some reference class, or (4) a series of classes that vary in relative communality with two reference classes, thereby defined as opposites. (p. 638)

On balance, Attneave considers the class conceptualization both "more convenient and versatile" but recognizes that we should not dismiss the possibility that both categorical and dimensional processes may exist in an "irreducible" form. In our approach to the judgment process, we consider that certain judgment tasks may evoke dimensional processes of judgment, others may evoke categorical processes of judgment, and still others may evoke both processes. Let us analyze several factors which might help us determine just when each type of judgment might ensue.

Stimulus Factors

What are the characteristics of the stimuli presented to the judge which may lead him to employ a categorical or dimensional judgment process? It would appear that an answer to this question must entail consideration of two aspects of the situation: (1) the *relative dimensionality* of any particular stimulus and (2) the *degree of sharing* or overlap of stimulus dimensions among the set of stimuli. Any given stimulus set may contain stimuli which are unidimensional (if such can be conceptualized in the social and clinical realms) or may contain stimuli which are multidimensional. It is difficult to determine the degree of precision with which we can empirically define social and clinical stimuli in terms of their relative dimensionality, as we shall note in subsequent chapters. At the very least we may be able to consider the *relative* differences among stimuli in terms of their dimensionality. Relations among the stimuli of a given set can be conceptualized in terms of the degree to which they share common dimensions. This may range from no shared dimensions among any of the stimuli to many or all shared dimensions among the stimuli (again, for simplicity's sake, we shall assume equivalent degree of overlap for all stimuli in the set).

Possible relations among these stimulus factors in terms of categorical and dimensional processes of judgment are considered in the following table.

		Each Stimulus Contains: Single Dimension	Each Stimulus Contains: Two or More Dimensions
Each Set of Stimuli	Shares No Dimensions	I Categorical	II Categorical
	Shares One or More Dimensions	III Dimensional	IV Dimensional and/or Categorical

If we consider first the case in which the stimuli in the set share no dimensions with each other (Cells I and II), it is apparent that identification of the stimuli will be of a categorical nature. The stimuli in the set will be experienced as discrete or nominal in nature, with little or no confusion in recognition, assuming that the attribute dimensions are accurately matched with the ideal stimulus. For example, if we assume that the set consists of only two stimuli, and the judge is asked to decide if these two stimuli are the same or different, so long as the judge can discriminate *among* the stimulus dimensions his judgment will be accurate. Thus, in a Cell I situation the judge may be asked to distinguish black from pink and under normal conditions of viewing will experience no difficulty in discriminating between these two categories of "color." In the Cell II situation the judge may be asked to distinguish between two stimuli in a set which share no dimensions, each stimulus containing two or more dimensions. For example, presented with a pink scarf and a black bowling ball, we would have no difficulty in distinguishing between them because each has unique defining dimensions or attributes (of color, texture, shape, etc.). However, in the judgment of social stimuli, such dimensional independence among the stimuli is less common. That is, we are more likely to encounter the situation covered by the bottom two cells of the preceding table in which one or more dimensional attributes are shared among the stimuli in the set.

Cell III represents the situation in which the single-attribute stimuli differ from each other only in terms of the scale value each possesses on a common dimension, as in distinguishing between stimuli representing two shades of pink. Analogously, the clinician may be asked to judge the degree of regression among a group of patients or the intensity of acting-out behavior among a group of delinquents. If we assume that such attributes as regression and acting-out are unidimensional (an assumption we shall examine further in subsequent chapters), the judgment process here is clearly a dimensional one of articulating differences along the common attribute dimension.

However, if we identify each of our stimuli in more extensive terms, it is perhaps more accurate to consider this last example as a judgment task involving discrimination among a set of multidimensional stimuli which share one attribute dimension. In this case, it becomes an instance of a Cell IV judgment, and the problem of analyzing the judgment process becomes more involved. It is clear that in the situations covered by Cells I and II, the process of *differentiation* (Chapter 1) is involved because the judge has to discriminate among or between the dimensional attributes of the stimuli. In the case of Cell III, the process of *articulation* is engaged in because the judge must discriminate among values on a single stimulus dimension. Cell IV, however, includes the judgment of stimuli which are subject to *both* differentiation and articulation, including as it does stimuli which are multidimensional and those which share one or more of these dimensions. Because it is likely that many if not most stimuli encountered in clinical and social judgment are of the Cell IV variety, a closer analysis of this situation is in order.

We have noted that in Cells I and II the judge is asked to *differentiate* between two or more stimuli since there are no shared dimensions. Thus, in Cell I one stimulus may contain dimension A and the other dimension B. In Cell II, one stimulus may contain dimensions A and B whereas the other stimulus contains independent dimensions C and D. In Cell III each stimulus contains the same dimension, but the scale values of each stimulus on this dimension differ (e.g., A1 and A2, where 1 and 2 represent different scale values). Here the judge must articulate the difference between A1 and A2. The Cell IV task differs from the Cell III case in that the stimuli differ not only in terms of the stimulus dimensions they contain but also in terms of their scale values. Consider the following four stimuli (W, X, Y, and Z):

W	X	Y	Z
A1	B2	C1	B2
B1	C1	D1	C1
C1	D1	E1	D2

If we compare stimulus W with each of the other three stimuli, we can consider how the dimensional process of articulation might be involved and how the categorical process of differentiation might be involved. In comparing W and X, two dimensions are shared, whereas only one dimension is shared by W and Y. Presumably, the discrimination between W and Y is easier to make than that between W and X. A more complicated relationship may exist, however, in that while X and W share two dimensions, B and C, each stimulus possesses a different value on dimension B. It is certainly possible that this difference could be considered by the judge to be just as important as a difference in dimensions. Thus, in considering the relation between W and Z, articulating a difference between B1 and B2 may be considered as important as differentiating between dimensions A and D.

Perhaps we can concretize these relationships by considering a clinical example which parallels the relations between W and X, i.e., two patients who may be assumed to have one attribute in common (C1) but differ both in terms of one common stimulus dimension (B1 and B2) as well as in terms of one unshared dimension (A and D). Such a judgment situation might arise in relation to determining which of two patients is an excited catatonic and which is manic. Both patients may share the attribute of extreme agitation and excitement (C1) and yet differ in terms of degree of bizarre ideation (B1 and B2). Furthermore, one patient may have a history of occasional schizophrenia in his family (A1), and the other may have some evidence of manic-depressive illness in his family (D1). The judge, having made these dimensional articulations, could then assign the patient to a diagnostic group on the basis of a categorical matching process.

As the number of attributes increases, however, and as they are increasingly shared among the stimuli to be judged, it is possible that the categorical matching process may become increasingly difficult because of the large number of dimensions which the judge must differentiate among and deal with simultaneously. Such conceptual overload may result in a "chunking" operation (Miller, 1956) whereby attributes are combined to form fewer elements in the stimulus; or this overload may force the judge to deal with one salient or common feature of the stimulus array. In the case of the four stimuli outlined above, attribute C1 is such a common feature.

Clearly, it is difficult to decide on a priori basis exactly how categorical and dimensional processes may interact in a Cell IV judgment. At the very least, these considerations highlight the importance in the systematic analysis of judgment processes of specifying as exactly as possible the dimensional characteristics of the stimuli. In subsequent chapters we shall present studies of clinical and social judgment in which stimuli are varied in terms of their dimensional properties. Such studies provide a start in this important problem of stimulus specification in behavioral judgment research.

Response Factors

Perhaps of even greater importance in analyzing judgment as a dimensional or a categorical process is a consideration of the nature of the response required of the judge. The reader will have noted that the above discussion of stimulus factors has carried with it explicit statements about the *kind* of response to be given by the judge. For example, we have used such responses as "same" or "different," "manic" or "catatonic," and "more" and "less" pink. If the response domain is clearly ordinal in nature, dimensional processes are more likely to operate in judgment. That is, a clinician may be asked to classify eight clients in terms of severity of emotional disturbance. With such a task, the judge must discriminate among the clients along a common response dimension, a process we call articulation. On the other hand, the judge may be asked to assign eight clients to eight different diagnostic categories. If we assume that each category has a unique set of defining attributes, it would seem likely that a categorical matching process would be involved in judgment. That is, criterial attributes of the various diagnostic categories would be matched against the attributes of each case in order to achieve the best fit between input and output. However, as in the case of stimuli discussed in the preceding section, the relative uniqueness of the defining attributes among the response categories is of possible importance. If one or more attribute dimensions are shared among the several response alternatives, the judge must either ignore this confounding common element or articulate degrees of difference of this attribute dimension among the response classes. In this latter instance, what might have been a categorical judgment process evolves into one with dimensional characteristics.

A number of factors could influence this transition or shift from a categorical to a dimensional basis in clinical judgment. One of these is the *comparative* basis of many judgments. Even in the case of the method of single stimulus presentation, as in the absolute judgment situation, it has long been recognized that an adequate theory must account for the comparative phenomena that have been observed. One clear example of this is the influence of various "anchor" stimuli which, although perhaps not actually present during a single stimulus presentation, can affect the judgment of that stimulus. We shall have more to say about these anchoring phenomena in clinical and social judgment in subsequent chapters. For the present it is sufficient to recognize that such comparative phenomena imply judgmental distinctions of *more* or *less,* i.e., some variable position on a dimension of judgment.

Another facter which could shift a judgment from a categorical-matching to a dimensional basis involves what we have previously referred to as conceptual "chunking" in the face of an overload of the cognitive system. The exact conditions which facilitate this grouping or consolidation of information in clinical and social judgment remain to be explicated and studied. However, we shall consider one factor—the possible limitations of the judge himself as a processor of information. Another factor which we shall discuss in later chapters is the built-in correlation among the various diagnostic response classes commonly used in clinical judgment. Whatever the factors may be, some suggestive evidence (Miller and Bieri, 1963) has been found which indicates that experienced clinicians, given the discrete classifications of standard psychiatric nosology, may resort to some underlying dimensional basis in discriminating among cases. A prime example of this underlying dimension of judgment is the continuum of maladjustment or degree of pathology. It is of interest in this regard that Menninger (1963) has recently criticized the value of standard psychiatric nosology and has advanced a classification of his own which appears to be a dimension of pathology, ranging as it does across five categories from least to most disturbed: "nervousness," "neurotic," "social acting-out," "psychotic," and "severely disturbed."

A final consideration on the response side concerns how the task presented to the judge may induce a particular *set*. That is, a recognition or identification task may invoke a categorical process in that the judge, in responding to the instructions (often implicit) "What is it?", is set to identify exemplary attributes of the noun category he is seeking. On the other hand, if the task is more one of *discrimination* among stimuli ("In what respect do the stimuli differ from one another?"), it is possible that the judge is set to articulate differences among the stimuli in terms of their varying values on a common attribute dimension. Such response sets, as we have suggested, are generated not only by specific task demands, such as the nature of the stimuli and the instructions to the judge, but are probably also importantly influenced by aspects of the social setting within which judgment occurs. These situational factors will be analyzed in detail in Chapter 8.

DIMENSIONAL AND CATEGORICAL PROCESSES IN CLINICAL JUDGMENT

For the moment, let us assume that the judgment classifications of clinical diagnosis are nominal in nature, such that the clinician's task is to determine which of the classifications in his diagnostic repertoire the attributes of the client match best. The first stage of the judgment process, then, once information is available (from whatever source), is to determine the presence or absence of potentially relevant attributes. Such judgments are likely to be dimensional in character. Let us take the attribute of interpersonal aversiveness as an example. The clinician determines if a particular client meets such a criterion essentially in the same manner, it would seem, as the subject in a psychophysical experiment determines if a light is "bright" or "dim." That is, the determination of interpersonal aversiveness is a *magnitude* estimation along a dimension which might range from very slight or no withdrawal tendencies to extreme withdrawal tendencies. The question which faces the clinician in judging this attribute is whether the level or intensity of the client's withdrawal tendencies is sufficiently *great* to warrant the designation of interpersonal aversiveness. We assume that the clinician is able to make a certain finite number of discriminations in his articulation of the dimension of withdrawal. The exact number of these reliable discriminations at times may not exceed three or four, but this problem will be analyzed in more detail in the next two chapters.

For the present, returning to our analogy of the judgment of the intensity of a light, we may attempt to specify those factors which determine if the light will be judged as "very bright," "bright," "moderate," or "dim." One important factor may be the *range* of the previous experience of the judge with lights of varying intensities of brightness. That is, we would have to know how extreme a range of prior stimulation the judge has experienced in his judgments of varying brightnesses. The effect of range is partially attributable to the operation of extreme stimuli as "anchors" or comparison stimuli, a problem we shall analyze in Chapters 5 and 6. Suffice it to say here that if the anchor with which a given stimulus is compared is less extreme for one judge than for another, we might expect systematic differences in their judgments of that stimulus. Because the clinician may be working in a setting with rather circumscribed kinds of cases, the range problem would appear to be particularly relevant as a factor in clinical judgment.

A second related factor which could influence the judgment of the brightness of the light is the *distribution* of prior judgments of brightness within the range experienced by the judge. One way in which these distribution effects have been conceptualized is in terms of the *adaptation level* they produce (Helson, 1964). As we shall note in Chapter 5, the exact metric for determining the adaptation level is the subject of some disagreement (e.g., Parducci, 1963). We may define it, however, as an implicit neutral or zero point on a dimension in relation to which a particular stimulus will be judged as bright or dim, for example. Again, considering the possible differences in the kinds of clients seen among clinicians, we would assume that distribution effects would be operative in their judgments. Indeed, Block (1964) has discussed in detail applications of adaptation-level theory to particular aspects of clinical practice.

We may finally note that *individual differences* in ability to discriminate levels of brightness may influence the judgment of the light. Given equivalent prior experience both in terms of the range and of the distribution of lights judged, two judges may so differ in their ability to articulate intervals along the brightness dimension that one judge could discriminate four intervals reliably while the other could discriminate eight intervals reliably. Notice that we are discussing how one light is judged at a time, as in absolute judgment, rather than how simultaneously presented lights are discriminated. This focus on absolute judgment in the present book reflects our belief that many if not most clinical judgments involve the judgment of a single client at a time. Although many practical considerations in the working situation of the clinician foster such an individualized approach to each client, we should also note that clinicians in psychology, psychiatry, and social work are often influenced by an approach to the client which emphasizes his "unique," individual personality structure. Such an idiographic emphasis, of course, does not vitiate the operation of more normative influences in judgment of the type we have been considering, but works on a "silent" level beyond the immediate awareness of the clinician as he attempts to particularize a given judgment about a client.

If we now return to the question of the interpersonal aversiveness of the client, we can say that the clinician is faced with judging the relative degree of withdrawal manifested in the client's behavior, and that this judgment will be influenced by the range and distribution of prior withdrawal behavior judged by the clinician, as well as by his ability to articulate levels of withdrawal on the aversiveness dimension. Now it could be argued that even in the matter of determining the presence or absence of a behavioral attribute such as interpersonal aversiveness, the judge is engaging in a categorical process in that he may have a set of implicitly defining attributes for such a dimension. Although this possibility cannot be denied, especially if the relevant attribute such as withdrawal is relatively multidimensional in nature, our assumption is that the judge may use a categorical matching process to establish the presence or absence of a dimension (e.g., this is withdrawal behavior and not dependency), but that the judgment of intensity along this attribute dimension is dimensional in nature.

Diagnosis and Dimensionality

We began this chapter with a consideration of categorical and dimensional phenomena in relation to the judgment of clinical diagnosis. As we noted in relation to Sullivan's skeptical analysis concerning the diagnostic criteria for schizophrenia, any given clinical category may evolve into subcategories which have a dimensional quality, such as the process-reactive continuum. It must be pointed out, however, that the evolution of subcategories from a superordinate category such as schizophrenia does not *ipso facto* involve a transition from categorical to dimensional judgment. Indeed, the subcategories may in time become new general classes within which further discrimination may take place. However, several considerations suggest that the judge may invoke dimensional attributes in evolving these subclasses. First, a dimension provides a common framework within which to construe the relations among different subclasses. We often note that some common element binds the subclass together; for example, although we may speak of a pseudoneurotic schizophrenia or a deteriorated schizophrenic, the generic class "schizophrenic" is retained. This suggests that a dimension of degree of schizophrenia may evolve ranging from slight schizophrenic tendencies ("schizoid") to extreme schizophrenic behavior ("deteriorated" or "burned out"). A related possibility is that once these subclasses have been formed, the judge may order them along a more general dimension which is not necessarily involved in the original classification of schizophrenia. In particular, this dimension could be one of pathology or maladjustment, such that the various subclasses would be ordered in terms of severity of illness or pathology.

Note that although the subclasses of schizophrenia may be ordered in terms of a dimension of degree of schizophrenia, these subclasses may represent different combinations of the criterial attributes of the larger set of schizophrenia. Such combinations would presumably differ in terms of their *number* and their *kind* of attributes. However, the functional utility of such categorical definitions of subclasses must be related to the cognitive economy of the individual judge in terms of the ease with which he can deal with both the unique configurations of sets of attributes and the subclasses which these sets represent. That is, it may be less of a cognitive strain to judge a patient in terms of an underlying dimension than to juggle conceptually a series of classes which have different combinations of attributes sampled from a common set.

Perhaps the closest analogue to this problem of the dimensional and categorical nature of clinical judgments is to be found in the field of somatotyping. While at one time the relatively discrete, nominal nature of body types was emphasized, more recent work like that of Sheldon has emphasized the essential continuity between one type and the next. Each person's body build may be considered to be defined by different values on each of three presumably independent dimensions. Although we abstract a category for each configuration of values, the "pure" ectomorph exists more as an ideal category and masks the essential continuity among the "mixed" types.

THE ROLE OF THEORY IN CLINICAL JUDGMENT

This analysis of the judgment process has centered on dimensional and categorical processes by means of the systematic consideration of stimulus and response factors. It is apparent that such an analysis emphasizes the similarities among the clinical, social, and physical judgment realms. There are, however, exceptional considerations that impinge upon the clinical judgment situation which merit some discussion. It is perhaps with respect to the potential impact of clinical theory that clinical judgment differs most from judgments in the physical and social domains. The clinical psychologist (certainly in his university training as a psychologist) aspires to learn about the systematic relations among the phenomena he studies, relations which we can subsume under the general rubric of "theory." It is the belief of the neophyte clinician (and his mentors) that these "laws" of behavior, however crudely formulated and substantiated, can appreciably influence the nature of his clinical judgments and thus of his clinical practice. This is not the place to engage in a detailed consideration of whether in fact theories of behavior such as psychoanalysis *do* form the basis for most clinical judgments. In general, we would probably agree with Meehl that the various theories of personality drilled into students during their graduate careers may have little relevance to the more implicit "clinical" theories used in the workaday world of clinical practice. However, whether the clinician is using an explicitly formulated theory of behavior in his approach to the clinical judgment situation, or whether he is using a more implicit, less highly formulated theory, such a conceptual structure can serve several functions.

On the input side, the clinical theory of the judge serves to highlight the distinctiveness of the attributes available in the stimulus to be judged. That is, the theory serves an *orienting* function and acts to reduce to a more manageable size the potential number of cues contained in the stimulus configuration. This economical function of the clinical theory in judgment probably operates through some sort of scanning mechanism in which the relevant attributes or dimensions of the stimulus can be separated from those which are irrelevant or redundant. The search for relevant input can be impeded or facilitated by the clinician in various ways. Such factors in his training as his level of theoretical sophistication, his level of experience, as well as the nature of his experience, may affect his ability to discriminate the relevant stimulus dimensions in the input.

Having served as an aid in the search for relevant stimulus dimensions, the clinical theory of the judge can also serve an *organizing* function in the utilization of these relevant attributes. In particular, the theory may help to determine which cues belong together and what the relative hierarchical ordering or weight of each dimension should be. This type of organizing role of clinical theory is probably most explicitly studied in research which analyzes how cues may be combined to form an overall judgment. Sometimes this kind of approach centers on a probabilistic associationism, in which the response which is chosen is presumed to be selected on the basis of a pooling of probability values for each cue in the stimulus complex (Mahrer and Young, 1961). A related approach is the multiple regression analogy in which optimal weights are attached to each cue in predicting a criterion response (Hammond, Hursch, and Todd, 1964).

Finally, on the output side, the clinician's theory may aid the judgment process by providing the possibility for new judgment categories. As clinical theories become more explicit, and perhaps as the individual clinician evolves and elaborates his own systematic understanding of his work, new categories of judgment are formulated. As we indicated above, this kind of categorical expansion due to the development of clinical theory can perhaps be observed in relation to the problem of schizophrenia.

RÉSUMÉ

In this chapter we have discussed two possible approaches to the judgment process—the categorical and the dimensional. The former viewpoint emphasizes judgment occurring through a process of matching discrete stimulus attributes with an "ideal" stimulus in order to achieve the best fit between input and output. Dimensional processes of judgment, in comparison, are invoked when magnitude judgments of stimuli along an intensity continuum are called for. Although the issue of the exact form of the interaction between categorical and dimensional approaches is deemed important for such basic psychological problems as the relation of perception to concept formation, our position is to emphasize the joint occurrence of both processes in clinical and social judgment. A specification of both stimulus and response factors in judgment in terms of *dimensional* properties leads to a clarification of possible relations of categorical and dimensional processes in judgment. In addition, we have discussed the possible importance of theories of personality is clinical judgment, even though their influence may be less than is commonly thought.

Having presented such a background in some of the psychological issues which have molded our concept of judgment, we turn next to a detailed consideration of information theory as one approach to the analysis of judgment which holds promise of subsuming both categorical and dimensional approaches.

chapter 3 INFORMATIONAL ANALYSIS OF CLINICAL JUDGMENT

INTRODUCTION

In our analysis of the clinical judgment situation, we have turned to information theory as a potential source of methods and concepts to guide our theoretical understanding. However, it should be pointed out that at present any *one* mathematical model cannot be used to study the judgment process in its entirety. Rather, mathematical models are being used to ask particular questions about the different aspects of the judgment process. One mathematical system may be appropriate for asking some kinds of questions but not others. Before considering in detail the application of information theory to clinical and social judgment in this and in the following chapter, let us consider briefly some assumptions underlying the use of mathematical models of judgment.

According to Torgerson (1958), there are two general classes of mathematical approaches that have been used to study judgment: (1) deterministic models and (2) probabilistic models. In deterministic models no provision for unsystematic or error variance is made. All the variation in responses is attributed to the variation in judges and stimuli. On the other hand, probabilistic models have built into them provisions for studying error variance as well as judge and stimulus variation in responses. With probabilistic models, statistical criteria of goodness of fit of the model to empirical data can be developed, whereas with deterministic models there is only an ideal approximation to empirical data.

Since a basic assumption in probabilistic models is that judgment behavior *is* probabilistic, much of the experimental procedure includes a design in which the experimenter and the judges have some notions of what the available alternatives are. Luce (1959) points out that all theories of choice behavior assume that there is a "mathematically well-defined set, the elements of which can be identified with the choice alternatives." The basic question is, "What is an alternative?" Unfortunately, it is difficult to conceptualize systematically the specification of alternatives, especially in the domain of clinical judgment with which we are concerned, and, as Luce indicates, this limitation of all theories of choice behavior at present makes their application difficult. However, within the limitations of the experimental delineation of stimulus and response alternatives, certain questions can be pursued in studying judgment. If we delimit the focus of attention, for simplicity, to stimulus variables and response alternatives, at least three aspects of judgment can be studied: (1) the combinations of stimuli to form a judgment; (2) the study of preferences for response alternatives; and (3) the relations between stimuli and responses. For each of these three aspects of judgment, different mathematical models have been constructed and have led to different kinds of questions. Let us consider some possible models that have been used for each of these judgment aspects.

In order to study the ways in which different stimuli are combined in arriving at a judgment, various models have been proposed. A typical model here is the *actuarial* model in which an attempt is made to derive a prediction of a particular outcome by combining various stimuli in an additive manner. Thus multiple correlational techniques are used to study the combinations of stimulus material that are most predictive of a given outcome. The concern with this particular model is to determine what variables out of a given set of variables should be combined with what weightings in order to make a judgment. For example, judges making predictions about whether or not a delinquent will recidivate may weigh various combinations of variables such as "severity of offense" and "age of offender" in order to arrive at their decisions. Clinical judgments of diagnosis based on patterns of MMPI scores can also be conceptualized in this manner. Representative of this approach is the research of Meehl (1959) and of Hammond, Hursch, and Todd (1964).

Another variant of this approach in the social perception area is exemplified by the work of Wishner (1960). By considering the intercorrelations among traits that form a stimulus complex, it was shown that accurate predictions could be made concerning the different impressions of personality which would be formed. With such actuarial approaches, the characteristics of the data must be such that they satisfy the conditions for using multiple correlational techniques. In addition, this particular model focuses on stimulus combinations but it tends to be less concerned with a study of the relations between response alternatives.

If one is interested in analyzing the aspect of judgment that is centered on preferential behavior among a series of alternatives, one might apply the mathematical formulations of Restle (1961) which we discussed in the previous chapter. In his set-theoretic approach, Restle restricts his mathematical analysis to a consideration of the choice between two alternatives, for he reasons that any set of alternatives can be analyzed repeatedly by two choices at a time. In order to make a choice between two response alternatives he assumes that there is an ideal situation for each alternative. If the set of elements in a response alternative matches an ideal situation, that alternative will be chosen. With Restle's system it is possible to study the relations of various alternatives to one another. However, as we have seen, the inherent limitation of this system resides in the way in which elements of a set can be defined and in the relations of the elements of a set to one another. It is difficult to match the elements of an ideal set to a set of elements in a particular response unless one can specify the nature of the elements in a set. The frequency of occurrence of one response alternative to another, however, can be studied in Restle's system. Furthermore, the response alternatives have only to be of a *nominal* order, i.e., the response categories need only be mutually exclusive and exhaustive.

A third consideration in studying aspects of the judgment process may focus on the relations between stimuli and responses under specified experimental conditions. Information theory represents such an approach. As in the other mathematical systems discussed, a basic empirical problem of information theory is in specifying a mathematically well-defined set of stimuli that can be identified with the choice alternatives. Attneave (1959) indicates that information theory assumes a stochastic process, i.e., one in which probability laws are applicable to a sequence of symbols. If the probability laws which characterize a stochastic process remain constant for all parts of a sequence of symbols, the process is said to be ergodic. Since ergodicity is usually necessary for the application of much of information theory, mathematicians have been concerned with rigorously proving the existence of ergodic properties. What this means is that the set of probabilities for assigning a set of stimuli uniquely to a set of response alternatives must remain constant as the stimuli are repeated. Information theory is consequently an inappropriate model for studying judgment as a learning phenomenon. However, the use of information theory can lead an investigator of the judgment process to ask questions concerning the nature of the relations between the specified stimulus and response conditions in an experiment in order to determine, for example, the relative efficiency of a clinician in processing information. As we shall see, a unique feature of information theory is that it provides a way for quantifying the amounts of information in the stimulus and response alternatives as well as the amount of information shared by stimuli and responses. It is to be emphasized that information concepts are not meaningful unless there is a definite set of possible alternatives available to the judge. While such a restriction makes it possible to quantify information, it also places constraints upon the types of clinical judgments which may be studied, excluding for example the more "free-floating" or open-ended judgments that we discussed in Chapter 1. However, as we shall see, in spite of these restrictions a wide range of clinical judgments can be approached within the information-theory model.

THE INFORMATION-THEORY MODEL

One fundamental issue to which this book addresses itself is the process by which the clinician translates the "raw" stimuli he receives from a client into one of many different kinds of responses, which we can call a clinical judgment, a judgment about what the clinician perceives that in some way explicates or describes or identifies the nature of the stimulus that confronted him. The judgment process can be conceptualized, then, as an act of *transmitting stimulus information.*

This elementary conception of the judgment process can be diagrammed as follows:

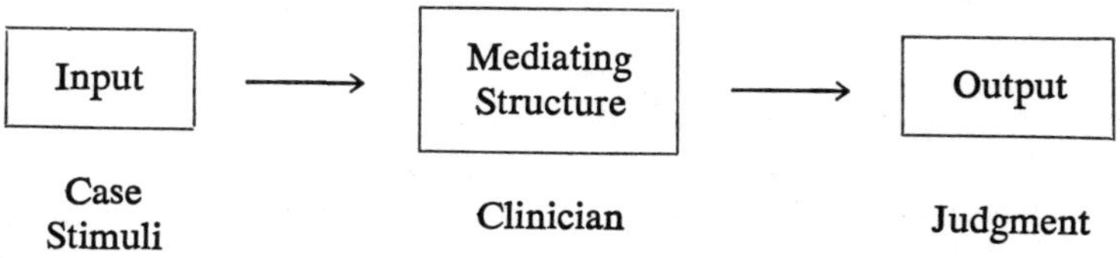

In some ultimate and fundamental sense, the precise nature of the mediating structure will probably be understood within the context of the physics, chemistry, and physiology of the brain and the central nervous system. It is clear, however, that psychological investigations can yield an understanding of the mediating structure at another level of abstraction and inference by means of treating it as a "black box." Such inquiries can never hope to examine directly the inner workings of the mediating structure. The inputs, to a certain extent, are observable; the outputs are also observable, but the mechanism of the mediating structure itself remains inaccessible to direct observation. Nevertheless, if we can describe in some systematic fashion the nature of the input, as well as that of the output, we can examine the transformation which occurs from the former to the latter and we can infer from this transformation something about the nature of the mediating process itself.

The purpose of this chapter is twofold: to discuss the nature of a mathematical and statistical model that permits the quantification of inputs and outputs, and to demonstrate how this model can provide a novel point of departure for examining the judgment situation and can generate new concepts and hypotheses about the process. This model goes by the name of *information theory*. It is our intent to present neither a detailed account of the historical development of information theory nor a proof of the formal mathematical theorems that underpin the theory, nor even a detailed account of the methodological application of information theory to psychological research. For such accounts the reader is referred elsewhere.*

Wiener, in his classic book (1948), first brought to popular attention the notion that information was a measurable commodity. Shortly after the appearance of this work, Shannon published his basic paper on the mathematical theory of communication (1948). Here, for the first time, the *amount* of information contained in a message ensemble was defined mathematically. The word "amount" is of extreme importance. In the traditional, engineering sense it bears no relation to the value, meaning, purpose, or kind of information in the ensemble. Thus the reader should note that our use of the word information will be related to this notion of *amount* rather than to the more common use of the word. G. Miller (1953) aptly cautioned us about this very technical definition of "information":

> Most of the careless claims for the importance of information theory arise from overly free association to the word "information." This term occurs in the theory in a careful and particular way. It is not synonymous with "meaning." Only the *amount* of information is measured—the amount does not specify the content, value, truthfulness, exclusiveness, history, or purpose of the information. The definition does not exclude other definitions and cer-

* See especially the classic paper by Shannon (1948), who was the prime developer of the theory, and Khinchin (1957), who worked out some of the undiscovered proofs. Attneave provides a rather detailed and lucid discussion of the applications of information theory to psychology, and it is strongly urged that his book (1959) be carefully examined. Garner's work (1962) not only includes a very thorough discussion of the statistical properties of the information measures and an extensive review of empirical research using the informational methodology, but also introduces some most creative and novel psychological concepts that stem from information theory. Other good sources for obtaining a background in this area are Luce (1961) and G. Miller (1956).

tainly does not include all the meanings implied by the colloquial usages of the word. (p. 3.)

Information theory is very much concerned with events that could have occurred but did not. Consider the task of a person who must make a choice between one or two objects as opposed to that of the same person who must choose one object among one thousand objects. All else being equal, it is clear that in the former instance the individual in question is faced with an easier problem than in the latter instance. The latter individual, once the choice has been made, has received more information about the object or the array of objects when there were a thousand alternatives confronting him than when there were only two alternatives. In this sense, information removes uncertainty. There is considerably more uncertainty in predicting which one of a thousand alternatives will be selected than in predicting which one of two will be selected. Thus uncertainty and information are interchangeable commodities; the amount of information in an event is exactly equal to the amount of uncertainty residing in that event before its occurrence, and this uncertainty, in turn, is a direct function of the number of possible events that could have occurred.

The application of this notion of information is quite straightforward and logical in communications engineering. It is of utmost importance, therefore, to know how much information there may be in an array of message symbols that are to be sent through a channel, for the design of the channel will, in part, be a function of this amount. (Another function will be the desired fidelity of the channel in transmitting the message sequence, and, as we shall see, this notion of transmitted information will be of considerable importance to us.) If the message ensemble consists of a series of letters of the English alphabet, the amount of information in any given letter is determined by the twenty-six alternative letters that can potentially be sent and by their probability of occurrence.

It is conventional to use the *bit* as the metric that defines a unit of information. The bit, which is a condensation of the phrase binary digit, is simply one binary choice or selection. An event that reduces the number of alternatives available by one-half would have exactly one bit of information in it. There is the same amount of information, then, in an occurrence that reduces one hundred events to fifty as there is in an occurrence that reduces four events to two. Every time the number of alternatives is reduced by one-half, one bit of information is gained. Conversely, every time the number of alternatives is doubled, the uncertainty in the array of alternatives is increased by one bit. The definition of the bit is rather arbitrary—it is a useful convention that the unit for quantity of information be expressed as a logarithmic function to the base 2.*

The amount of information, then, in an array of symbols is the logarithm, to the base 2, of the number of alternative symbols in the array—*provided that they occur with equal probability*. If the symbols occur with unequal probability, the amount of information is determined by the Shannon formula:

$$H = -\sum^{i} p_i \log_2 p_i \qquad (1)$$

where H stands for the Shannon measure of information and is a function of the probability of occurrence of each ith alternative. Since most of the data in psychological research occurs in the form of relative frequencies rather than as a priori probabilities, it is convenient to have a formula geared to such relative frequencies. Thus, by substituting $(n_i)/N$ for p_i in the equation above, the Shannon measure of information can be defined as

$$H = \log_2 N - \frac{1}{N}\sum^{i} n_i \log_2 n_i \qquad (2)$$

where N is the total number of symbols in the message array and n_i is the frequency of each specific ith occurrence.

Since we shall be discussing psychological issues and data drawn from psychological research for the remainder of this chapter, it is appropriate at this time to discard our use of the terms message, ensembles, and symbol occurrences and to begin to use the language of stimulus and response. Having made this rather abrupt shift in orientation and language usage, we can proceed with our discussion of the properties of information.

Consider now an experiment in which we deal with a series of stimuli and a series of responses. The stimuli (X) carry values of x from x_1 through x_i to x_n, and the responses (Y) carry values of y from y_1 through y_j to y_n. It is possible to determine the amount of information in the stimuli as follows:

$$H_x = \log_2 N - \frac{1}{N}\sum^{i} n_i \log_2 n_i \qquad (3)$$

where H_x is the amount of information in the stimuli.

* However, in some engineering instances it is more convenient to use a unit expressed in logarithms to the base 10, in which case the metric is called a *Hartley*, named in recognition of the early pioneering work of R. V. L. Hartley (1928), on information transmission.

The amount of information in the responses is determined in a similar manner, this time considering the array of response alternatives:

$$H_y = \log_2 N - \frac{1}{N}\sum^{j} n_j \log_2 n_j \tag{4}$$

The amount of information in the joint occurrences of stimuli and responses—the equivalent of the information located in the total stimulus-response system—can be computed. Again, the computation is familiar:

$$H_{xy} = \log_2 N - \frac{1}{N}\sum^{i}\sum^{j} n_{ij} \log_2 n_{ij} \tag{5}$$

where H_{xy} is the amount of information in the total system. If the amount of information in the stimulus array and the amount of information in the responses were completely independent of each other, we would expect that $H_x + H_y = H_{xy}$. To the extent that this identity does not hold, we have a measure of the overlap, or relationship, or predictability between stimulus and response. This relationship, commonly referred to as the amount of transmitted information, is determined quite simply:

$$T_{x;y} = H_x + H_y - H_{xy} \tag{6}$$

where $T_{x;y}$ is the amount of transmitted information.

By means of such quantifications, then, we have a model which permits us to examine the amount of information in an input (H_x), the amount of information in an output (H_y), and the amount of information that is held in common by input and output ($T_{x;y}$). The ideal channel or, in our earlier language, the mediating structure that permits the most faithful transformation of input into output would be described by the following relationships:

$$T_{x;y} = H_x = H_y = H_{xy}$$

It is necessary for us to consider two additional informational measures, both derived from the functions we have already discussed. In the event that perfect transmission does not occur the "error" may be traced back to either the input or the output or both. Thus, if there is stimulus information that is uncertain when the response is known, i.e., stimuli that have no relation to the responses or, in the language of the communication engineers, when there is equivocation of transmission, uncertainty can be determined as follows:

$$H_y(x) = H_x - T_{x;y} \tag{7}$$

where $H_y(x)$ is stimulus equivocation. The amount of uncertainty in the responses when the stimuli are known, or the ambiguity of the responses, or the "noise" is determined by

$$H_x(y) = H_y - T_{x;y} \tag{8}$$

where $H_x(y)$ is response ambiguity.

Thus stimulus equivocation can be thought of as the amount of stimulus information that does not get through the channel—information that is somehow lost by the subject. Response ambiguity is best described as irrelevant responses—response information that has no relationship whatever to the stimulus.

The reader is again urged to examine Attneave's book (1959) with care for a more detailed and illustrated discussion of the relationship between these informational variables. It should be noted that an informational analysis is not restricted to the simple stimulus-response model. The three-variable analysis is of considerable interest (where X, again, may be the stimulus, Y the response, and Z may be either subjects, another stimulus, another response, and so on). Indeed, the analysis may handle n variables although the number of different informational functions that generate from analyses of additional variables increases at a horrifying pace (Quastler, 1955, p. 143).

McGill (1954, 1955) has ingeniously shown that the multivariate information analysis is isomorphic to an analysis of variance. An analysis of variance, however, requires that the criterion variable, at least, be of a metric nature. The informational analysis makes no such demand and requires only nominal data for any or all of the variables under consideration. Thus informational analysis has great generality but is a less powerful tool when dealing with ordinal data.

The resemblance between a bivariate and multivariate informational analysis and a correlation analysis will probably be apparent to the reader. The distinction between the two, however, is quite important. As Garner (1962) points out, a partial or multiple correlation yields measures of the *degree* of relatedness between variables while an informational analysis yields measures of the *amount* of relatedness. Thus two pairs of variables may have the same amount of association and yet differ in their degree of association. In Figure 1 such a contingency exists between the pair of variables A_1,B_1 and the pair A_2,B_2. Thus pair A_1B_1 and pair A_2B_2 have the same amount of association as reflected in the fact that the area of overlap in the two instances is identical, yet the degree of association between the two pairs is quite different. By the same token, two pairs of variables may have the same degree of association and yet differ in their amount of association, as illustrated in Figure 2. In this instance approximately 30 per

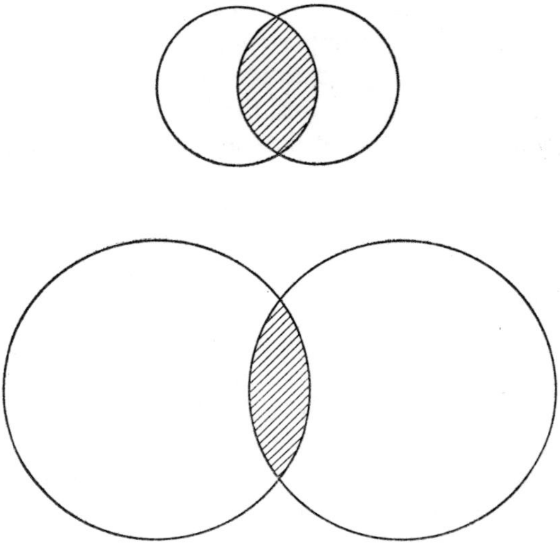

Figure 1.

cent of each variable is held in common with the other one of the pair yet the amounts are quite different, as is reflected in the absolute magnitude of the areas of overlap.

The preceding discussion treats information theory and its application to psychological research primarily in terms of a statistical methodology

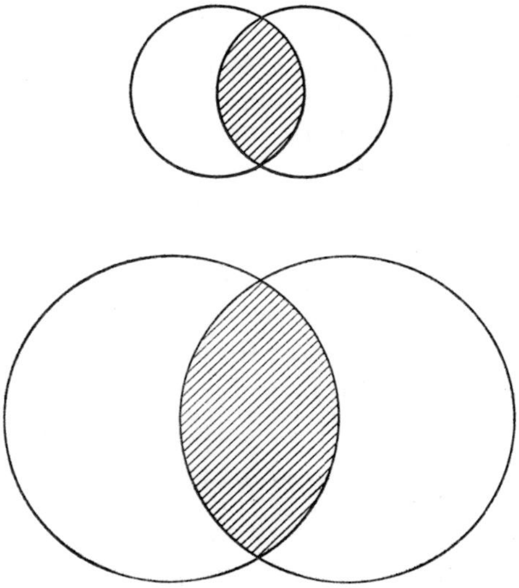

Figure 2.

for the analysis of data and the design of experiments. As such, information theory is of considerable importance. It provides a metric, the bit, which can be universally applied to almost all stimulus-response situations. As Berlyne (1957) points out, the informational analyses may be appropriately used in any kind of data analysis where a stimulus can be reasonably partitioned from a response. Moreover, the nature of the informational analysis is of an extremely general kind because of the nonparametric nature of the informational functions. The measure of transmitted information, $T_{x;y}$, can be transformed into chi square (Miller and Madow, 1954; McGill, 1954), and the extent to which two variables are related can then be tested for its significance.

Although the statistical properties of information theory are themselves worthy of considerable attention, it is likely that information theory will be of a more general interest to the behavioral sciences. Indeed, the book by Garner (1962) proposes that the amount of information in a stimulus array (or more precisely, the amount of uncertainty residing within the array) may be a determinant of the psychological meaning of those stimuli to an individual. Note that Garner's extension of the concepts of information theory leads back to the more colloquial definition on information, a rather marked departure from traditional usage in communications. In any event, Garner addresses himself to the meaning of meaning and proposes that uncertainty and structure (the nature or the form of that uncertainty) are crucial variables of meaning. Mention should also be made of new studies in the area of concept formation and the important place that information-theory concepts have in these studies (Archer, Bourne and Brown, 1955; Bourne and Haygood, 1959; Hunt, 1962; Walker and Bourne, 1961). Finally, the concept of channel capacity and its insightful application to studies in psychophysics should be noted, although we will discuss this notion in considerable detail in the following pages.

We are suggesting that information theory provides something more than a model for experimental design and a novel meta statistics for the analysis of data; it also provides new concepts, new points of view, and new insights into age-old psychological problems. It is of particular value in providing a point of departure for the investigation of the clinical judgment process, and it is to these issues that we now turn our attention.

INFORMATION TRANSMISSION AND CHANNEL CAPACITY

If we revert back to our original model of the judgment process in which the mediating structure has as one of its several functions the task of transforming inputs into outputs, it becomes clear that a very important attribute of this structure is its ability to discriminate among the array of stimuli that constitute the input. As we indicated earlier, the *process* of discrimination is not subject to direct scrutiny by means of the information theory model; however, the ability of the mediating structure to discriminate among the stimuli is subject to rather precise measurement. Consider the following problem: If we momentarily restrict ourselves to a discussion of unidimensional stimuli, we find a judge who is confronted with a series of such stimuli and whose task is to make some assignment of each stimulus to one of a series of available response classes. The assignment may be based upon a quantitative assessment of the stimulus or it may be based upon a qualitative assessment—the information theory model is essentially indifferent to these two kinds of activities.* Suppose, then, that a subject were presented with a series of auditory tones that varied along the dimension of pitch and his task was to make an assignment of each auditory stimulus to a category of pitch. Such an assignment would logically require a discrimination of a given stimulus from another in the series or from a standard tone (which may be implicit in the subject) or from an anchor (which, again, may be implicit). A very important question can be raised as to how many such discriminations can be made by the subject before he begins to confuse the tones.

There are at least two variables that are thought to have some pertinence to this question: (1) the number of stimuli in the series and (2) the nature of the response task. Thus it may be hypothesized that the ability of the subject to make discriminations among stimuli along a single dimension should increase as the number of stimuli to be judged increases. Clearly, the number of such stimuli will set an upper bound on discriminative capacity: if there are only two stimuli in the series, then only two discriminations can be made; if there are four stimuli, then only four discriminations can be made; if there are *n* stimuli, then only *n* discriminations can be made. Granted, then, that the number of stimuli in the series does place an upper bound upon discriminative capacity, is it true that a judge can make *n* discriminations among a series of *n* stimuli? Here again, the obvious answer would be "not necessarily." In order to reach the upper bound set by *n*, there should at least be the requirement that the stimuli in the series differ from one another by a *j*nd. Obviously, if there is no noticeable difference between each of the stimuli in

* The experimenter, however, may not be indifferent to these two distinct judgment functions. As has been pointed out by Cronbach (1955), the use of informational statistics may be inappropriate when the experimenter is fundamentally interested in the ordinal properties of the data. In such an instance the more conventional statistical and experimental procedures would be more powerful instruments for explicating these properties.

the series in regard to all of the rest, there can be no reasonable expectation that a subject will be able to make *n* discriminations.

Suppose, however, that all the stimuli in a series are separated from one another by at least a *j*nd. Would we expect discriminative capacity to be equal to the number of stimuli? It would seem that another prerequisite must exist in the experimental task; the response requirements of the subject must be sufficiently flexible to allow for the maximum number of potential discriminations. Clearly, if the subject is allowed only a dichotomous response, he can do no more than make two discriminations regardless of how large *n* is. A stimulus can be either an *A* or a *B*. If the response system is expanded to consist of *n* possible categories of response (equal to the number of stimuli), could we then expect a judge's discriminative capacity to show no limit other than *n?*

This, it would seem, is the acid test—a large series of stimuli along a unitary dimension, all separated from one another by at least one *j*nd, and the provision of a response system that allows for as many response classes as there are stimuli. There are, however, further considerations. From one point of view the "best" discriminator would be the subject who operates as some sort of a random machine. That is, as each stimulus comes up it is randomly assigned to one of the categories in the response reservoir. Thus if the series of stimuli is presented to the subject over and over again, the laws of probability would lead us to expect two things: (1) the random operator would use all the possible judgment categories, and (2) he would use each category almost equally often. It is no accident if the reader notes that the statistic H_y, discussed earlier, would be an ideal measure of this kind of discriminative ability. H_y takes into account two variables: both the number of categories used and the frequency with which each category is used. Terwilliger (1962) refers to this latter characteristic as *balance*. Thus the random operator would perform maximally in regard to both the number of categories used and the balance—the extent to which each category of response is used equally often.

There is something intuitively unsatisfactory about the claim that the random operator is the "best" discriminator. Although his responses indicate that he makes the maximum number of discriminations—that is, he places them into all the available response classes—and that he uses all response classes equally often, by what perverse logic can he be thought to be the "best" discriminator? What would seem to be needed is some index of his *reliability* in regard to the discriminations he makes. Thus we would want our "best" discriminator to be perfectly consistent in placing identical stimuli into the same response class. With this additional criterion, the random operator would fare badly. The probability that he would place a replicated stimulus in the same response category as its predecessor would be equal to the reciprocal of the number of categories available. The statistic H_{xy}, discussed earlier, gives us an index of reliability. To the extent that stimulus and response have a high probability of joint occurrence they are reliably associated with each other, and this will be reflected in the value of H_{xy}.*

What we have been discussing thus far in our elaboration of the notion of discriminative capacity are two aspects of the problem:

1. *Balanced variability*—the extent to which the stimuli are judged as being located in a number of different categories and the frequency with which these categories are used. This component is reflected in the statistic H_y.
2. *Reliability*—the extent to which the stimuli are judged consistently. This component is reflected in the statistic H_{xy}.

These two components of discriminative ability are embedded in the informational statistic, $T_{x;y}$. It will be recalled (Eq. 6) that $T_{x;y}$ is defined as:

$$T_{x;y} = H_x + H_y - H_{xy}$$

As was mentioned earlier, this statistic goes by the name of transmitted information. If we were interested in comparing the discriminative ability of two judges we would do well to design our experiment so that H_x, the amount of uncertainty in the stimulus, would be constant for both judges. Variations in $T_{x;y}$ could thus occur only as a consequence of the two components discussed above—balanced variability and reliability.

Implications of Psychophysical Research

Given these considerations, we can return to our original problem of discriminative capacity and to the question of whether or not this capacity is only limited by n_s, the number of discriminable stimuli in the series, and by n_r, the number of available response categories.

For certain kinds of unidimensional physical stimuli, the question has been answered empirically, and the details of these empirical findings will be discussed in the next chapter. Suffice it to say for the moment that the number of reliable discriminations which can be made for stimuli that vary along a single dimension *does not* increase linearly as the number of stimuli increases. The prototype of the curves generated in psychophysical studies is illustrated in Figure 3. The general form of the

* The absolute magnitude of H_{xy} varies inversely with the joint occurrence of stimulus and response. As reliability increases, H_{xy} decreases in size.

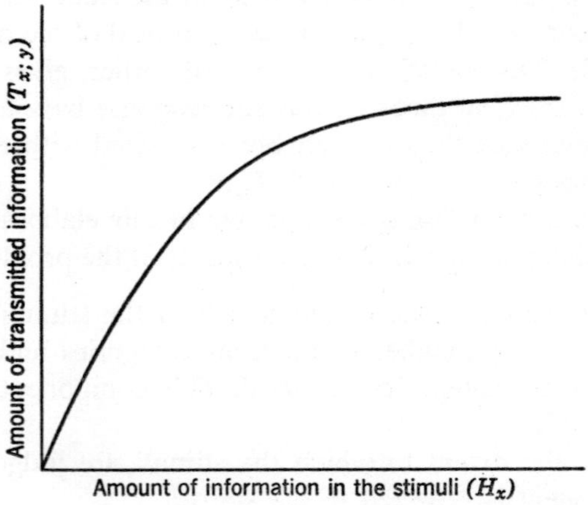

Figure 3.

curve is generated under conditions in which the number of response categories is set equal to the number of stimuli, as well as under conditions in which the number of response categories is smaller. For unidimensional stimuli, it has been established that the value of the asymptote is approximately 2.5 to 3.2 bits—for a wide range of different stimulus dimensions (G. Miller, 1956). This is roughly equivalent to a range between five and nine discrete discriminations.

To be clear in our terminology, $T_{x;y}$ (transmitted information) is a value obtained for a *specific* number of stimuli and a specific number of response alternatives. As the number of stimuli (H_x) to be judged is increased over a series of experiments, the point at which the transmitted-information curve reaches an asymptote is referred to as the *channel capacity* of the subject. Channel capacity is a psychological concept that refers to the capacity of a subject to discriminate in a reliable and consistent manner among stimuli that are drawn from and range across a single dimension. It is explicit in the notion of channel capacity that this discriminative ability cannot be increased either by adding more stimuli to the series or by adding more response categories, over and above a certain minimum number, to the response task. It is of extreme importance to note that within the context of the notion of channel capacity, discrimination is very specifically defined; it refers to the subject's ability to make different categorical assignments of the stimuli and to do this with reliability or consistency. Note also that the concept does not concern itself with the accuracy or validity of the responses. A subject's responses may be completely "wrong" when measured against some external criterion, but this is irrelevant to the notion of channel capacity as discussed above.

In anticipation of subsequent discussion, we are making a distinction between two classes of variables that may have an effect on variations in information transmission. *Task variables* are seen as variations in the nature of the judgment task itself; manifestation of domains of stimuli and responses, amount of information in the input, etc., may be included in this class. *Subject variables,* on the other hand, refer to variation among judges and may include such things as their personality and cognitive characteristics. A subject may vary in his ability to transmit information over a variety of judgment tasks, and a group of subjects may vary in their individual information transmitting abilities within a given experimental task.

INFORMATION TRANSMISSION IN REGARD TO DIFFERENT KINDS OF JUDGMENT TASKS

From the foregoing considerations it is clear that the concepts of information transmission and channel capacity are only pertinent to the so-called absolute judgment task, yet this is by no means the only kind of discriminative task with which people are confronted either in real life situations or under experimental conditions. Consider the rank-ordering task. It is apparent that if a subject were presented with a series of stimuli and were asked to rank order them along an intensity dimension, he would, in effect, be forced to make the maximum number of discriminations. The subject would have no choice but to assign one, and only one, stimulus to a category of rank and he would have to use all the categories of rank. Within the statistical argument presented earlier, a subject's H_y under these conditions would be maximal and invariant. True, if he were asked to replicate the rank-ordering task his reliability, as reflected in H_{xy}, would not be constrained by the experimental method—but then we concern ourselves only with this one aspect of his "discriminative" ability. The rank-ordering task may be of extreme methodological and substantive interest, but we maintain that it is not directly relevant itself to discriminative ability within the context of information transmission.

By the same token, a paired-comparison task forces a subject to make discriminations between stimuli. Confronted with two stimuli, the judge is asked to determine which of the two stimuli has more or less of a specified attribute. Whether or not the stimuli are subjectively discriminable, the subject is constrained to make a choice. On the basis of judgments of all pairs of stimuli in the array, the stimuli are then ranked—leading once more to a maximum H_y. Again, it should be noted that the task of paired comparisons may be quite important for certain methodological purposes and for certain substantive inquiries but has little relevance to the notion of transmitted information as previously defined.

It is in the absolute-judgment situation where the concepts of information transmission and channel capacity have the most direct relevance. A stimulus is presented—a categorical judgment is called for. Another stimulus is presented—another judgment is called for. And so on, through the entire series of stimuli. Under these conditions of judgment, the subject is not compelled by the experimental task to use all available response categories, nor does he have an opportunity to directly compare stimuli in the series. No two stimuli ever appear simultaneously in the perceptual field. Now it may be argued with considerable justification that there is never really any such thing as a *pure* absolute-judgment situation, that there is always some implicit standard or anchor available to the judge. Nonetheless, it would seem that the so-called absolute-judgment task is as close as we can get to the kind of experimental procedure that would bear most directly on the notion of channel capacity.

Furthermore, we would argue that the absolute-judgment task most closely approximates the condition of judgment that most often occurs in the clinical situation. Since an essential theme of this book is concerned with clinical judgment, it is important that special note be made of the logical similarity between the absolute-judgment situation and the clinical situation. In clinical practice judgments are invariably made on the basis of case stimuli that appear sequentially. A rank-ordering task or a paired-comparison task does not approximate what usually occurs in the day-to-day events of clinical practice. More will be made of this later. For the moment it is sufficient to note that the absolute-judgment task is the one that has most immediate relevance to the daily circumstances of clinical judgment—indeed of almost all kinds of social judgment.

The Range of the Stimulus Materials and Its Relation to Information Transmission

An important consideration may be raised at this point in regard to the range of stimuli and its effect upon discriminability. It would appear to be intuitively obvious that the discriminability inherent in an array of stimuli would be, in part, a function of the range of the sensory continuum from which the stimuli are drawn. Thus we would expect that a series of auditory stimuli drawn from the range of 100 to 500 cps would be less easily discriminated in terms of pitch then a series of the same number of stimuli drawn from the range of 100 to 8000 cps. (In both instances, we will assume that the stimuli are equally spaced on a log scale along the continuum, and that in any case they are separated from one another by at least a *j*nd.) The empirical data that relate to this issue will be presented in the following chapter. For the moment we may note that the evidence is, to a certain extent, equivocal, but there is reason to believe that within the domain of physical stimuli the effect of increasing the range of the sampled stimuli on channel capacity is rather slight.

The illustration of tone discrimination cited above was actually drawn from an experiment by Pollack (1952). His findings are neatly summarized by Attneave (1959) as follows:

> . . . the subjects' behavior suggested that they had about five pigeonholes into which they could sort tones by pitch, and that these same pigeonholes (but no more) could be freely rearranged along the pitch continuum to accommodate almost any distribution of stimuli. (p. 69)

This, indeed, is a rather remarkable finding which lends support to the concept of channel capacity as a theoretical construct useful for an understanding of discriminative behavior.

The above considerations concerning range may be applicable only to the discrimination of physical stimuli. Some tentative evidence that range is an important variable in the discrimination of behavioral stimuli will be presented subsequently.

INFORMATION TRANSMISSION AND STIMULUS DIMENSIONALITY

It should be kept firmly in mind that thus far our discussion of information transmission and channel capacity has been relegated strictly to *unidimensional* stimuli, that is, stimuli that vary along one attribute. The isolation of a relatively pure dimension in regard to physical stimuli is a comparatively easy task. Thus, if our interest is in the channel capacity of an individual judge for the attribute of loudness of tones, stimuli would be generated that varied *solely* in regard to decibel count. Other potential attributes of a series of tones, such as pitch, timbre, intervals between presentation, and length of presentation, would all be held constant and invariant.

We have noted that the concept of information transmission has been invoked in regard to discrimination within a unitary stimulus dimension. We may very well ask what happens to discriminative ability when multidimensional stimuli are involved, since clinical and social stimuli are probably of this sort.

This question has been explored in some detail in psychophysical research, and a beginning, tentative understanding has been achieved, although there has been relatively little systematic work on this problem within the realm of social and behavioral judgment situations. A brief survey of the empirical findings in regard to this issue will be found in the following chapter. For the present, we may note that within the realm of physical stimuli discriminative ability does increase as the dimensionality of the stimulus to be judged increases. However, the following considerations are important:

1. The increase in information transmission is not additive. That is, if the $T_{x;y}$ for dimension *A* is 2.00 bits, and the $T_{x;y}$ for dimension *B* is 2.00 bits, the information transmission for the compound stimulus dimension, *AB,* will not be 4.00 bits but closer to 3.00 bits.
2. The increase in $T_{x;y}$ for the compound dimension occurs at the expense of discrimination per dimension. By an ex post facto analysis of what occurred in the judgment of the compound stimulus dimension, *AB,* it will be found that dimensions *A* and *B* were discriminated less well than they would have been if they were presented singly.

The fact that discriminative capacity increases as the dimensionality of the stimulus increases brings the judgment behavior of human beings more in line with the observations of everyday experience, where it is rather obvious that man can make more than five to nine discriminations of complex-multidimensional stimuli. It is therefore no great feat of judgment for an individual to be able to recognize instantly one of several hundred faces, or one of several thousand words of the English language. Consequently, the empirical fact that discriminative capacity increases as the dimensionality of the stimulus increases begins to account for the rather versatile judgment ability of the human organism.

By introducing the notion of the dimensionality of the stimulus, we begin to become aware of the possibility of two rather distinct cognitive processes in the judgment situation. The first is the previously discussed process of discrimination within a given stimulus dimension. We have chosen to call this judgment process *articulation*—the ability of a judge to make reliable and error-free distinctions among an array of stimuli that vary along one attribute dimension. It is within the context of articulation, then, that the notions of transmitted information and of channel capacity have been traditionally applicable. The second judgment process relates to the ability of a judge to make distinctions among several stimulus dimensions, and this process we have chosen to call *differentiation* (Miller and Bieri, 1963).*

* MacKay (1950), within the framework of information theory, draws a distinction between *metron* content which is equivalent to the information within a single dimension and Gabor's concept of *logon* content, the information among a group of dimensions. This "translation" of metron and logon content is rather free, but the resemblance to the notions of articulation and differentiation is most significant.

In order to make this distinction clear, consider the following example, which is constructed within the context of a social judgment situation. Suppose two clinicians were confronted with a series of behaviors that were composed of two orthogonal dimensions, aggression and dependency. (The illustration suffers, thus far, from two possible limitations: aggression and dependency are probably only *relatively* independent dimensions, and they are far from being unidimensional.) Furthermore, suppose that each of these two dimensions was composed of four different classes. Aggression can have the quality of *A, B, C,* or *D;* and dependency can have the quality of *Q, R, S,* or *T*. Given these stimulus characteristics, then, there are sixteen possible kinds of behaviors, as indicated in Table 1.

Table 1. The Sixteen Possible Behaviors Generated from Two Behavioral Dimensions Each Consisting of Four Classes

	Dimension	
Behavior	Aggression	Dependency
1	*A*	*Q*
2	*A*	*R*
3	*A*	*S*
4	*A*	*T*
5	*B*	*Q*
6	*B*	*R*
7	*B*	*S*
8	*B*	*T*
9	*C*	*Q*
10	*C*	*R*
11	*C*	*S*
12	*C*	*T*
13	*D*	*Q*
14	*D*	*R*
15	*D*	*S*
16	*D*	*T*

Suppose, furthermore, that we presented our two clinicians with these sixteen behaviors and asked them to classify each one on the basis of its uniqueness. From this experiment we obtained from Clinicians X and Y the data of Table 2.

In both instances Clinicians X and Y saw the sixteen behaviors as being of four unique kinds, but their perception of these four classes of behavior was predicated upon fundamentally different processes. Because Clinician X perceived that these behaviors were made up of only one dimension, aggression, the dimension of dependency was totally ir-

Table 2. Classification of the Sixteen Behaviors by Clinicians X and Y

Clinician X			
Class 1	Class 2	Class 3	Class 4
(1) *AQ*	(5) *BQ*	(9) *CQ*	(13) *DQ*
(2) *AR*	(6) *BR*	(10) *CR*	(14) *DR*
(3) *AS*	(7) *BS*	(11) *CS*	(15) *DS*
(4) *AT*	(8) *BT*	(12) *CT*	(16) *DT*

Clinician Y			
Class 1	Class 2	Class 3	Class 4
(1) *AQ*	(3) *AS*	(9) *CQ*	(11) *CS*
(2) *AR*	(4) *AT*	(10) *CR*	(12) *CT*
(5) *BQ*	(7) *BS*	(13) *DQ*	(15) *DS*
(6) *BR*	(8) *BT*	(14) *DR*	(16) *DT*

relevant for him. However, within the dimension of aggression he was able to make four discrete discriminations.

Clinician Y, on the other hand, clearly operated on the basis that the behaviors consisted of two dimensions; he classified them on the basis of both dependency and aggression. Within each dimension, however, he was only making two discriminations. For Clinician Y, aggression consisted of two types: *AB* and *CD;* that is to say, he confused *A*'s with *B*'s and *C*'s with *D*'s. Furthermore, dependency consisted of only two types, *QR* and *ST;* he confused *Q*'s with *R*'s and *S*'s with *T*'s.

Thus, we would say that Clinician X was a "good" *articulator* but a "poor" *differentiator* because he was able to make rather fine discriminations within a given dimension but he had a rather limited ability (in this instance, at least) to discriminate among dimensions. Clinician Y, on the other hand, we would say was a "good" *differentiator* but a "poor" *articulator*. He was able to perceive a larger number of dimensions but he could make only a limited number of discriminations within each dimension.

Although there is no empirical evidence which supports the assumption these two aspects of discrimination behavior are independent of each other, for speculative purposes it may be fruitful to conceive of four types of judgment behavior that can be explicated from the following fourfold table:

		Articulation	
		High	Low
Differentiation	High		
	Low		

The "best" (most discriminating) judge would obviously be the individual who is high on both articulation and differentiation. He would be characterized as having a relatively large number of dimensions available to impose upon the objects to be judged and at the same time would have the ability to make rather fine discriminations within each dimension. It is instructive to note that with a relatively small number of dimensions and with a relatively small number of articulations within each dimension, it is possible to make an extremely large number of unique judgments about events—be they physical objects or behavioral entities. If a judge had seven dimensions available to him and could make seven discriminations within each dimension, there would be 806,736 unique identifications possible. If there were eight dimensions and eight discriminations, 16,777,216 such identifications would be possible. The "poorest" judge would be the low articulator–low discriminator. He would be an individual who would have a limited number of dimensions available to bring into a judgment situation and who could break down each dimension into only a limited number of classes.

The individuals who occupy the low articulator–high differentiator and the high articulator–low differentiator cells of the above matrix would be judges who are rather more difficult to describe as being either "good" or "poor." If one were to assume that the ability to differentiate is a more powerful judgment characteristic than the ability to articulate, the number of unique objects generated from these two characteristics could be easily computed. N (the number of unique objects) is equal to the number of articulations, a, raised to the power of the number of differentiations, d, i.e., $N = a^d$. These relationships, which demonstrate the increasing importance of differentiation as a judgment characteristic, are more easily seen in Table 3.

On the basis of the preceding discussion, it becomes clear that the differentiation-articulation paradigm may become a useful apparatus for examining individual differences in judgment behavior. Although empirical research in this most important question of variation among judges

Table 3. Comparative Power of Differentiation and Articulation

Differentiation	Articulation	Number of Unique Objects	Differentiation	Articulation	Number of Unique Objects
2	2	4	2	2	4
2	3	9	3	2	8
2	4	16	4	2	16
2	5	25	5	2	32
2	6	36	6	2	64
2	7	49	7	2	128
2	8	64	8	2	256
2	9	81	9	2	512
2	10	100	10	2	1024

is almost nonexistent, in Chapter 7 we shall consider research in judgment in which both articulation and differentiation are considered (Rigney, Bieri, and Tripodi, 1964).

Furthermore, it becomes a matter of some interest whether or not the discriminative functions of differentiation and articulation can be related to stages in the cognitive development of the human organism. As the young child or infant begins to cognize his external world, which discriminative function does he first develop? Does he first differentiate adults into "mommies" and "daddies" without making distinctions within these domains, or does he first make distinctions between "good" people and "bad" people without an earlier differentiation into domains of people? Moreover, one can speculate about possible aberrations or arrestations in the development of these cognitive attributes and about their potential role in the development of some forms of mental illness, e.g., schizophrenia.*

The Elaboration of the Dimensionality Issue: Relevancy and Redundancy

There are further issues to which we might address ourselves when we consider the effect of the dimensionality of the stimulus materials upon the discriminative capacity of the judge. Specifically, we shall discuss the *relevancy* and the *redundancy* of the stimulus dimensions. These considerations begin to take us into a discussion of the nature of the response system and the interaction between stimulus variables and response variables. In anticipation of the argument which will follow, we should

* The work of Harvey, Hunt, and Schroder (1961) and of Wolfe (1963) begins to extend these notions concerning cognitive development in children.

note that although the demarcation of stimulus from response in the area of physical stimuli is a difficult task, it is infinitely more manageable than in the realm of social and behavioral stimuli. We therefore find ourselves confronting the thorny question of stimulus definition and trying to define attributes of a complex stimulus by a method which is independent of a judge's response. In psychophysical research these questions can be dealt with, more or less adequately, by a body of knowledge drawn from physics; in clinical and social judgment research there is, unfortunately, no such reservoir of independent measurement instrumentation to tap (Hunt and Jones, 1962).

The two concepts of relevancy and redundancy may best be illustrated by the following example. Suppose that we were able to construct a series of clinical stimuli each one of which contained the dimensions of educational achievement, occupational status, and degree of ego strength. Furthermore, suppose that these stimuli were presented to judges who had the task of forming a clinical judgment for each stimulus. For the sake of discussion, we shall say that the dimension of ego strength is *relevant* to the judgment system of clinical diagnosis, whereas the dimensions of education and occupation are *irrelevant*. Thus relevancy is essentially an indication of criteriality as used in concept formation; that is, certain elements of a stimulus are criterial for, or define, the concept (in this case, a clinical diagnosis). Redundancy, on the other hand, refers to the correlation between stimulus dimensions—whether or not those dimensions are relevant. In the example above, educational achievement and occupational status are highly correlated, almost to the extent where one could predict one from the other with fair certainty. We would consequently say that the dimensions of education and occupation are *redundant*. If there were no correlation we would say that they were *nonredundant*. Therefore, in this illustration we have a multidimensional stimulus composed of three dimensions, one of which is relevant and two of which are irrelevant—the irrelevant dimensions being redundant. These issues are discussed in more detail below.

Relevancy. Needless to say, it is not a simple matter to ascertain which dimensions are relevant and which are irrelevant in complex, clinical judgment situations. In order to make one of the standard nosological judgments of psychiatric diagnosis, it thus becomes rather difficult to identify the specific case stimulus dimensions which are seen by a particular judge as being salient to such a judgment. Some clinicians would indeed maintain that *all* case dimensions are relevant. This contention is predicated on the rather reasonable hypothesis that dimensions of behavior *interact* with each other so as to produce an extremely relevant, complex stimulus (Mahrer and Young, 1961). Thus age, sex, occupation, marital status, etc., by themselves may be rather irrelevant to psychiatric diagnosis, but as a cluster of interacting dimensions they may be most important.

The foregoing complications in considering the relevance of stimulus dimensionality become much less distressing in the study of physical stimuli. Within the context of judging multidimensional physical stimuli, the relevancy of the component dimensions becomes a rather simple thing to ascertain or indeed to manipulate on an a priori basis. Consider Table 4, which lists the eight unique stimuli that can be generated by

Table 4. Two Subjects' Responses to Eight Stimuli Generated from Three Dimensions, Each One of Which May Take One of Two Values

Dimensions *ABC*	Subject 1	Subject 2
000	W	W
001	W	X
010	X	W
011	X	X
100	Y	W
101	Y	X
110	Z	W
111	Z	X

three dimensions—each one of which can take one of two values. Here we have three stimulus dimensions, *A, B,* and *C*—each one of which can take the value of 1 or 0. It is rather clear by looking at subject 1's responses that the only dimensions that were relevant for this subject were dimensions *A* and *B*. Dimension *C* was totally disregarded—or at least it played no role whatsoever in determining the response. Subject 2, on the other hand, used dimension *C* as his only relevant dimension; dimensions *A* and *B* for this subject were irrelevant.

One can ask, therefore, how this variable of relevancy affects a judge's discriminative ability. Do irrelevant dimensions within the stimulus serve as a detriment to discriminative ability? Do they aid it? What is the optimum number of relevant dimensions in a stimulus for maximum discriminability? To what extent does the interaction between the number of relevant and irrelevant dimensions affect discriminability? These questions remain unanswered for the question of discrimination, but some tentative insights which use the concept of relevancy have been applied to the problem of concept formation. Bourne and Haygood

(1959) find that an increase in the number of relevant dimensions improves performance in concept formation problems but that the improvement is related to the number of irrelevant dimensions. In their studies, Bourne and Haygood were also manipulating the redundancy of the variables, a concept which we shall discuss in the following section. Their findings will have to be seen within the context of a relevancy-redundancy frame of reference.

Redundancy. As was suggested earlier, redundancy is a concept that refers to the degree of correlation that exists among stimulus dimensions. In order to illustrate this notion further we shall draw upon an abstract example. Suppose we have four dimensions, *A, B, C,* and *D,* and each dimension is able to take one of two values, 1 or 0. Table 5

Table 5. The Sixteen Possible Stimuli That Can Be Generated from Four Dimensions, Each Taking One of Two Values

Stimulus Number	Dimension *A*	*B*	*C*	*D*
1	0	0	0	0
2	0	0	0	1
3	0	0	1	0
4	0	0	1	1
5	0	1	0	0
6	0	1	0	1
7	0	1	1	0
8	0	1	1	1
9	1	0	0	0
10	1	0	0	1
11	1	0	1	0
12	1	0	1	1
13	1	1	0	0
14	1	1	0	1
15	1	1	1	0
16	1	1	1	1

shows the sixteen possible stimuli that can be generated under these conditions. Suppose, then, that from this series of stimuli six were sampled for experimental use with the ensuing subjects' response (Table 6).

In this example the relevant dimensions for subject 1 were *A* and *B*. It must be noted, however, that *A* and *B* are perfectly correlated, i.e., they are completely *redundant* in the sense that the subject could have used either dimension *A* or dimension *B* as a rationale for his response. Thus dimension *A* has the value of 0 only when dimension *B* has the

Table 6. Two Subjects' Responses to a Sample of Stimuli Drawn from Table 5

ABCD	Subject 1	Subject 2
0100	X	R
0101	X	S
0110	X	T
1001	Y	S
1010	Y	T
1011	Y	U

value of 1, and *A* has the value of 1 only when *B* has the value of 0. Note that dimensions *C* and *D*, although irrelevant to the response, are not at all redundant (in the special sense in which redundancy is here used). That is to say, by knowing the value of dimension *C* one cannot predict the value of dimension *D*. The reader can see that subject 2 used dimensions *C* and *D* as his relevant dimensions and there was no correlation or redundancy between these two dimensions. However, *A* and *B* for subject 2 were irrelevant dimensions. These examples illustrate our use of the concept of redundancy, which refers to the extent of correlation between dimensions—the greater the correlation, the greater the redundancy. It should be noted, however, that redundancy can have other meanings, an idea which is discussed in great detail by Garner (1962).

The effect of the redundancy of the stimulus dimensions upon discriminability has not been systematically studied. However, Bourne and Haygood (1959) found that concept formation is facilitated by an increase in the number of redundant, relevant variables, but is impaired by an increase in the number of redundant, irrelevant variables. In a further study, there was found a *linear* decrement in performance with increased irrelevant information and an *exponential* decrement in performance with increased relevant information. Although these studies indicate that even in relatively simple judgment situations the influence of relevancy and redundancy may be complicated, it is evident that the outline for studying these variables in the clinical judgment situation is present. As we have indicated, there is almost no empirical data stemming from the application of these variables to the study of the judgment process. Thus far, the few studies that have investigated the problem of the discriminability of clinical stimuli have *assumed* that the stimulus information was relevant and have ignored the whole question of redundancy.

THE DIMENSIONALITY OF THE JUDGMENT SYSTEM AS IT BEARS ON INFORMATION TRANSMISSION

Just as it is possible to consider the effect of the dimensionality of the stimulus on discriminability, so it is possible to consider the effect of the dimensionality of the response on the judgment system. Within the domain of physical stimuli, the dimensionality of a response may be rather simple to determine or control: for example, if a subject is presented with auditory stimuli that vary according to pitch he may be asked to respond on a pitch continuum, perhaps by indicating a particular interval on a cycle-per-second dimension within which he judges the stimuli to fall. Or, if he is judging the position of a pointer on a line he may be asked to reproduce the point on a graphic scale. In any event, there is, typically, a one-to-one correspondence between the nature of the physical stimulus and the nature of the expected response.

When multidimensional physical stimuli are used in judgment research the response is frequently a series of unidimensional judgments. Thus, Beebe-Center et al. (1955), in their studies of the discrimination of taste intensities, used as stimuli compound saline and sucrose solutions. The response that was called for, however, was a series of two judgments: one of saltiness and then one of sweetness. It is difficult, indeed, to conjure up a single multidimensional response that would incorporate within it attributes of both salt and sweet. Some multidimensional physical stimuli can be accompanied by response systems of equal dimensionality. Klemmer and Frick (1953), for example, used as a stimulus a dot in a square, and the response demanded of the subjects was to reproduce the stimulus. Here the stimulus consisted of two dimensions, a dot that had both horizontal and vertical coordinates and was accompanied by a response of the same order of dimensionality—a reproduced dot in a square.

As far as we have been able to determine, no systematic investigation has been undertaken to examine the effect of varying the dimensionality of the stimulus *and the response* upon discriminative ability. We can again construct a fourfold table.

The table represents a factorial design for a study which would clarify this issue considerably. The isolated cell represented by the letter *A* has been amply investigated, and cells *C* and *D* have been more or less looked at, but not as part of the same experiment. Cell *B*, however, which has a unidimensional stimulus with an accompanying multidimensional response, has hardly been tapped. Indeed, within the realm of physical stimuli it is difficult to imagine the form which such an S-R condition would take. Conceptually, it would take the form of a stimulus

		Stimulus	
		Unidimensional	Multidimensional
Response	Unidimensional	*A*	*C*
	Multidimensional	*B*	*D*

which consists of a point on a line, with a response of a dot in a square, a rather peculiar kind of response given the stimulus but one which nevertheless is theoretically feasible. It is clear, however, that there is a relative simplicity attached to S-R conditions in psychophysical experimentation. There is, first, a very direct correspondence between the stimulus and response, and, second, to a certain extent the stimulus can be defined independently of the subject's response. Within the realm of social and behavioral stimuli, however, it is extremely difficult to conceptualize the stimulus-response condition; even the most delimited segment of an individual's behavior is highly complex and multidimensional. How can such a stimulus be defined? And what kind of judgment can be called for?

In the clinical situation the stimulus is usually a human being who is observed over a substantial segment of time in a variety of interacting circumstances. The judge may be asked to make a clinical diagnosis based upon the standard psychiatric nosology. Here, indeed, is a multidimensional stimulus coupled with a multidimensional response. Or the judge may be asked to respond to the same stimulus in regard to the patient's degree of aggressivity—again a multidimensional response—but probably less so than a judgment of clinical diagnosis.

On the other hand, the stimulus may be a rather brief, written case vignette or a TAT response, again multidimensional in nature but probably much less so than ongoing behavior in an interview situation. And, again, judgments may be called for that are more or less multidimensional—a judgment of the degree of pathology or a judgment of the particular kind of defense mechanism employed by the patient.

Within the context of social stimuli, therefore, it is quite reasonable to think in terms of stimuli and responses that vary in their relative dimensionality and to study how these variations in input and output dimensionality affect the judge's ability to discriminate behavioral stimuli. In the following chapter we shall present data on this problem. However, it should be noted again that the dimensionality of the particular stimulus and response systems often must be ascertained on an a priori, rational basis. One such basis could consider dimensionality of a response system to be a function of its inclusiveness. That is, if two dimensions such as aggression and dependency can be included within a common dimension of pathology, the dimension of pathology can be considered to be of greater dimensionality than either of the other dimensions. A further consideration revolves around the issue of the orthogonality of different judgment systems which, of course, is similar to the problem discussed earlier of the redundancy of stimulus dimensions. It is a most difficult task to elicit dimensions of clinical judgment that are independent of each other. Indeed, we shall subsequently present evidence which suggests that there is a common underlying dimension that serves as a basis for a large variety of different clinical judgments and that this dimension is some sort of evaluative dimension of pathology or maladjustment.

NOMINAL VERSUS ORDINAL JUDGMENT SYSTEMS

Finally, it is necessary to consider the whole question of nominal versus ordinal judgmental dimensions. It must first be noted that there are few commonly accepted or used judgmental systems that consist of a set of nominal categories; one possible exception is the psychiatric clinical diagnostic system of the American Psychiatric Association. Thus the large bulk of clinical judgments consists of loosely organized, informal, and private assessments which are strung together in narrative form and which may or may not be of a nominal character. If they are not, they may take the form of "rather aggressive," "quite intelligent," "very weak ego," etc. This use of the qualifying adjective implies that aggression, intelligence, and weak ego are ordinal dimensions.

Now it makes some difference in the quantitative assessment of discriminative capacity by means of the informational statistic, $T_{x;y}$, whether or not the variables in question are nominal or ordinal. Although the measure of transmitted information can be computed in either case, we have seen that $T_{x;y}$ is insensitive to ordinality and will consequently tend to underestimate the amount of shared information with ordinal data. This may or may not be important, depending upon the interpretation one tends to give to discriminative capacity or information transmission. Thus, if one chooses to think, as we have, of information transmission as the maximum number of discriminations that can be made *before the subject begins to confuse the stimuli,* then it can be argued that $T_{x;y}$ is an appropriate statistic even with ordinal data. The question of discrimination is consequently framed in the following way: how many discriminations can be made before the subject begins to make errors? The *magnitudes* of the errors are ignored.

Needless to say, the experimenter may choose to consider a less stringent measure of discrimination—in which case the use of the informational statistic will not take advantage of the entire potential of ordinal data. However, within the context of information transmission as elucidated here, any error is treated as a maximum error. The confusion of one stimulus with another, no matter how slight, is taken as a signal that discriminative ability is being taxed and that some limit has been reached. Thus, whether the response systems are nominal or ordinal may be a significant variable for some experimental and some practical situations. In the studies of judgment that will be discussed in the following chapter, both kinds of response systems have been used—in studies of the discrimination of physical stimuli and in studies of the discrimination of clinical stimuli. In both instances it appears that the concepts of information transmission and channel capacity are reasonable conceptual variables.

SUMMARY

In this chapter we began by presenting a model of the judgment process which treated the stimulus as an input, the response or judgment as an output, and the mediating structure or judge as a communications channel. We discussed information theory as a statistical and methodological apparatus within this paradigm as a means whereby inputs and outputs could be quantified. We found the informational statistic, $T_{x;y}$, to be an index of the association between input and output—that is, a measure of the amount of information in the response which was reliably associated with the information in the stimulus. This analysis was seen to form an isomorphism with an analysis of variance or a correlational analysis, and to have the advantage of being extremely general in application. After presenting the concept of information transmission as a measure of discriminative ability we identified two of its aspects, balanced variability and reliability. We argued that the concept was most reasonably applicable in the absolute-judgment situation, the type of judgment framework which was thought to be most nearly analogous to the clinical task.

We discussed the concept of information transmission in relation to stimulus variables where the range of the stimulus was thought to be an important variable in the clinical judgment situation. After considering the problem of stimulus dimensionality in some detail, we used the concepts of *differentiation* and *articulation* as distinct cognitive variables which might throw light on the discrimination of multidimensional stimuli. The dimensionality of the stimulus problem was further elaborated to include a discussion of the *relevancy* and *redundancy* of the dimensions. Finally, we considered the dimensionality of the response system and concluded that this rather neglected aspect of judgment research was of paramount importance in the explication of discriminative behavior.

chapter 4 EMPIRICAL RESEARCH RELATING INFORMATION THEORY TO CLINICAL AND SOCIAL JUDGMENT

The ability to discriminate among behavioral stimuli appears to have important ramifications in both the clinical and social judgment realms. For the clinician this ability may relate particularly to his skill in making crucial diagnostic judgments concerning disposition and treatment of his patients. For the student of social attitudes this ability may have importance in clarifying how differences in the discrimination of issues along an attitude continuum influence one's judgment of these issues in certain situational contexts. We may investigate those possible characteristics of the judge himself which may relate to differences in ability to discriminate. Informational analysis is of value to such problems, and our discussion in this and subsequent chapters will present methods and empirical evidence which indicate how such an analysis can be implemented.

Because the majority of the research on judgment using the information-theory model falls within the domain of investigation of psychophysics, it is necessary that we briefly review aspects of this work before proceeding to the realm of clinical and social judgment. As a preface to this review, we would call attention again to the detailed presentation of Garner (1962), who has discussed this material in a viable, creative manner. We shall present our own studies of clinical and social judgment which use the informational approach in some detail.

THE EXPERIMENTAL MODEL

Whether their focus is on judgment of physical stimuli or judgment of behavioral stimuli, most of the studies we shall discuss in this chapter have used a basically similar experimental approach. This relatively simple model consists of the following three methodological steps:

1. The selection of an array of stimuli to be judged. This selection is made according to one or more of several criteria, including a particular domain of stimuli (pitch of a tone, loudness of a tone, aggressive behavior, etc.), the distribution along a continuum from which the stimuli are sampled (manipulating range or interstimulus distance), the number of stimuli, and the relative dimensionality of the stimuli.
2. The selection of a response system. This again is made according to certain criteria, including the use of nominal or ordinal scales, the number of response alternatives, the presence of anchors, and the relative complexity of the response categories.
3. The judgment of the stimuli. In the studies with which we shall be concerned the method of single stimuli (or absolute judgment) is the method of judgment used. The stimuli in the series to be judged are usually randomized, and judgments are replicated several times.

STUDIES OF CHANNEL CAPACITY IN THE DISCRIMINATION OF UNIDIMENSIONAL PHYSICAL STIMULI

During the early 1950's, shortly after information theory was introduced into psychology by Garner and Hake (1951), a large series of experiments was performed on the discriminative ability of the human judge. At present we have data that indicate the characteristic channel capacity for all five of the senses.

Auditory stimuli were among the first to be studied in detail. Pollack (1952), using the new information-theory model, studied the ability of a human judge to discriminate auditory tones that varied in regard to pitch and found an asymptote at 2.30 bits. That is, regardless of how many tones were presented to the judge, he could discriminate only approximately five of these before he began to confuse the tones and make errors of identification. In the same experiment Pollack looked into the question of how the range of stimuli might affect channel capacity. Thus he obtained the value of 2.30 bits from a series of stimuli sampled from a range of 100 to 500 cps. When Pollack extended the range to encompass tones from 100 to 8000 cps, he found only a slight gain of 0.2 bit in information transmission. A further consideration is worth noting in regard to this experiment *and will be true of all the other data on channel capacity reported in this chapter*. The value of 2.3 bits is an *average*

$T_{x;y}$, that is, it is the mean channel capacity for a group of subjects and consequently masks individual differences in discriminative ability that may be of extreme importance. For example, we would not expect an individual who is tone deaf to be able to achieve a channel capacity of 2.3 bits for pitch discrimination; conversely, we would expect an individual with "perfect pitch" to surpass the value of 2.3 bits.

Garner (1953) studied the ability of human beings to discriminate the intensity or loudness of tones. Sampling stimuli within the range of 15 to 110 db, he obtained a $T_{x;y}$ of 2.1 bits—a figure that is slightly lower than Pollack's finding for the discrimination of tones that vary in pitch.

Hartman (1954) analyzed the problem of the effect of practice or learning on discriminative behavior by using auditory stimuli that varied along a pitch continuum and found an increment in channel capacity that was a function of learning. However, the increment rapidly leveled off, which suggests that a subject has to achieve a familiarity with the stimuli and the experimental task before the concept of channel capacity can be properly considered.

A great many investigations have been carried out on the discrimination of unidimensional, visual stimuli. Hake and Garner (1951) presented subjects with stimuli that consisted of a pointer on a line and obtained a channel capacity of 3.1 bits. A similar experiment was performed by Coonan and Klemmer with almost identical findings (unpublished study cited by G. Miller, 1956). The Hake and Garner experiment is noteworthy in that they studied the effect of the number of response alternatives available to the judge and its affect on channel capacity and found that an unlimited number of responses had no effect.

The ability to discriminate squares of varying sizes was studied by Eriksen and Hake (1955a), who found a channel-capacity value of 2.1 bits. This study, coupled with the Hake and Garner experiment of 1951, throws considerable light on the effect of the number of response alternatives upon discriminative behavior. Eriksen and Hake varied the number of stimuli and the number of responses in a factorial design and found that channel capacity tends to diminish in those instances where the number of response categories is fewer than the number of stimuli. Thus, in order to obtain an optimum measure of transmitted information, the number of responses should equal the number of stimuli—but according to Hake and Garner when the number of response categories exceeds the number of stimuli no increase in channel capacity can be obtained.

For the discrimination of spectral hues, a channel capacity of approximately 3.6 bits has been obtained independently by Chapanis and Halsey (1956) and Conover (1959). This is not the largest value obtained, however, for a visual stimulus. Muller, Sidorsky, Slivinske, Alluisi, and Fitts (1955) obtained a value of 4.5 bits for visual stimuli which consisted of a line that could be rotated in a 360° angle. Subjects were asked to judge the angle of the inclination of the line. According to Garner (1962) this is the highest value yet obtained for a single sensory dimension, and he attributes this large channel capacity to the presence of powerful psychological anchors that accompany such stimuli (i.e., the presence of implicit horizontal and vertical anchors).

The only published studies in discrimination of taste intensities are by Beebe-Center, Rogers, and O'Connell (1955), who found remarkably similar values of channel capacity for sucrose and saline solutions, 1.69 and 1.70 bits, respectively. These values appear to be the lowest obtained for physical stimuli and correspond to approximately three perfect discriminations of taste intensities.

Engen and Pfaffmann (1959, 1960) found a value almost as low for the discrimination of odor intensities, a value of 1.9 bits. For odor *quality,* however, they obtained a surprisingly high channel capacity of 3.5 bits.

Finally, we report the findings of Geldard for the discrimination of tactile sensations (unpublished study, cited by G. Miller, 1956). Using vibrations placed on the chests of subjects, Geldard found an ability to discriminate approximately four tactile intensities (2.00 bits), five durations of sensation (2.32 bits), and seven locations of tactile sensations (2.81 bits).

The foregoing discussion represents only a partial sample of the many studies that have been done within the realm of unidimensional, physical stimuli. These findings are summarized in Table 1.

It was a cluster of considerations much like those represented in Table 1 that prompted George Miller (1956) to write his classic paper, "The Magical Number Seven, Plus or Minus Two." Discussing some of the above findings, Miller wrote:

> Although there is no question that the differences are real and meaningful, the more impressive fact to me is their considerable similarity. If I take the best estimates I can get of the channel capacities for all the stimulus variables I have mentioned, the mean is 2.6 bits and the standard deviation is only 0.6 bits. In terms of distinguishable alternatives, this mean corresponds to about 6.5 categories, one standard deviation includes from 4 to 10 categories and the total range is from 3 to 15 categories. Considering the wide variety of different variables that have been studied, I find this to be a remarkably narrow range. (p. 86)

In any event, it would seem clear that the concept of channel capacity is a rather meaningful notion when applied to the discriminative ability of

Table 1. Channel Capacities for Unidimensional Physical Stimuli [a]

Stimulus	Channel Capacity in Bits	Investigator
Auditory		
Intensity of tones	2.1	Garner (1953)
Frequency of tones	2.3	Pollack (1952)
Visual		
Spectral hues	3.6	Chapanis & Halsey (1956)
		Conover (1959)
Point on a line	3.1	Coonan & Klemmer [b]
		Hake & Garner (1951)
Size of squares	2.1	Eriksen & Hake (1955)
Angle of inclination of a line	4.5 [c]	Muller et al. (1955)
Taste		
Sucrose solutions	1.7	
Saline solutions	1.7	Beebe-Center et al. (1955)
Olfactory		
Odor intensity	1.9	Engen & Pfaffmann (1959)
Odor quality	3.5	Engen & Pfaffmann (1960)
Tactile		
Intensity	2.0	
Duration	2.3	
Location	2.8	Geldard [b]

[a] Studies listed are those which obtained the highest value for the particular stimulus in question.

[b] Unpublished study, cited by G. Miller (1956).

[c] Garner (1962) suggests that the large value obtained for this type of stimulus is probably a consequence of the presence of strong psychological anchors.

a subject who is confronted with an absolute judgment task. Clearly, a judge's ability to discriminate among an array of unidimensional, physical stimuli is not infinite—on the contrary, the scores elicited over a wide range of experimental situations reflect a rather limited ability to make such discriminations.

STUDIES OF INFORMATION TRANSMISSION IN THE DISCRIMINATION OF "UNIDIMENSIONAL" SOCIAL STIMULI

Next we may consider the discrimination capacities of clinical judges in contexts crudely analogous to those we have just discussed. How discriminating is the judge of social stimuli? The studies that we shall present in answer to this question do not allow us properly to speak of "channel capacity" but rather of "information transmission," as we distinguished these two terms in Chapter 3. However, an occasional mixing of these terms will occur for semantic purposes. As we indicated in the previous chapter, the definition and specification of a behavioral stimulus in terms of its dimensionality is a complex matter and one that can be only partially resolved. In this section we shall consider behavioral stimuli that may be assumed to vary in terms of their *relative* dimensionality; that is, they are thought to be less dimensional in nature than other stimuli in the particular experiment under discussion. For example, we shall discuss a study in which aggressive and dependent stimuli were judged. In one phase of the experiment the subjects had to make judgments about the aggressive behavior, and in another phase they were required to make judgments about the dependent behavior. Obviously, these two "dimensions" of behavior were not unidimensional, but they were presumed to be *less* dimensional than the stimuli presented in a third phase of the research—stimuli that consisted of combined aggressive *and* dependent behavior.

A further introductory consideration must be discussed. For the first time we shall be confronted with the concept of a *group channel capacity;* that is, in some of the research to be reported, scores of $T_{x;y}$ were computed that were based upon *pooled* subjects' responses. By so doing, the experimenters were considering the ability of subjects *as a group* to transmit information from stimulus to response. Thus, in this instance, H_y would indicate the balanced variability of the group as a whole, H_{xy} would indicate the agreement among judges, or the inter-judge reliability, and $T_{x;y}$ would consequently be an index of the group's channel capacity. It is apparent that a $T_{x;y}$ obtained in this manner must have different characteristics from a $T_{\overline{x;y}}$ obtained by *averaging* a group of individual $T_{x;y}$'s. For example, since it is reasonable to expect that intra-individual reliability in judgment will be greater than inter-individual reliability, individual scores of transmitted information should be higher than group scores.

An important consideration which dictates the use of a group $T_{x;y}$ in certain experimental situations has to do with possible sequential effects in judgment due to such factors as memory and learning. It will be recalled that in order to obtain a score of $T_{x;y}$ for an *individual* judge it is necessary to judge the stimuli more than once; otherwise there is no conceivable way to get a measure of H_{xy} or internal reliability. In the judgment of physical stimuli such sequential presentations may pose no real problem. In the social judgment situation, however, the replication of the stimulus may offer the opportunity for a subject to *remember* his response to a behavioral stimulus. This may be especially likely if the social stimulus is quite complex, as in the first study to be discussed below. In regard to the computation of a group channel capacity, these considerations of sequential effects are of no relevance because the "replications" are made by other subjects.*

AN INFORMATIONAL STUDY OF CLINICAL JUDGMENT

The first study of clinical judgment which used the information theory model (Miller and Bieri, 1963) had two major purposes. The first of these aims was to determine if information transmission would vary as a function of specific types of input and output conditions. The second aim, to be considered later in this chapter, was to determine if information transmission would vary as a function of the increasing dimensionality or complexity of the information available to the judge. Turning first to our initial aim, we were interested in determining if a particular kind of clinical information could be discriminated best in relation to a particular kind of clinical judgment. Toward this end we chose to study three domains of input considered to be typical of information used by clinicians; these were developmental history, current behavior, and interview behavior. As response categories, the domains of clinical diagnosis, object relations, and defensive structure were selected as representative of the kinds of judgments that could be made on the basis of the varieties of input mentioned above.

The Design

Because each type of stimulus material was to be judged in relation to each type of response system, a three-by-three factorial design was required. In order to obtain a measure of information transmission for each of the nine cells of this design, it was necessary to generate a new matrix in which specific stimuli, within a given stimulus domain, were cast along one axis of the matrix and specific responses within a given judgment system were cast across the other axis. To illustrate, suppose

* One could use only one replication in order to avoid these memory effects. A limited number of replications, however, presents important problems in terms of correcting the obtained value of $T_{x;y}$ for bias. The informational measure $T_{x;y}$ is a *biased* estimate of the "true" information transmitted, and Miller and Madow (1954) have worked out the following correction for this bias: unbiased $T^{x;y} =$ biased $T_{x;y} -$ (degrees of freedom)/(1.3863n). With large matrices and a small number of replication, it is impossible to use this correction because of the difficulty in estimating the appropriate number of degrees of freedom. The reader is urged to examine the works by Miller and Madow, Miller (1955), and Attneave (1959) for a more thorough discussion of this problem.

we were to isolate the cell in the design which is located by the coordinates of developmental history and clinical diagnosis. In order to generate information measures, we would need a series of developmental histories and a series of alternative clinical diagnoses. Judges would then be given the task of assigning a specific clinical diagnosis to each of the developmental histories.

We arbitrarily decided to use exactly eight specific stimuli within each of the three stimulus domains mentioned above, as well as eight response alternatives within each judgment area. In this manner each cell of the three-by-three factorial consisted of a matrix composed of eight stimuli and eight responses, as represented in Table 2.

Table 2. Matrix of Judgment

		Domains of Clinical Stimuli		
Judgment System		Developmental History 12345678	Current Behavior 12345678	Interview Behavior 12345678
	1			
	2			
	3			
Object Relations	4			
	5			
	6			
	7			
	8			
	1			
	2			
	3			
Defenses	4			
	5			
	6			
	7			
	8			
	1			
	2			
	3			
Clinical Diagnosis	4			
	5			
	6			
	7			
	8			

The Stimulus Conditions

There seemed to be no completely satisfactory rationale for determining the defining properties of the three main stimulus domains of developmental history, current behavioral material, and interview material. In order to preserve as clear a distinction as possible between developmental information and current behavioral information we decided to use age boundaries as the essential point of distinction. Consequently, the first gross distinction was that a developmental history was to include data about the client up until the age of his early adolescence whereas a current behavioral history was to concern the client's recent and current situation, which was set at approximately 35 years of age. Interview material would, of course, contain current behavior but would be essentially contentless in regard to specific factual data that referred either to his present situation or his developmental years. Because of the extensive nature of the design, it was desirable that the stimulus materials be easily administered and that they be of modest length. Consequently, we decided that the stimulus materials would be in the form of brief written case vignettes constructed according to the predetermined criteria mentioned below. Although this decision implied that the stimulus materials might be somewhat "artificial," we decided that the use of completely fictitious case vignettes would not be so very different from the reduction and abridgment of actual case records. Since the vignettes were to be constructed *de novo,* as it were, we could be fairly precise in determining the actual content of the case material. We made a major effort to insure that the vignettes would be plausible and relatively interesting to the judges and constructed the vignettes according to the following prescriptions: (1) each vignette was to be approximately one paragraph in length or about ten typewritten lines, (2) all the vignettes were to refer to adult males of approximately 35 years of age, and (3) the presenting problem of the client was to be controlled by the elimination of all cues as to the nature of the presenting problem. These, then, were the general guidelines for the construction of the case vignettes. The specific content of the vignettes within each of the stimulus domains was governed by the following content guides.

Developmental History Vignettes. Each developmental history vignette included data about the client up to the age of his early adolescence. There was information in the vignettes that pertained to each of the following areas:

1. The ordinal position of the child in his family.
2. A general statement about the personalities of each parent. If there

are no parents, a general statement about the personality of a parent surrogate.
3. When applicable, a general statement characterizing the nature of the parental interaction.
4. When applicable, a general statement that would reveal something about each parent's relationship to the child.
5. When appropriate, a statement about sibling interaction.
6. Data about the school performance of the child, as well as teachers' and peers' assessments of the child.

The developmental histories, then, were constructed so as to include all of the above data, although the order of this information could vary from case to case. In addition, in order to make the case "come alive," we included some sort of episode or "slice of life" about the client as a child. An example of a case vignette within the domain of developmental history is given below:

> Mr. 4 was the older of two children. The other child was a girl, 5 years younger than he. The father, a passive withdrawn man, spent most of his time involved in his own work and had little to do with Mr. 4. The parents' marriage was fairly stormy. The mother was a conscientious young woman, somewhat prone to indulge and overprotect Mr. 4. He had asthma as a child. The care and discipline of the children fell completely to the mother. Mr. 4 was thought of as a "momma's boy" throughout his early years. He was a quiet, "model" child in school and a favorite of his teachers. He did very well academically. Once, when he was 13 years old, his mother caught him putting on some of his sister's clothing. He never had too many friends in school, and spent most of his time voraciously reading, or working for hours on end on his stamp collection. (Miller and Bieri, 1963, p. 319)

Current Behavioral Vignettes. Each current behavioral case vignette was constructed to provide data about the current functioning of the client. All of the vignettes included information about the following:

1. The marital status of the client and the number of his children, if any.
2. If married, a statement as to the nature of the marital relationship and an illustrative incident referring to the mood of the marriage. If not married, a statement as to the nature of his relationship to a person close to him.
3. The relationship of the client to his children, when applicable, and an incident illustrative of this relationship.
4. Kind of employment.
5. Functioning on the job as assessed by superiors or peers.
6. The nature of the client's relationship to co-workers.

Each of the current behavioral case vignettes included all of the above data, but the order of presentation varied from case to case. An example of a case vignette within the domain of current behavioral history is given below:

Mr. 22 is married and he has three children. He claims that he has little interest or feeling for his wife any more and try as he might he finds little pleasure in her company. He will come home from work and usually sit in front of the TV set, remaining there until time for bed. When his wife tries to talk to him he sometimes becomes irritated and curt with her. He knows he has no reason to be this way yet, "I can't help it, I feel so guilty—she's a good wife and mother—yet being nice to her doesn't come naturally—I have to force myself to be nice." He is fond of the children and spends considerable time with them. He owns a clothing store and spends long overtime hours there. His employees like him and think of him as a good boss. Other business men consider him to be an honorable, decent man.

Interview Material Vignettes. Each interview vignette was constructed to provide data concerning the manner in which the client behaved and reacted during the first few moments of a therapeutic interview. All the vignettes included information about the following:

1. The time of arrival for his appointment.
2. The dress and physical appearance of the client.
3. The general demeanor of the client, including his mannerisms, tone of voice, and motor activity.
4. The behavior of the client upon his immediate contact with the therapist.
5. At least one interactive segment between client and therapist.

An example of an interview vignette is given below:

Mr. 1 was in the office 5 minutes ahead of time. He was dressed neatly in comfortable clothes. He shook hands with the worker and sat leaning forward in his chair. He began in a halting manner to say, "I really don't know where to begin. I've never had to tell this to anyone before." The worker smiled sympathetically. Mr. 1 offered her a cigarette. When she refused he asked her if she minded if he smoked, and lit up when she nodded that she didn't mind. He began to tap his foot nervously and exclaimed, "I really feel terribly embarrassed and ashamed about the whole thing." He then stopped and frowned and there was a long pause before he blurted out—"Do I really have to say it?" Worker was silent. He then said, "Maybe it would be better if you asked me some questions."

Pathology Ratings. Once the above content guides were formulated and a large number of case vignettes were constructed within each of the three stimulus domains, a serious sampling problem became evident. It was impossible to define either the nature of the universe from which the vignettes were constructed or the precise means by which this universe was sampled. It was clear that the case vignettes were not randomly selected. Moreover, it was not self-evident in what precise manner the vignettes within any stimulus domain were different from each other, if, indeed, they were different. Since this entire sampling problem could not be satisfactorily resolved, we decided to devise a substitute means by which we could be certain that the cases differed at least on an empirical basis. Consequently, the case vignettes were judged by an independent group of experienced social caseworkers as to where they fell on a global pathology scale. By this means the experimenter could be assured (1) that the case vignettes within any given stimulus domain were distributed on a pathology dimension, and (2) that the ranges of these distributions were similar among the three stimulus domains.

An initial pretest, based upon the large reservoir of case vignettes originally constructed, was conducted with a group of experienced caseworkers. As a result of this pretest, some cases were rewritten, some were kept intact, and many were discarded. New vignettes were added for the second round of pretesting, and as a result of this second pretest more were discarded, others were kept, and still others were changed. After several more cycles in this process the basic case stimuli were finally arrived at: eight vignettes within the domain of developmental history, eight vignettes within the domain of current behavioral history, and eight vignettes within the domain of interview materials.

The Judgment Categories

Object Relations Alternatives. In order to construct an eightfold typology of object relations, we decided to outline what we considered to be the more clinically meaningful dimensions of this judgment area and to build the judgment alternatives from various combinations of these dimensions. The following five dimensions of object relations were considered to be important:

1. Mature—Infantile
2. Longstanding—Brief
3. Many—Few
4. Intense—Superficial
5. Formed with ease—Formed with discomfort

Given these bipolar dimensions, it was possible to generate many different kinds of object relations. After asking a small group of experienced caseworkers to examine the various possibilities, we settled upon the following eight object relation types:

A. Mature object relations can be formed comfortably with a variety of different people. These include both long-standing, intense relations as well as social relations of a less involving nature.
B. Intense and long-standing object relations of maturity can be formed without undue difficulty. However, they are restricted in number and variety. On a less involving social and casual level, mature relations are easily formed.
C. A variety of long-standing and intense object relations can be formed. However, they contain some infantile elements. Mature relations of a casual and social nature are easily formed.
D. Only a restricted number of long-standing and intense object relations can be formed, and these always contain a great many infantile elements. A variety of more casual and social relations are formed easily.
E. Only with considerable discomfort can a very few intense object relations be formed. These may be long-standing but are of a very infantile nature. A few object relations can be formed readily on a casual and social level.
F. No long-standing and intense object relations of any kind can be formed. The more casual, social kind of relations can be formed without difficulty and can be numerous, but they are always shallow and of an infantile nature.
G. The only kind of object relations that can be formed are superficial and few in number. These are undertaken with great discomfort, and are infantile in nature as well as short-lived.
H. There is no capacity to form object relations—even of a most tenuous and transient kind.

No claim is made that this typology is completely satisfactory or that it samples adequately the universe of possible types of object relationships. However, it was judged by a small group of experienced clinicians who actually tested it out against the case vignettes as being clinically meaningful, relatively mutually exclusive, and allowing for a "best fit" for a wide range of different cases. In fact, spontaneous comments from judges as to the value of this typology were not uncommon.

Defensive Structure Alternatives. Many of the same problems encountered in constructing object-relationship types were met in developing a meaningful response system concerning defensive structure. At first, we made an attempt to construct a typology of defenses on the basis of combinations of specific defense mechanisms. This approach, however, was abandoned because we felt that the limited information in the case vignettes that were to be judged would not support such specific kinds of judgments. As a result we decided to consider the adequacy of the defensive structure as a whole and move away from a consideration of specific defense mechanisms. Within this more global conception of the defensive structure, adaptation to change and the control of anxiety were seen as possible foundations upon which a typology could be built. It became clear, however, that this simple approach would not in itself permit the construction of eight alternatives that would be clearly different from one another. Another ego function, reality testing, was consequently melded with defenses. In essence, then, the judgment area of defenses became one that consisted of two highly related ego functions, defensive structure and capacity for reality testing. With this expanded definition of the judgment area, the following dimensions were generated as bases upon which to elaborate specific responses:

1. The way the defensive structure protects against anxiety
2. The way the defensive structure permits adaptation to external change
3. The effect of stress upon the functioning of the defensive structure
4. The capacity of the ego to test reality

Having formulated these dimensions, we constructed various types of defensive structure and gave them to experienced clinicians to examine and test out. As a result of such pretesting the following eight types of defensive structure were chosen as response alternatives for the research:

I. Defenses continually break down and flood the individual with a constant stress of anxiety. No adaptation to change is possible. Reality testing is practically nonexistent.
J. Defenses are extremely weak and function moderately well only under extremely favorable external conditions. Adaptability and reality testing are always very poor.
K. Defenses are extremely weak and inflexible. By avoiding novel and stressful situations, anxiety is successfully controlled. Capacity for reality testing is moderate.
L. Defenses permit easy adaptation to even extreme changes in life. They are so successful in preventing anxiety that it is almost never felt. Important aspects of reality testing are very poor.
M. Adaptation to change and good control of anxiety are possible under favorable circumstances. External stress causes a breakdown in defenses with a consequent flood of anxiety and impaired reality testing.
N. Defenses permit adaptation to most changes in life. However, there

is always a chronic flow of mild anxiety even under the best conditions. Reality testing is usually adequate.

O. Defenses permit adaptation to even extreme changes in life situations. Some common situations provoke mild anxiety, however. Reality testing is always good.

P. Even under the most extreme external stress, defenses permit adaptation and protect against undue anxiety. Common situations provoke no anxiety. Reality testing is always excellent.

Again, it should be noted that the above typology of defensive structure was not seen as a definitive classification system. It did, however, have considerable appeal to the caseworkers who acted as pretest subjects. They saw the alternatives as providing a possible "best fit" for a wide range of cases and as being, for the most part, mutually exclusive.

Clinical Diagnosis Alternatives. Since typologies of clinical diagnoses do exist, the task became one of selecting from the many different existent schemes those diagnostic entities which would be familiar to the judges and which would be appropriate for the research design. We examined several different clinical diagnostic schemes. The American Psychiatric Association (1952) classification system contains a great many different clinical entities, but it was quite clear that our judges would, for the most part, be knowledgeable about only some of the clinical categories included in this typology. The classification system of Fenichel (1945), as obtained from his chapter headings, more nearly approaches the general typology that we felt to be commonly used by the social caseworkers who eventually comprised our sample of judges. Consequently, after examining these two schemes along with several others, we selected the following composite clinical diagnostic typology for the research:

R. Normal
S. Situation neurosis or traumatic neurosis (reactive to a specific, current, environmental stress)
T. Anxiety hysteria
U. Obsessive-compulsive neurosis
W. Character disorder or character neurosis (excludes psychopath or sociopath)
X. Psychopath or sociopath
Y. Borderline psychosis
Z. Psychosis

Procedure

Members of a group of experienced clinicians, all of whom were social caseworkers employed predominantly in psychiatric settings, were assigned randomly to the three conditions defined by the three stimulus domains. Eighteen judges were in each of the three stimulus conditions. Within each domain, the eight specific stimuli were randomized and presented to each judge one at a time. The subject then made three judgments about each stimulus: a judgment as to the "case's" ability to form object relations, a judgment as to his defensive structure, and a clinical diagnosis. The specific judgments were selected from the three groups of alternatives described above.

Findings

The findings for this study are reported in Table 3. The statistic reported is a group $T_{x;y}$ and thus represents the information transmitting ability of the groups of judges.

Table 3. Group Scores of Transmitted Information for Three Types of Clinical Stimuli and Three Types of Clinical Judgment [a]
(Miller and Bieri, 1963)

	Responses			
Stimuli	Object Relations	Defenses	Clinical Diagnosis	Mean
Developmental history	1.16	1.07	0.93	1.05
Current behavior	1.26	0.99	1.02	1.09
Interview excerpts	1.02	0.88	1.04	0.98

[a] All scores have been corrected for bias, using the Miller-Madow correction. (By permission, American Psychological Association)

In terms of the major question which we posed, it must be concluded that all nine combinations of the input-output pairings yielded approximately the same values of group information transmission. While object relations and current behavior information produced the largest values of $T_{x;y}$, the differences are less striking than the relative homogeneity of the scores. Although in this particular study we could obtain no direct measure of individual channel capacity because judges did not replicate their judgments, it was nevertheless possible to obtain a rather good *estimate* of individual transmitted information. Thus, we examined the individuals' scores of H_y—which were directly obtainable from the data—and subtracted a constant term (calculated from what is an average loss as a result of error in similar clinical judgment situations) and arrived at an approximation which, although probably imprecise, serves illustrative purposes. The data reported in Table 4 were obtained in this manner.

Table 4. Estimated Scores of Individual Transmitted Information for the Data in Table 3

(Miller and Bieri, 1963)

Stimuli	Responses: Object Relations	Defenses	Clinical Diagnosis	Mean
Developmental history	1.74	1.81	1.73	1.76
Current behavior	1.81	1.63	1.69	1.71
Interview excerpts	1.72	1.74	1.85	1.77

Again, the homogeneity of the scores in Table 4 is noteworthy, although this time one could argue that the similarity of scores could be a consequence of the *constant* term used in making the estimate. Be that as it may, we have made an initial approximation of a channel capacity for clinicians to discriminate among an array of behavioral stimuli. The mean values in Table 4 indicate that judges were able to make three to four reliable discriminations among the eight cases presented.

In a more recent study, Miller and Bieri (1964) have obtained data on *individual* information transmission for two different dimensions of behavior, aggression and dependency. The stimuli selected for study consisted of brief, written descriptions of either aggressive or dependent behavior. An example of one of the aggressive stimuli was:

> He told the waitress that she was a clumsy ox and should be fired, after she spilled a bowl of soup over him.

An example of one of the dependent items was:

> Whenever he had to find another job, he always relied on his wife to make contacts for him.

Subjects received eight dependent or eight aggressive stimuli to judge. It is clear that these stimulus materials were much briefer than those used in the previously mentioned research. The choice of judgment system also differed from the 1963 study. In the present instance, an eight-category numerical rating scale of maladjustment comprised the judgment system in contrast to the verbal categories of the previous judgment system. In order to obtain a measure of individual information transmission the experimental task was given to a judge on two occasions separated in time by approximately two weeks.

The results of this study were that judgments of both aggression and dependency yielded equivalent amounts of information transmission (1.84 and 1.83 bits, respectively).* It should be noted that these values are similar to the estimated scores of information transmission reported in our earlier study (Table 4).

Tripodi and Bieri (1964) obtained scores of individual information transmission relative to judgments of three dimensions of social stimuli: aggressive behavior, social withdrawal behavior, and body anxiety symptoms. Their study is reported in greater detail in Chapter 7. On the basis of replicated judgments on an eight-point maladjustment scale, the following individual scores of transmitted information were derived: 1.98 bits for aggression, 2.02 bits for social withdrawal, and 2.01 bits for body anxiety.

Several additional studies have shed further light on the ability of judges to discriminate social stimuli. Atkins (1964), in a study primarily concerned with anchoring effects (Chapter 6), had judges rate items concerning fraternities for degree of favorableness. Using a fifteen-category scale ranging from extremely favorable to extremely unfavorable, four replications were made of a series of twenty-one statements. The mean score of individual information transmission for these items was 2.65, or somewhat more than six perfect discriminations. It should be noted that in this study Atkins had the same judges discriminate sizes of squares and that, with the same number of replications, a mean $T_{x;y}$ score of 2.34 was obtained for individual judges. Finally, we may note that Bieri and Atkins (1965), using the same aggression items as Tripodi and Bieri (1964), obtained a mean information transmission value of 2.12 bits based on six replications of judgments. Observe that this mean score is close to the 1.98 bits obtained in the Tripodi and Bieri study.

The results of these studies are summarized in Table 5. We observe that over a variety of social dimensions, discriminability of social stimuli varied from about 1.70 bits to 2.65 bits, a range of about three to six discriminable stimuli. Caution must be exercised in regarding these values in Table 5 as indices of a "channel capacity" for the discrimination of social stimuli. Only a limited number of differing types of stimulus domains were sampled, and it is quite conceivable that other kinds of

* This study was also concerned with the effect of range on channel capacity, and these scores are averages for four conditions of range. The detailed scores will be presented in a subsequent portion of this chapter.

Table 5. Measures of Information Transmission for Social Stimuli

Stimulus	Transmitted Information in Bits	Investigator
Developmental histories	1.76 [a]	Miller & Bieri (1963)
Current behavioral material	1.71 [a]	Miller & Bieri (1963)
Interview excerpts	1.77 [a]	Miller & Bieri (1963)
Aggression items	1.84	Miller & Bieri (1964)
Dependency items	1.83	Miller & Bieri (1964)
Aggression items	1.98	Tripodi & Bieri (1964)
Social withdrawal items	2.02	Tripodi & Bieri (1964)
Body anxiety items	2.01	Tripodi & Bieri (1964)
Attitudes toward fraternities	2.65 [b]	Atkins (1964)
Aggression items	2.12 [b]	Bieri & Atkins (1965)

[a] Estimated.

[b] The maximum possible $T_{x;y}$ is 3.91 bits. For the other studies in this table, the maximum possible value of $T_{x;y}$ is 3.00 bits.

social stimuli might yield higher values of information transmission. In addition, these studies did not employ a wide variation of types of responses, although the Miller and Bieri (1963) study did contain three response systems of clinical judgment. In regard to a notion of channel capacity, however, it should be noted that three studies in Table 5 did use the same stimulus dimension (aggression). It is instructive to compare the results of the Bieri and Atkins (1965) study with those of the two earlier studies using aggression stimuli. In spite of the larger number of items, the larger number of replications, and the larger number of response categories used, the slightly larger mean $T_{x;y}$ score obtained by Bieri and Atkins represents less than one additional discriminable stimulus compared to the Miller and Bieri (1964) study. Thus the fact that the scores obtained do not even begin to approach the maximum values possible under the given experimental conditions suggests that for the type of response demanded in these studies an upper limit of information transmission was being approached.

Most of the mean values of information transmission in Table 5 are close to 2 bits, indicating that about four perfect discriminations were achieved. The higher mean value for the discrimination of attitude items (2.65 bits) is noteworthy because it indicates that between six and seven stimuli were discriminable. In part, this greater discriminability of attitude items may reflect the fact that attitude dimensions are bidirectional, ranging from negative to positive, and contain a zero point in the neutral center of the scale which may serve as an additional anchor to aid discrimination. Such a scalar characteristic is missing from the unidirectional intensity dimensions represented by the other social stimuli in Table 5, which range from very little of an attribute to an extreme amount of that attribute. Further consideration of the relation of discriminability of a stimulus dimension to anchoring phenomena will be found in Chapter 6.

STUDIES OF CHANNEL CAPACITY IN THE DISCRIMINATION OF MULTIDIMENSIONAL PHYSICAL STIMULI

Thus far we have considered the ability of judges to discriminate among relatively simple dimensions in both the physical and behavioral stimulus realms. Next we shall turn our attention to the problem of how judgments may be affected by increasing the relative complexity of the stimulus. Initially, let us present some data gleaned from a large variety of studies concerned with the effect of increasing the dimensionality of a physical stimulus upon discriminative ability. We shall cite only enough studies to indicate what seem to be certain specific principles in regard to this issue.

Pollack (1953) performed an experiment in which he asked for judgments of auditory stimuli that varied in respect to both pitch and loudness. For this two-dimensional stimulus he obtained a value of 3.1 bits, a value which should be seen in contrast to the previously obtained values of 2.3 for pitch when presented alone and 2.1 for loudness when presented alone (see Table 1). By means of an informational analysis of the responses to these compound stimuli, Pollack ascertained that the dimension of pitch contributed 1.6 bits to this total and the dimension of loudness contributed 1.3 bits. (The difference of 0.2 bit can probably be accounted for by the *interaction* of pitch and loudness.) Thus we find evidence that information transmission does increase with the dimensionality of the stimulus but increases at the expense of information transmission per dimension.

Pollack and Ficks (1954) undertook another experiment with auditory stimuli in which they varied as many as seven dimensions at one time. With a complex auditory stimulus composed of seven orthogonal dimensions, they obtained a $T_{x;y}$ of about 7.00 bits—the equivalent of 128 *perfect* discriminations. This indeed begins to approach the level of discriminative ability which one intuitively feels approximates the capacity of the human organism.

Eriksen and Hake (1955b), using the three dimensions of brightness, size, and hue of visual stimuli composed of Munsell paper, were able to obtain a channel capacity of 4.11 bits. This value should be contrasted with the findings previously cited of Chapanis and Halsey (1956) and Conover (1959) of 3.6 bits for spectral hues, and with the value of 2.34 bits for brightness and 2.84 bits for size which Eriksen and Hake (1955a) obtained. Thus we again see an increase in channel capacity when the dimensionality of the physical stimulus is increased. The Eriksen and Hake finding is especially noteworthy in that they combined the three stimuli in a perfectly correlated manner—that is, they were totally redundant in the sense of redundancy described in Chapter 3. Each hue was presented with a particular brightness and a particular size, and, as Garner (1962) points out, such a procedure in no way increases stimulus uncertainty. In spite of this complete redundancy in the stimulus, information transmission increased substantially.

Klemmer and Frick (1953) used a visual stimulus which consisted of a dot in a square—a stimulus which has two dimensions—and obtained a channel capacity of 4.4 bits. This can be contrasted with the finding of 3.1 bits for a point on a line (Table 1). Osborne, Quastler, and Tweedell (1955) in a similar experiment used the same type of stimulus and obtained an identical value of 4.4 bits for this multidimensional stimulus. It should be noted that Klemmer and Frick were able to obtain a channel capacity of 7.8 bits from stimuli which consisted of a 3 x 3 grid *with from one to four dots in each grid.* This extremely dimensional stimulus again yields scores of discriminative ability that begin to approach what we reasonably feel to be the true capacity of the human being.

Engen and Pfaffmann (1959, 1960), varying both intensity and quality of olfactory stimuli, obtained a value of 4.03 bits, in contrast to the previously mentioned values of 1.9 bits for odor intensity alone, and 3.5 bits for odor quality.

Finally, Beebe-Center, Rogers, and O'Connell (1955), varying both the saltiness and sweetness of solutions, obtained a value of 2.25 bits for the compound taste stimulus. This again contrasts with the 1.7 bits obtained for these dimensions when presented alone. A further finding of Beebe-Center et al. was that although discriminative ability increases with the dimensionality of the stimulus, this increase is at the expense of discrimination per dimension—a finding identical to that of Pollack.

The foregoing considerations begin to generate what seems to be a set of principles in regard to the discriminability of physical stimuli as a function of an increase of stimulus dimensionality:

1. Discriminative ability increases as the dimensionality of the stimulus increases. It has been amply demonstrated that this occurs in the jump from one to two dimensions, and from two to three dimensions. With seven dimensions we have also seen a marked increment. We are not at all certain, however, that the *rate* of increment is constant as new dimensions are added to the stimulus. Indeed, it is likely that the rate of increase diminishes, and it may well be that discriminative ability, when plotted against an axis of increasing stimulus dimensionality, will also reach an asymptote. But this hypothesis demands empirical data that do not yet exist.

2. The increase in channel capacity as a result of increased stimulus dimensionality is not additive. Thus Beebe-Center et al. find a value of 1.7 bits for sucrose and saline solutions independently; however, they do not find a value of 3.4 bits for the compound stimulus—rather it is 2.25 bits.

3. The increase in channel capacity as a result of increased stimulus dimensionality occurs at the expense of discriminability per dimension.

4. There will be an increase in channel capacity even though the stimulus dimensions are perfectly redundant—that is, even though there is no real increase in the amount of information contained in the stimulus.

Are these principles of discrimination behavior that seem rather clear-cut in regard to physical stimuli also applicable to the discrimination of social stimuli? It is to this question that we next turn our attention.

STUDIES OF INFORMATION TRANSMISSION IN THE DISCRIMINATON OF MULTIDIMENSIONAL SOCIAL STIMULI

In the study by Miller and Bieri (1963) discussed earlier, where estimated individual measures of information transmission of 1.76 bits for developmental history, 1.71 bits for current behavior, and 1.77 bits for interview excerpts were obtained, compound stimuli consisting of combinations of these stimuli were also presented to clinicians for judgment. Thus a developmental history and a current behavioral description were combined to form what was assumed to be a more multidimensional stimulus. Similarly, current behavior was combined with interview data, developmental history with interview data, and, finally, all three types of stimulus were combined with one another. This yielded a total of four different domains of multidimensional stimuli, each domain again consisting of eight specific "case" stimuli. This method of combining dimensions in a correlated manner was *consistent* in that stimuli of comparable pathology values were combined with one another. The results for the judgment of these stimuli are reported in Table 6.

Table 6. Estimated Scores of Individual Information Transmission Obtained from Multidimensional Behavioral Stimuli [a]

(Miller and Bieri, 1963)

Stimulus Combinations	Estimated $T_{x;y}$
Developmental and current	1.73
Developmental and interview	1.74
Current and interview	1.71
Developmental and current and interview	1.71

[a] Estimated scores are averaged over the three different response conditions.

These data are in marked contrast with those reported previously for physical stimuli in which a direct and invariant increase in channel capacity occurred with an increase in the dimensionality of a *physical* stimulus. In this instance there is no indication that any increment at all occurred. It must be noted, however, that the data reported in Table 6 are *estimates* and that the process of estimation may have erased trends in the data.

It will be recalled (Table 3) that mean group channel capacity measures of 1.05, 1.09, and 0.98 bits were obtained for developmental, current, and interview materials, respectively. If we compare these values with those presented in Table 7 for combined information, there does seem to be an increase in discriminative ability as the "dimensionality" of the stimulus increases from one to two types of information, at least as far as the group as a whole in concerned. The addition of a third kind of information, however, does not yield an increment in discriminative ability.

On the basis of this one study, then, the effect of increasing the complexity of the stimulus in social judgment is equivocal. While an increment in discriminability is observed for group measures of information transmission, this increment is not observed for *estimates* of individual information transmission. However, the study of Tripodi and Bieri (1964) does provide for direct assessment of individual information transmission as a function of increasing stimulus dimensionality. The method and results of this study will be presented in detail in Chapter 7. Briefly, it was observed that information transmission did *not* increase

Table 7. Scores of Group Channel Capacity Obtained from Multidimensional Behavioral Stimuli [a]

(Miller and Bieri, 1963)

Stimulus	$T_{x;y}$
Developmental and current material	1.28
Developmental and interview material	1.11
Current and interview material	1.17
Developmental and current and interview material	1.25

[a] Scores are averaged over the three different response conditions. (By permission, American Psychological Association)

as the dimensionality of the stimulus increased from one to two dimensions (in fact, a *decrease* was observed). However, there was a significant increase in information transmission when stimulus dimensionality increased from two to three dimensions. One further aspect of this study is of interest in the present context. Tripodi and Bieri point out that multidimensional stimuli may be combined in either a *consistent* or *inconsistent* manner. In this latter condition, for example, high pathology items are combined with low pathology items. Significant decrements in information transmission were found under conditions of inconsistently combined stimulus dimensions in comparison with judgments of consistently combined information. It is apparent that even in the case of stimulus information which is contradictory, one further aspect of the nature of the stimulus must also be specified. That is, the *quantity* of information within each dimension may be equivalent or disproportionate. In the Tripodi and Bieri study mentioned previously, the quantity of information (defined as the number of items of information in each dimension) was equal when stimulus dimensions were combined. However, if disproportionate quantities of each dimension were combined in an inconsistent manner we would expect that the relative proportion of each dimension would be of importance. Bieri (1962) has reported that judgments of contradictory information vary as a function of the ratio of the amount of inconsistency in the stimulus. In making trait judgments about persons described as both dominant and submissive, for example, it was observed that judges weighted the relative amounts of each type of information in arriving at their over-all assessment. Interestingly, it was also observed that males, in comparison with females, required proportionately less dominant information than submissive information in judging a man to be dominant and required *more* submissive information before judging a male to be submissive.

We have observed, then, that the increasing complexity of a behavioral stimulus apparently does not bear a direct relation to an increase in discriminability. In order to analyze this problem further, it is instructive to consider two additional facets of the judgment task: the nature of the response system and the range from which stimuli are drawn.

THE EFFECT OF THE NATURE OF THE RESPONSE ON DISCRIMINABILITY

Unfortunately, there has been comparatively little systematic research focused on the possible effect of variations in the nature of the response systems on discriminative ability and channel capacity.

Probably the first such investigation was that of Bendig and Hughes (1953), which was concerned with the effect of the number of rating-scale points on information transmission. Using as stimuli the names of twelve foreign countries, Bendig and Hughes had subjects respond to these stimuli on 3-, 5-, 7-, 9-, and 11-point rating scales according to the subject's degree of knowledge about these countries. The experimenters also systematically manipulated the number of anchors on the scale. For the scales with three anchors (the optimum condition insofar as anchoring is concerned) they obtained scores of 0.41, 0.51, 0.56, 0.56, and 0.59 bit for each response condition (3, 5, 7, 9, and 11 points). These were scores of group information transmission, and in this sense they revealed, in part, the extent to which a group of subjects agreed with one another as to their knowledge of specific foreign countries. In this context the rather low scores obtained were not unreasonable. In any event, the investigators concluded that information transmission increases as the number of response alternatives increase, although we might add that the magnitude of the increment is rather slight. That is, the increase in information transmission from five response alternatives to eleven alternatives was only 0.08 bit—a rather modest retrieval of information for doubling the size of the response scale. A similar study by Bendig (1954), using as stimuli different foods and again manipulating the size of the response scale, yielded comparable results.

These two studies should be seen in conjunction with Garner's (1960) work in the same area. Using samples of handwriting as stimuli and variously sized scales of handwriting legibility as responses, he also found a slight increment in information transmission as the number of response alternatives increased. Again, we should note the extremely modest increment: approximately 0.38 bit for four categories as opposed to approximately 0.50 bit for twenty categories.

The reader will recall the Eriksen and Hake (1955a) study, which varied the number of stimuli and the number of response alternatives in a factorial design and which concluded that $T_{x;y}$ only reaches a maximum when the number of response categories is equal to the number of stimulus categories. However, it should be noted once more that in the most extreme condition, where twenty-one stimuli were judged on a 5-point scale and on a 21-point scale, the retrieval gained by more than quadrupling the size of the scale was only 0.6 bit.

In our own work, we also observed a rather slight increase in $T_{x;y}$ as a function of an increase in number of response categories. When aggression items were judged using a fifteen-category scale, Bieri and Atkins (1965) found a mean $T_{x;y}$ score of 2.12 bits, whereas in two previous studies the same items judged on an eight-category scale yielded values 1.84 and 1.98 bits (Table 4).

These considerations lead us to conclude that the number of response alternatives does have an effect on channel capacity, and the effect takes the following form:

1. Channel capacity will increase up until the point at which the number of rating categories equals the number of stimuli.
2. The rate of increment, however, may be quite small.
3. The addition of response categories beyond a number that is equal to that of the stimuli has no effect on channel capacity (Hake and Garner, 1951).

We should mention the study by Alluisi and Muller (1958), which analyzed the compatibility of stimulus and response and its effect on channel capacity. Using seven response codes which differed in terms of their compatibility with the stimulus, these investigators found that the more compatible code yielded the best results. Thus arabic numerals, the most overlearned and directly compatible response system, were found to be greatly superior to a novel, abstract color code.

Within the context of investigations that bear directly on clinical discrimination, Miller and Bieri (1963) found variable scores of information transmission as a consequence of differing response systems. In particular, they noted through a multivariate analysis that there was subsumed under the responses of object relationships, defenses, and clinical diagnosis some common underlying response dimension—and they hypothesized that this may well have been a dimension of "global pathology."

We suggested in Chapter 3 that one could consider the dimensionality of the response system as well as the dimensionality of the stimulus in attempting to elicit meaningful variables that pertain to discriminative capacity. The study by Miller and Bieri (1964) used as one of its response domains a judgment system of global pathology. This response was considered to be more dimensional than that of aggression or dependency because it could subsume both of the latter dimensions. The pathology dimension did yield the most consistent increment in channel capacity when multidimensional stimuli were used. Table 8 shows these findings, averaged over all the conditions of range.

Table 8. Scores of Channel Capacity as a Consequence of Increasing the Dimensionality of the Response System
(Miller and Bieri, 1964)

Stimulus-Response Condition	$T_{x;y}$
Aggressive-dependency on aggression	1.76
Aggressive-dependency on dependency	1.86
Aggressive-dependency on pathology	1.92

We must re-emphasize, however, that the response system of pathology is only *assumed* to be more dimensional than that of aggression or dependency. Although there is considerable justification for this assumption stemming from rational considerations we quite properly should show empirically that such is the case, and we cannot claim to have made such a demonstration by means of Table 8. In any event, we consider the nature of the response system in terms of its dimensionality, its range of alternatives, and its compatibility to be of extreme importance when considering the ability of judges to discriminate among an array of stimuli—whether they be physical stimuli or social stimuli. In spite of some suggestive leads that can be ascertained from the studies cited in the preceding discussion, only a start has been made in understanding the interplay of response variables and discrimination.

THE EFFECT OF THE RANGE OF STIMULI ON CHANNEL CAPACITY

We have previously mentioned the studies by Pollack (1952) in which he found that increasing the range from which physical stimuli are sampled did not have an appreciable effect upon channel capacity. A similar finding was reported by Eriksen and Hake (1955a), where the average difference was discovered to be only 0.16 bit for squares which ranged in size between 2 and 42 mm. and squares which ranged from 2 to 82 mm. Rather similar findings have been reported by Alluisi and Sidorsky (1958). Thus with regard to physical stimuli we can conclude that although the range effect is present, its consequences are rather negligible.

Miller and Bieri (1964) examined this issue with regard to behavioral stimuli of aggression and dependency sampled from different ranges of the maladjustment continuum. They used four conditions of range: (1) eight stimuli sampled from the "mild" range, (2) eight stimuli sampled from the "extreme" range, (3) eight stimuli sampled from the "middle" range, and (4) eight stimuli sampled from the entire maladjustment continuum. These four range selections were made according to the data indicated in Table 9 below. Thus, out of an original sixteen stimuli that spread themselves across the entire range of either aggression or dependency, eight stimuli were selected in four ways.

Table 9. Selection of the Four Conditions of Range from an Original Array of Sixteen Stimuli

Range Condition	Stimuli Selected
Range I (mild)	1,[a] 2, 3, 4, 5, 6, 7, 8
Range II (extreme)	9, 10, 11, 12, 13, 14, 15, 16
Range III (middle)	5, 6, 7, 8, 9, 10, 11, 12
Range IV (entire)	1, 3, 5, 7, 9, 11, 13, 15

[a] Stimulus No. 1 would be the least aggressive or dependent stimulus and No. 16 would be the most aggressive or dependent.

Table 10. The Effect on Channel Capacity Caused by Different Conditions of Range from Which the Stimuli Are Sampled

(Miller and Bieri, 1964)

Range of Pathology Sampled	$T_{x;y}$
I (mild)	1.82
II (extreme)	1.86
III (moderate)	1.72
IV (full)	1.96

The findings from this aspect of the experiment are given in Table 10. These results indicate that the variable of range does have an effect on discriminability, but again the effect is small. It does not appear to be as negligible, however, as the range effects we have noted to occur in the discrimination of physical stimuli. The changes in discriminative capacity, moreover, are in the expected direction. Thus, middle-range stimuli (condition III) are the least discriminable, stimuli drawn from the entire continuum (condition IV) are the most discriminable, and stimuli drawn from either extreme (conditions I and II) are midway in terms of their discriminability.

There seem to be at least two considerations that may explain these findings. First, there are no clear-cut behavioral anchors available for midrange stimuli as there are for stimuli that range over an entire behavioral continuum. In the case of full-range stimuli along aggressive and dependent behavioral continua, we may consider the extreme stimuli to be rather dramatic, unequivocal end anchors, a state of affairs less characteristic of extreme physical stimuli. Thus, the range IV condition had two such end anchors, ranges I and II each had one such anchor, and range III had none. (We shall consider the operation of such anchor conditions upon judgment in detail in the next two chapters.)

Second, we can consider the effect of interstimulus distance upon the range findings. Although we cannot say that the original sixteen stimuli were separated from one another by equal intervals it seems reasonable to argue that ranges I, II, and III were relatively similar in this regard. Range IV stimuli, on the other hand, probably had larger interstimulus distances than did those in the other three ranges. Thus we may confound two variables, range and interstimulus distance, and we cannot be sure how each may account for the relatively greater discriminability found in our range IV material. However, the greater importance of range in terms of the operation of end anchors is suggested by the findings that ranges I and II were discriminated more accurately than range III despite the assumed equivalence of interstimulus intervals in these three ranges.

CONCLUSIONS

In this chapter we have examined those studies which have used the information-theory model to elucidate the problem of discriminative ability in judgment behavior. We have tried to show that the concepts of information transmission and of channel capacity are particularly useful in relation to the problem of discriminability in judgment.

In regard to the judgment of physical stimuli, we have noted that the average human observer can make only a limited number of discriminations among unidimensional stimuli. Indeed, this capacity seems to be limited to approximately seven discriminations. We must re-emphasize, however, that this is an *average* value and conceals rather wide and important variations among individual judges.

In contrast to physical stimuli, the precise explication of the relative dimensionality of behavioral stimuli was a more difficult problem. To the extent that such behavioral stimuli were assumed to be relatively unidimensional, we observed an even more limited capacity for discrimination (between three and six perfect discriminations) than in the case of physical stimuli. In regard to physical stimuli, there seems to be a direct relation between an increase in stimulus dimensionality and an increase in information transmission. The findings in regard to the discrimination of behavioral stimuli, on the other hand, show no such uniform relation. In fact, under certain conditions of increased stimulus dimensionality a decrement in discriminability may be observed. Furthermore, we have found that in the discrimination of physical stimuli, the range variable—although it has some effect—is of no major consequence. With behavioral stimuli, on the other hand, we have seen that the range from which the stimuli are drawn may be a more significant consideration. This finding was thought to be a consequence primarily of the influence of end anchors in the case of behavioral stimuli.

Thus it appears reasonable to assume that processes of judgment operate differently in the judgment of physical stimuli than in the case of social and clinical judgment. In this connection it is interesting to note that some tentative evidence is available to the effect that a judge's ability to discriminate behavioral stimuli *cannot* be predicted from his ability to discriminate physical stimuli. Miller and Bieri (1964) had their subjects judge two kinds of physical stimuli (the length of lines and the intensity of gray hues). Information-transmission scores were computed for these tasks. A zero-order correlation was found between $T_{x;y}$ for the physical stimuli and $T_{x;y}$ for the behavioral stimuli. Furthermore, there was no correlation between a subject's ability to discriminate one kind of physical stimulus and his ability to discriminate the other kind of physical stimulus. Interestingly, however, there was a rather high positive correlation between a subject's ability to discriminate one kind of behavioral stimulus and his ability to discriminate another type of behavioral stimulus. That is, if a subject tended to have a high $T_{x;y}$ score in the judgment of aggressive stimuli he was likely to have a high $T_{x;y}$ score in the judgment of dependent stimuli.

Several lines of research activity are suggested by the work covered in this chapter. First, one implication stemming from the studies of clinical discrimination cited is that the nature of the *response* system may be of major importance. We have seen that if the response demanded is more complex or inclusive, a judge will be able to discriminate among stimuli more accurately than if the response system is relatively simplistic or noninclusive. On the other hand, the study by Miller and Bieri (1963) indicates that even such presumably complex response categories as "psychotic" or "obsessive complusive" may, in certain judgmental contexts, be used as relatively simple categories of judgment along a dimension of maladjustment. These observations would suggest that there may well be *limits* upon the conceptual ability of the judge in terms of the degree of inclusiveness of judgmental categories that can be utilized. Further inquiry into the nature of these limits is certainly needed.

Another area of investigation concerns the nature of individual differences in discrimination behavior. We have repeatedly noted that the average values of information transmission conceal substantial variation among individual judges. What personality, experiential, and cognitive correlates are associated with such variation? Our own work has suggested the importance of differences in individual cognitive structures, and we shall present this evidence in detail in Chapter 7.

Finally, it should be noted that most of the conceptions discussed in Chapter 3 regarding redundancy and relevancy have yet to be broached in relation to clinical discrimination.

Such, then, are the initial studies of clinical and social judgment within the general framework or informational analysis. It is evident that the major focus of these studies is upon the *discriminability* aspect of judgment. The information-theory model centers our attention upon those characteristics of the input and the output systems that influence the ability of the judge to discriminate among the stimuli available to him. This is certainly only one aspect of the judgment process, but an important one in our view. From our discussion of the research we have completed it is evident that characteristics of the nature of stimulus dimensions may influence discriminability of behavioral stimuli, perhaps even more so than in the case of physical stimuli. In the next two chapters we shall turn to a more detailed analysis of this problem from the viewpoint of anchoring effects in judgment.

chapter 5 ANCHORING EFFECTS IN JUDGMENT

The term "anchoring," as it is applied to judgment, carries many of the same implications as its nautical counterpart. Just as a ship that is anchored is *fixed* in one place and is expected not to drift substantially with the tides and waves, so an anchored stimulus (often called "an anchor" for short) is one which is presumed for one reason or another to be stabilized in its position. Furthermore, just as an anchored ship or buoy can function as a point of *reference* in locating the position of one's own ship, for example in a channel, so does an anchored stimulus appear to serve an orienting function with respect to other stimuli. *The effect of the presumed fixed position of one stimulus, the anchor, upon the judged position of another stimulus is termed an anchoring effect.*

This definition of an anchoring effect is merely descriptive, and it raises a host of questions and problems, as we shall see. What sort of effects may an anchor be observed to have on the judgment of other stimuli? Does the presence of an anchor affect the judgment of all other stimuli presented or only of some? In what kinds of judgment tasks are anchoring effects found? What seem to be the critical attributes of these tasks? Is the anchor "presumed to have a fixed position" by the subject, by the experimenter, or by both? At the level of psychological theory, what sort of models of the judgment process have been offered to account for the effects observed, and can one evaluate their relative merits? Since there are several different measurement criteria by which one can assess anchoring effects, how can these measurements be compared? Finally, in what ways can one expect the judgments regarding human attributes to be similar to or different from the judgments regarding "sensory" attributes of psychophysical stimuli, as far as anchoring effects are concerned?

Our purpose in writing this chapter is to alert the student of clinical and social behavior to the phenomenon of anchoring effects in judgment and to discuss some of the problems that face the researcher interested in investigating these effects.

PARAMETERS OF THE JUDGMENT TASK

Anchoring effects are observed when a subject is given the task of making absolute judgments about stimuli. In such a task, two conditions necessarily obtain and a third usually does but is not essential to the definition.

First, the stimuli to be judged will be selected to differ from one another *ordinally,* i.e., in terms of quantitative degree along some attribute dimension. We do not here present a set of stimuli which are *nominally* different kinds of things, such as a tone and a light and a buzzer, but rather those which are the same kind of thing and merely differ by degree in some respect, e.g., a series of tones which differ in pitch, or a series of lights which differ in brightness, or examples of behavior which exemplify different degrees of dependency.

Second, in responding to these stimuli the subject is not to compare these stimuli to one another directly, but rather is to place each stimulus *absolutely* where it appears to lie on the response scale provided for judgment. We may contrast this to the task of making simple comparative judgments, in which the subject is presented with two or more stimuli at once (or in quick succession) and asked about the difference *between these stimuli* in ordinal terms. In a task of comparative judgment the subject might be asked, "Is A louder than B or softer than B?" or "Pick out a weight that is exactly halfway in heaviness between the weight of A and the weight of B" or "If we call the brightness of this A light 10 units, tell me when I have adjusted this other light B to a brightness of 20 units." In all these cases the subject is explicitly asked to use one stimulus (or more) as a standard of comparison in judging another. The "response scale" to be employed by the subject need not be constant from the judgment of one stimulus to the judgment of the next because it is not defined apart from the standard of comparison provided for each judgment. In making absolute judgments, on the other hand, all stimuli in the series are to be judged in reference to a common ordinal response scale.

We will note here that either of two broad classes of response scale may be used for judgment, a *rating* scale of equal-appearing intervals, or else a *magnitude* or ratio scale assumed to have an absolute zero point. These are often referred to as different "levels of measurement," whether our measuring device is a physical instrument or our unaided subjective judgment. Most of our physical measuring instruments employ ratio scaling. A ruler is one example of a ratio scale: it has an absolute zero point such that the number "1" on this scale refers to one (inch) unit above zero, and each successive number not only indicates an equal additional increment of distance magnitude (the difference between 1 inch and 2 inches equals the difference between 2 inches and 3 inches, etc.), but also indicates a multiple of our basic magnitude unit (3 inches equals three units magnitude above zero). If we ask our subject to judge lengths of lines on a magnitude scale we are asking him to refer his numerical judgments to a constant *unit magnitude,* whether we specify inch units or whether he is free to establish his own implicit notion of what is to constitute a base unit. One of the few examples of a physical instrument which does not employ ratio scaling but merely equal-interval scaling alone is the thermometer. On a Fahrenheit scale, for example, we have selected a certain arbitrary zero point which is *not* assumed to correspond to no temperature. Since zero on this scale is already some positive magnitude of temperature, 1 degree F does not represent a base unit of magnitude but only a base *unit of magnitude increment* above an arbitrary starting point of measurement. We can say then that the difference between a temperature of 1 degree F and 2 degrees F equals the difference between 2 degrees and 3 degrees, etc., but we cannot say that a temperature of 3 degrees is a multiple, three times the temperature of 1 degree. This would be analogous to beginning our inch measurements arbitrarily at 10 inches on our original magnitude scale, the ruler, and calling 10 inches "1," 11 inches "2," 12 inches "3," and so on. The inch increment here remains constant, but it is apparent that the 12 inches we are calling 3 increments is not three times as great an extension as the 10 inches we are calling 1.

Turning to judgments, whenever we ask a subject for simple ratings we are asking him to use his successive response categories, e.g., a range of numbers as if they represented perceived equal increments on the stimulus side, but we do not require him to judge stimulus magnitudes in reference to an absolute base unit. We might, for example, present him with a series of ten lines which vary in length between 5 and 20 inches and ask him to rate the length of each line by using any number between 1 and 10. Now since we are not asking him to represent absolute magnitude units there are a variety of response alternatives we may allow him to use which imply simply equal-interval distinctions: our scales may be either unidirectional or bidirectional, and categories may be either numerical or verbal. A unidirectional numerical scale might consist of the integers 1, 2, 3, 4, 5, 6, 7, 8, 9, 10. Such a scale could have any range of numbers at any intervals one chooses (e.g., 1, 5, 10, 15, etc.). In studies which utilize informational analysis one usually provides as many scale values for responding as there are different values of stimuli to be judged. Sometimes one provides more stimulus values than response values, and then it is necessary for the subject to use each rating to represent a range of values in the stimulus series. A bidirectional numerical scale will increase in both plus and minus directions from a middle zero point, e.g., −4, −3, −2, −1, 0, +1, +2, +3, +4.* It is most often on such a scale that the subject is allowed to utilize an unlimited number of response alternatives, using as extreme plus or minus numbers as he wishes. Both unidirectional and bidirectional scales may be composed of verbal rather than explicitly numerical response categories. A unidirectional scale might run from the category of "not at all (loud)" at the low end to "very, very (loud)" at the high end. A bidirectional scale might run from "very, very (soft)" at one end, through a neutral category such as "neither (soft) nor (loud)," to "very, very (loud)" at the other extreme of the scale. Again, with verbal categories both the range of different responses and the fineness of discrimination implied between each category and the next may vary from one scale to another. The important thing is that the difference in magnitude between each response category and the next appear to the subject to be equal throughout the scale range.

Usually, when absolute judgments are called for, stimuli are presented for judgment one at a time, i.e., by the *method of single stimuli,* and the subject receives a random-order sequence of the range of stimulus values to be judged. This is not, however, an essential condition to the making of absolute judgments. Several stimuli may be present in the field at the same time as long as each stimulus is judged "in its own terms."

To summarize, then, in the process of making absolute judgments the subject is presented with a series of stimuli which differ from one another in degree along some attribute dimension and is asked to make an ordinal judgment of each stimulus as it appears (whether shown alone or in the presence of other stimuli) in reference to a given response scale rather than directly in reference to other stimuli in the series presented. This response scale may require of the subject a level of measurement equivalent to equal-interval ratings or to ratio judgments of magnitude.

* As we noted in Chapter 4, attitude dimensions represent such bidirectional scales in social judgment.

CHARACTERISTIC RESPONSE TENDENCIES IN THE MAKING OF ABSOLUTE JUDGMENTS

Before we consider the effects upon absolute judgments which have been specifically attributed to the presence of anchors, it may be useful for us to review what in general may be expected of the subject responding to this task.

Magnitude Estimations and the Psychophysical Law. In judging stimulus dimensions for which physical values can be said to increase quantitatively from a zero value (e.g., length, area, numerousness, duration, heaviness, lightness, brightness, loudness), there is evidence that discriminability decreases for increasing magnitudes (Weber's law). The mathematical statement of the relation between the subjective judgment of stimuli and their actual magnitudes was stated as a *logarithmic* function by Fechner. More recently, Stevens (1957) has proposed that this function is more accurately considered to be a *power* function. Most generally speaking, what a psychophysical law indicates is that we judge magnitudes psychologically in terms of ratios, not simply in terms of fixed physical units. If we pile up a number of bricks, for example, we perceive that placing a second brick on the first not only adds one unit to the height of the pile but also doubles its height, whereas adding an eighth brick to a pile of seven does not "add as much" to the pile, psychologically, because this addition does *not* double the height of the pile. Thus, for increasing fixed units of magnitude we tend to underestimate the magnitude perceived; i.e., discriminability decreases for increasing magnitudes. If we present lengths of line increasing by equal increments from 1 to 20 inches and we allow our subject to use an inch magnitude scale in judging each line, we can expect that he will judge the 20-inch line to be less than 20 inches.

Rating Scales and the Regression Tendency. If we take the same dimensions for which we have obtained magnitude estimations and ask the subject to judge the stimuli on an equal-interval rating scale, what we shall find characteristically is that ratings will form a curve that is concave downward in relation to the curve of ratio or magnitude estimation. One can observe there that the perception of the stimulus magnitudes to be rated will be affected by the psychophysical relationship but that judgments will also be referred to the response domain available. Thus, at the upper and lower ends of the range of stimulus values to be judged responses will approximate those expected on the basis of magnitude estimation alone, but between these extremes there can be seen a regression tendency. The rating curve will arch in relation to the curve of magnitude estimations. In relation to magnitude estimates, lower-value stimuli will be rated too high, and higher-value stimuli will be rated too low, i.e., judgments "regress" toward the mean of the rating scale used. This tendency of most judges to use the middle categories of the rating scale more frequently than the end categories has been called the "central tendency effect." According to Johnson (1955), "This phenomenon of central tendency is another manifestation of the regression effect that always occurs when two series of data are not perfectly correlated" (p. 354). We might add that there is some disagreement among psychologists as to the reason for the central tendency or regression tendency effect in the use of scalar ratings; here we merely wish to point out that it can be expected to occur.

Stevens (1957), who has studied judgments across a wide variety of stimulus dimensions, has found that there are some attributes for which a discrepancy between magnitude estimations and scalar ratings will not be found, but rather for which the former will resemble the latter in its response characteristics. It is Stevens' view that in these cases the stimulus dimension is such that input differences are not perceived as magnitude differences psychologically. For example, even though tone pitch is a function of wave frequency physically speaking, we do not perceive a given note as if it were a certain magnitude above zero, but rather we locate its position on a psychological dimension extending from maximum lowness to maximum highness. In this case the "natural" response for a subject to use in representing his perception is a rating scale. A ratio scale of magnitude estimation is meaningless to him here and will be used as if it *were* simply an equal-interval scale. Similarly, visual inclination of a line is perceived in terms of some position on a dimension extending from vertical to horizontal as its limits. Such dimensions, on which a stimulus is judged in terms of "where" it lies, Stevens calls "metathetic" continua. He speculates that discrimination between stimuli on such dimensions is possible mediated by a physiological process that is substitutive (or metathetic): "We progress along the continuum by substituting excitation for excitation, i.e., by changing the locus of excitation" (p. 154). Differences between stimuli on these dimensions are seen to be qualitative differences. (Stevens also refers judgments of "what kind of," i.e., nominal judgments, to metathetic dimensions.)

On the other hand, Stevens suggests, there are also "prothetic" continua for which discrimination is mediated by an additive or prothetic process at the physiological level. "We progress along the continuum by adding excitation to excitation." On these dimensions we do perceive a given stimulus, for example the brightness of a light or the loudness of a tone, as if it were a certain magnitude above zero. Since the stimulus along such a quantitative dimension will be perceived by the subject in terms of "how much" it is, Stevens reasons, it is appropriate to use magnitude or ratio estimations which are direct measures of perceived intensity, and it can be expected that scaling methods (which measure "where" a stimulus is on a dimension) may give us results which depart from these magnitude estimations. To repeat, for magnitude dimensions on the stimulus side, Stevens considers magnitude estimations to be a more appropriate and therefore "true" measure of the subject's ordinal judgment.

One need not agree with Stevens' conclusions (or with his physiological speculations) and yet can legitimately question the relationship one can expect, as far as response tendencies, between the sort of stimulus dimension one presents to the subject for judgment and the sort of response scale one requires him to use in judging. In terms of mathematical operations, we recall, ratio scaling *presumes* equal-interval scaling; nine times one base unit on a ratio scale means nine times one unit of constant "substitutive" measure on an equal-interval scale $(1 + 1 + 1 + \ldots)$. Ratio scaling further assumes that an absolute zero point exists. Psychologically, the question seems to be whether or not, or perhaps in what instances, the subject is able to apply either level of scaling to the same stimulus materials, and whether he uses each independently of the other, revealing each level's own peculiar response bias.

Channel Capacity. We should perhaps mention here that it is in the making of absolute judgments that the measure of information transmission is applied. Thus, we may note that one characteristic "response tendency" is that transmission of information, as measured by $T_{x;y}$, does not increase linearly as the number of stimuli to be judged (and the number of points on the response scale) is increased. Rather, as we have seen, there appears to be an asymptotic value or channel capacity in our ability to make reliable absolute judgments along a single dimension of stimulus variation.

Midrange Variability. More specifically, we can say at this point that the limitation in making reliable discriminations pertains particularly to our ability to judge the stimuli falling toward the center of a presented array. The fact that there appears to be a constant error in the ratings of more extreme stimuli toward the center of the response scale does not mean that midrange stimuli are judged more reliably, but means merely that the direction of error or variability in judging midrange stimuli tends to be random. The fact is that as stimuli approach the midpoint of the series presented they are judged with increasing variability on the response scale. In a later section we shall review an experiment by Eriksen and Hake (1957) which suggests that this variability appears to reflect a subject's difficulty in using midrange response values rather than his difficulty in discriminating between midrange values in the stimulus series per se. This is not to say, however, that the stimulus series presented does not play a decisive role in defining the assignment of response ratings.*

Stimulus Values and Adaptation Level. A background to the phenomenon of adaptation level in judgment can be found in the realm of visual perception. If one looks at a sheet of paper painted so that it gradually changes from very dark gray at, for example, the left edge to a very light gray at the right edge, the sheet will appear to the observer as a uniform shade of middle gray, a gray that is an average of this range of input values. This has been called the assimilation phenomenon in perception. Such a perceptual "averaging" can be obtained only when the change in input value is so gradual that one can *not* notice any difference in intensity between each increment and the next. (The term assimilation, as we shall see, has since come to be used more broadly to indicate any instance in which the difference between two stimuli is either not noticed at all or is underestimated.) In working with absolute scalar ratings of various physical stimuli (weights, brightnesses, etc.), Helson (1959) proposed that a process analogous to that of the assimilation effect occurs in which the various values of the stimuli presented successively to the subject are neurologically pooled to form a certain "adaptation level" (AL) for the perceiver. AL will then be the stimulus input value which appears to the subject as neutral on his response scale, for example a weight that seems to be neither heavy nor light or one that is judged about 5 on a heaviness scale of 1 to 10. Specifically, Helson postulated that the magnitude corresponding to AL corresponds to the geometric mean of all the stimulus values presented to the subject. In addition to taking into account these values in the *stimulus series* being judged, the calculation of AL will provide weightings for the values of any *background stimuli* present when judgments of the series are made as well as provide the value of stimuli previously judged by the subject (*residual stimuli*).

Johnson's generalization theory (1955) earlier developed similar predictions, although he proposed that in some instances it is the arithmetic mean of stimulus values, rather than their geometric mean, which best represents the subject's subjective neutral point (AL) on the response scale. In general, what these authors are suggesting is that it is the *entire distribution of stimulus values* comprising the subject's psychological

* For example, in the study of discriminability of clinical stimuli (Miller and Bieri, 1963) discussed in the previous chapter, midrange stimuli were more poorly discriminated than were extreme stimuli, even though different non-numerical response systems were used.

field (along the judged dimension) which serves to define for him the meaning of his response scale and the scalar value to assign a given stimulus. It is in relation to the subject's AL that a particular stimulus will be judged heavy or light, large or small, bright or dim, etc. One may note that in using a mean to predict the centering of the response scale, greater weighting is given to the more extreme stimuli in the distribution. The special importance of the extreme stimuli in the making of absolute judgments has long been recognized. In Volkmann's opinion, "The center of the stimulus-range has no special functional significance whatever. . . . It is the end stimuli that control the principal properties of the absolute (response) scale" (1951, p. 283).

More recently, Parducci (1963) has demonstrated that judgments represent a compromise between the range of stimuli presented and the relative frequency with which different parts of the response scale are used. Midpoint judgments on the response scale correspond to a value which can best be represented as a compromise between the median and the midpoint of the stimulus series, and only with certain stimulus distributions will this value correspond to Helson's geometric mean. The midpoint of the range is simply that value which lies exactly halfway between the values of the extreme stimuli on either end of the distribution. If, for example, the lightest weight presented in a series is 1 gram and the heaviest is 99 grams, the midpoint of the stimulus series is 50 grams. If the midpoint value alone were important in centering the scale it would mean, in this instance, that a subject judging the weights of stimuli in this series using a seven-point scale would give a stimulus of about 50 grams the response rating of 4 (i.e., neither heavy nor light, but neutral). To also take into account the median of the series (the value dividing the stimulus distribution in half) would mean that if in the above example there were more stimuli in the series falling above 50 grams than falling below 50 grams, the subject's neutral point would be somewhat above 50 grams. What is to be noted here is that Parducci, unlike Helson, was separating the scale-centering function of the stimulus distribution in general from the scale-centering function of the two stimuli (which represent the highest and lowest values in the series presented) in particular. By independently manipulating the interval spacing and the frequency distribution of sets of stimuli presented to subjects, Parducci assessed the role of each of these factors and concluded that, although the median tends to have slightly more weighting the subject's scale center seems generally to represent a compromise between range and frequency considerations.

The fact that a subject's response scale is found to be centered at the geometric mean of the stimulus series (or at any other statistical measure of central tendency) does not necessarily mean that the subject himself mentally calculates this geometric mean or that his neurological processes carry out a similar mathematical operation. Nor does it necessarily follow that AL functions as a standard of comparison for the subject's judgments because stimuli above this point will be judged accordingly higher on the response scale in relation to the neutral category, and stimuli below this point judged in lower categories. Although such statistics are surprisingly useful in predicting the outcome of a subject's judgments they raise rather than answer the question of what psychological processes may be involved in such an outcome. It is at this point that theory begins and that it is possible for all these "adaptation level theorists," Helson, Johnson, Parducci, and others, to agree upon the empirical appropriateness of a given statistic in defining AL although they diverge in their conceptualization of the psychological process to be associated with it. For the moment we shall postpone the questions of theory. The most striking fact of a subject's behavior in making absolute judgments is that, even when he is provided with an ostensibly unlimited range of response scale, and despite the fact that he knows intellectually that there is potentially a very broad range of possible values along the stimulus dimension being judged, he nevertheless will articulate the meaning of the responses he may use in terms of the actual stimuli he encounters.

DEFINITION OF AN ANCHOR

Under conditions of absolute judgment, the subject has the problem of coordinating a series of graded stimulus inputs with a series of graded available response outputs. The response scale is considered to be anchored if it is connected at one or more points to a representative stimulus. A stimulus then is called an anchor when it is joined to the response scale which the subject must utilize and it serves as an example of what input is to be associated with a particular value on the response scale.

Now it appears that in the earliest uses of this term an anchor was said to be introduced for the subject when the experimenter explicitly added a new stimulus to the series being presented and told the subject its response value. Thus Volkmann (1951), in reviewing the effects of an anchor upon judgment, describes the introduction of an *end anchor* as one of presenting an auxiliary stimulus equal to the bottom-judged stimulus and telling the subject that this stimulus is to represent the bottom category of his scale. An anchor stimulus which is auxiliary to *any* stimulus value in the series to be judged, within the series as well as at either end, can similarly be introduced; it may even lie beyond the range of the judgment series of stimuli. For reasons which will soon be clear, we shall call such a stimulus a *designated anchor,* although it would seem that these two words are redundant in meaning. What we may say of a designated anchor is that the experimenter has performed an operation—that of telling the subject the anchor's response value—which defines the stimulus as being anchored independently of whatever subsequent effect this operation may have upon the subject's judgments.

After such a designated anchor was introduced certain predictable anchoring effects upon judgment were indeed observed. With this knowledge, a reverse process of defining the introduction of an anchor by its characteristic effects became plausible, and the term "anchor" came to refer to an inferred psychological status of a stimulus for the subject, and not directly to the explicit operation of the experimenter in designating it verbally. First of all, it was soon noted that one can introduce an auxiliary stimulus beyond the range of the stimuli already being judged, and that this stimulus would have a comparable effect upon judgments even when the experimenter did not verbally designate its response value. Such an *extra-range anchor* may be introduced into the series merely as a background stimulus, not itself judged by the subject, but will nevertheless induce anchoring effects upon judgments of the series stimuli. What we have here is a stimulus that is being defined as an anchor not because it is explicitly designated as such but because its introduction can be observed to affect judgments in a manner similar to that of the designated anchor. Because its effect is *as if* it were designated, we infer that this stimulus has a more-or-less definite value on the subject's response scale and we therefore term such a stimulus an *implicit anchor*. An experiment by Brown (1953) does suggest that in order to function as an effective anchor upon series judgments, an undesignated background stimulus must be not merely in the same "geographical environment" as the series stimuli but in the same "psychological field." Brown's subjects repeatedly lifted a background anchor which was either heavier or lighter than the series of weights they judged, but this anchor was in the form of a tray on which the stimulus weights were loaded. After the subject had judged each weight he was asked incidentally to pick up its tray and move it out of the way. The physical lifting of this psychologically irrelevant anchor did not affect judgment of the series' weights. At the same time, even when we utilize more apparently relevant background anchors and when their introduction into the series does modify judgment of these stimuli, the fact remains that judgment of the background anchor is not called for. Whether the subject himself judges it as having a particular value, at this point we have no way of knowing. We know that we introduce the auxiliary stimulus (beyond the series) and it has an effect upon other judgments like that of a designated anchor, and this can now serve as our definition of an anchor.

As a second step, we may introduce the new stimulus beyond the series and specifically ask the subject to judge its value along with the other stimuli he has already been judging. Indeed, when we do this we find that it is judged with a high reliability, indicating that it does have a fairly definite value on the subject's response scale, even though this value was not designated by the experimenter. We can now define an anchor as a stimulus introduced into an ongoing series which shows predictable effects upon the judgment of the previous stimuli and which we have reason to think the subject perceives as having a fairly clear response value itself (either by experimenter designation or by the subject's own judgment of it). It will be recalled that we are speaking here of the subject's judgment of an introduced anchor lying beyond the range of series values, such as a weight of 500 grams or of 100 grams introduced into a stimulus series ranging between 250 and 350 grams. Here the anchor has become part of the judgment series, but (a) lies outside its range and (b) is introduced only after judgments of the other stimuli have been obtained without its presence.

It is only a final step in our thinking to dispense with these last two conditions and define an anchor exclusively in terms of its own psychological clarity of value and its effects upon the judgment of other stimuli. Thus we come upon the use of the term "natural anchor." If we return to the original judgments of a series of stimuli we can observe that the most extreme stimuli in this series are responded to more reliably than stimuli toward the center of the series, and that end stimuli appear to show some of the effects upon the judgment of other stimuli in the series which have been observed for introduced anchors; therefore we will call the end stimuli in the series *natural anchors*. The reader may note here that the effects of these natural end anchors, unlike those of introduced anchors, cannot be assessed against judgments under a condition of no anchoring. We have come to a point where there can never be a true absence of anchoring according to our definition. What we can do here is to demonstrate that the judgment of a particular stimulus input value will be a function of its position in respect to the ends of the series. Within a range of stimulus weights of 100 to 200 grams, a weight of 200 grams will function as an anchor and be judged with maximum reliabilty relative to other stimuli in the series. Within a range of 150 to 250 grams, this same 200-gram weight will not function as an anchor but will be subject to effects of the new end anchors.

KINDS OF ANCHORING EFFECTS

The presence of an anchor stimulus has been observed to affect the judgment of other stimuli both in terms of decreasing or increasing *variability* of judgment and of *shifting* judgment either toward the value of the anchor—assimilation effect—or away from the value of the anchor —contrast effect.

Variability of Response. Under "normal" conditions of making absolute judgments, it can be observed that the variability of responses evoked by a given stimulus is maximal for stimuli toward the center of the presented series and minimal for stimuli approaching the extremes in value; variability of response forms a more-or-less normal curve across the range of stimulus values presented for judgment. Now insofar as we consider the end stimuli in the series to constitute natural anchors, variability of judgment increases with the distance of a stimulus from an anchor and is maximal for stimuli equidistant from both anchors, i.e., falling in the middle of the series. Or we may say conversely that reliability of judgment increases as the value of the stimulus to be judged approaches that of either anchor. The same input value of stimulus, e.g., a weight of 10 grams, will be variably judged on the response scale when it falls toward the middle of the stimulus values selected for judgment and will be judged more reliably when stimulus values are selected so that this weight falls toward either end of the distribution.*

It has been suggested (Eriksen and Hake, 1957) that the source of variability of midrange judgments stems from a response ambiguity rather than a stimulus ambiguity. These authors cleverly selected a stimulus series of values having itself no endpoints—a circular continuum of twenty hues. Each color was to be rated on a response scale of 1 to 20. They told one group of subjects to judge the color red as "1" and an orangish red as "20," thereby explicitly anchoring the response scale at these stimulus values. An accurate matching of stimuli and responses for this group would place the color green around 10 on the response scale. A second group was anchored for "1" at the color green and at a bluish green for "20," which would place the color red around 10 on their response scale. Both groups were then given the task of making absolute judgments for each of the 20 colors in the entire circle presented in random order. The results demonstrated clearly that variability of judgment increases for stimuli that are midrange in terms of one's given *response* scale, around the color red for group one and around the color green for group two. The same bluish-green hue which was judged with maximum reliability by group two was judged with maximum unreliability (variability) by group one.

* One word of caution. As sensory magnitudes (brightness, loudness, weight, etc.) are increased by equal physical increments, they become increasingly difficult to discriminate (Weber's law). In order to correct this sensory bias and obtain the above curve of variability it is necessary to select for absolute judgment stimuli which increase by logarithmic increments along the dimension to be judged in order that they be equally discriminable under conditions of paired comparison.

Now it may be noted in regard to the above experiment that although the authors attribute their findings to natural anchoring properties of the extremes of the response scale, in practice they presented their subjects with two designated anchors which *also* corresponded to the ends of the response scale. Their inference may not be altogether justified, since it can be observed that the introduction of *any* designated anchor, whether within or corresponding to an end of the response scale, serves to reduce variability of judgment of stimuli in its vicinity. That is, we may ask what would have happened to judgments in group one (so far as variability is concerned) if these subjects had been told initially that a purplish blue is "4" and blue is "5" on the response scale, i.e., designating anchors at values other than the ends of the scale.

To review, judgment of stimuli midrange in a stimulus series is maximally variable, whereas reliability increases as one approaches the end stimuli in the series which appear to function as natural anchors for judgment. If in addition we explicitly designate the response value for an end stimulus, we shall obtain an even smaller variable error in judgment over a wide range of stimulus values around this anchor. If we designate the response value for a midrange stimulus we shall similarly increase reliability, and here the *reduction* in variability will be even more striking since initial variability in this range is higher than in the vicinity of a natural end anchor.

Along with decrease in variability of judgment around an anchored stimulus value, two other phenomena have been observed (Volkmann, 1951) which suggest that anchoring the value of a stimulus within the judgment series aids the subject in representing presented stimulus values on his response scale. There is an increase in *accuracy* of judgment over "a wide range" of stimuli extending in value away from the anchor, although it is observed also that there is a decrease in accuracy outside this range. If reliability (low variability) is seen as a minimum of random error or spread of responses in judging a stimulus, accuracy can be seen as a minimum of constant error, each in relation to what the "best" response to a stimulus should be. Our criterion of accuracy is, of course, more stringent in ratio scaling than in equal-interval scaling. In the latter, judgments are accurate insofar as they preserve the ordering of stimulus values and represent the relative differences between successive values. The other phenomenon observed is an increase in the number of response categories which the subject is willing to use in judging the stimuli, i.e., in his *fineness of discrimination,* and along with this an increase in both the speed and the confidence with which he makes judgments.*

* Recent research by Johnson and King (1964) illustrates the influence of end anchors upon judgmental accuracy and central tendency effects.

Taken together, all these measures would seem to indicate that anchoring has the effect of increasing the *validity* of judgment, at least in the vicinity of the anchored stimulus value. This statement, however, must be qualified. First of all, "the vicinity of the anchor" is not clearly prescribed, and since judgments may *not* be more valid beyond this range we cannot say that anchoring improves judgment for the stimulus series as a whole. Next, even within the vicinity of an anchor, a reduction in response variability may be more striking than any reduction in constant error; there is some dispute with respect to an anchor as to whether and in what range of values increased accuracy per se will be observed.

To illustrate the phenomena we have been describing as well as the appearance of assimilation and contrast effects which will be discussed below, let us turn to a classic study of anchoring effects by Rogers, Volkmann, Reese, and Kaufman (1947). In this experiment subjects were asked to adjust the inclination of a succession of lines to specified angles of tilt, ranging from −10 degrees to +100 degrees with respect to the vertical. After recording the subjects' responses, a line tilted +30 was introduced as a designated anchor and a second series of judgments was obtained. The introduction of this anchor was observed to have the following effects: errors of estimation decreased for lines ranging from +5 to +40 degrees, while below +5 and above +40 degrees error actually increased. In terms of the direction of errors made, with introduction of the anchor there was a tendency for inclinations between +7 and +30 degrees to be overestimated and for those from +30 to about +55 degrees to be underestimated, i.e., a tendency for judgments in an area of about 25 degrees on either side of the anchor to be assimilated toward the anchor value. Below +7 degrees there was a tendency to underestimate the inclination, i.e., to judge tilt in a direction away from or contrasting to the anchor value. To repeat, these constant errors could be observed despite the general reduction of error regardless of its direction.

Assimilation Effects. The conditions under which assimilation of judgments toward the value of the anchor stimulus will occur are not altogether clear. The Rogers et al. study suggests that this is a distance phenomenon; it is the judgment of stimuli in the proximity of the anchor which show assimilation toward the anchor. The anchor in this study fell within the range of judgment stimuli. In a study by Sherif, Taub, and Hovland (1958) a similar effect was obtained with the end stimulus value designated as the anchor. Here the stimuli to be judged were gram weights, and judgments were made on a six-point rating scale. With the introduction of a high end anchor not only did subjects apply response category 6 to more stimulus values but they also tended to overuse categories 5 and 4, and to increasingly underuse categories 3, 2, and 1, thus showing an overestimation of stimuli (assimilation toward the high anchor) throughout the entire stimulus range. A similar general assimilation trend was observed with introduction of a low end anchor for a new series of weights and judgments obtained on a five-point rating scale. On the other hand, with the same five-point rating scale applied to another series of weights, introduction of a low end anchor produced both overuse of response category 1 (assimilation) and also a slight increase in use of category 5, i.e., a contrast effect in the judgment of stimuli beyond a certain distance from the anchor, specifically toward the far end of the series. In all these cases assimilation toward a designated anchor is obtained, but the relation between assimilation and distance from the anchor of the stimulus so judged is not clear. To confuse the matter further, we know that in the absence of a *designated* end anchor, judgments do not assimilate toward the endpoints of the judgment scale, i.e., toward those values of the most extreme stimuli in the series which we call natural anchors. On the contrary, it is a characteristic tendency in making absolute judgments to underuse the extreme response categories of a scale and, in effect, to assimilate judgments toward the middle values of the scale (the central tendency effect). Extreme stimuli in the series (*including* the natural end anchors) are not judged to be as extreme as they actually are; low magnitudes are overestimated in value and high magnitudes are underestimated.*

Finally, as we shall discuss in the next section of this chapter, assimilation effects have been obtained, at least in the judgment of social and clinical attribute dimensions, under the condition of sequentially alternating high and low natural end anchors. When the same midrange stimulus is presented for absolute judgment first in the context of a stimulus at the high extreme of the dimension and then in the context of a stimulus at the low extreme of the dimension, again with the high anchor, and so on, there appears to be a temporal trend toward judging this middle stimulus in the direction of the presented anchor (i.e., of increasing assimilation), *even though* the stimulus value of the judged item remains at a fixed distance from the anchors.

Contrast Effects. We have already mentioned instances in which introduction of a designated anchor within or at an end of the judgment series of stimulus values results in some contrast in the judgment of stimuli far removed from the position of the anchor. Even more striking (and consistent) contrast effects are obtained when an anchor stimulus, whether designated in value or not, is introduced beyond the range of

* We are speaking here of constant errors. It will be recalled that random error is maximal for midrange values.

values of the judgment series. To take a hypothetical example, if the subject has been judging a series of weights ranging in value between 75 and 140 grams and rating these weights on a six-point scale of heaviness, and an anchor value of 195 grams is introduced into the series, one is likely to observe a noticeable decrease in the subject's use of category 6; judgment of the heaviest stimuli in the original series is likely to shift down to a lower response category. Generally speaking, the further removed from the series or more "remote" the introduced anchor, the greater will be the contrast effect observed. That is to say, there is an increasing recession away from the anchor in the response categories utilized as the value of the anchor is further removed from the stimulus series. There does appear to be some limiting distance of remoteness beyond which an anchor value ceases to affect other judgments.

There is some disagreement at both the theoretical and empirical levels as to how far beyond the range of stimulus values an anchor must be in order to achieve a minimum of contrast effect. In two of the series run by Sherif, Taub, and Hovland the introduction of an anchor weight slightly below the lowest stimulus value resulted in *overuse* of the lowest rating response category in judging the series (i.e., assimilation).

Another condition under which contrast effects have been observed is that in which a given stimulus value is presented to be judged in alternating contexts of higher and lower values. If a given length of line must be rated on a scale of perceived lengths, the line will be given a higher rating when it is presented along with shorter line lengths to be judged and given a lower rating when presented in a context of longer lengths, relative to the rating given it when both shorter and longer lines are included in the judgment series. When the subject is presented with alternating high and low contexts of lines across a series of trials, his judgments of the critical stimulus can be observed to shift down and up in a direction contrary to the given context (Miller and Engen, 1960). A similar effect was obtained by Campbell, Lewis, and Hunt (1958) for judgments of tone pitch. Using line length, Krantz and Campbell (1961) obtained this result, which was not significant, only for judgment in inches (i.e., a magnitude judgment). With a response in ratings, these authors found that the judgments which showed contrast to the initial anchor context tended to be maintained despite the change of context, moving only slightly away from the new opposite anchor. In these studies the term "anchor" is used synonymously with "contextual stimulation"; i.e., we do not know whether the critical stimulus is being contrasted specifically to *an* anchor, the far end stimulus in the presented context, or whether it is being contrasted to the entire contextual distribution of stimulus values. In our own studies (in contrast to those of Campbell et al.), we have eliminated the filled range of values between critical stimulus and most extreme anchor value, and have presented only the extreme anchors together with the critical "moderate" stimulus.

In general, we may state as an empirical finding that a stimulus of "average value" * in a series of stimulus values will tend to be given a midrange value on the response rating scale provided for the subject, and that when the stimulus series is extended by introducing a more extreme (anchor) value at one end, judgment of this midrange stimulus will be shifted on the response scale in a direction away from the position of the anchor, i.e., will show a contrast effect. Whether this contrast effect is a result of the increase in absolute *distance* between anchor and critical stimulus or whether it is a result of a change in the relative distance of this critical stimulus from both extreme values in the series, that is, of a shift in the subject's *centering* of the series is a matter of theoretical controversy. In the next section we shall review these two alternative theories of anchoring.

THEORIES OF ANCHORING

As we have said, theories of anchoring may be grouped in two broad categories, those which we may call centering theories and those which we may call distance theories.

Centering Theories of Anchoring. According to any adaptation-level theory, scalar judgments will be some function of the values of the stimuli presented to the subject and an anchor will be expected to modify the scalar judgment of stimuli insofar as it can be predicted to cause a shift in the value of AL. Specifically, any predicted shift in AL due to introduction of the anchor should be in the direction of the anchor's value, and consequently stimuli within this area of shift should be judged in a direction away from, or in contrast to, the position of the anchor. Suppose that a subject is judging weights on a thirteen-point rating scale of increasing heaviness, such that a rating of 7 corresponds to "neither light nor heavy" or AL. In an initial series of stimuli, he tends to assign the rating of 7 to a weight of 28 grams. After a heavy anchor weight is introduced in the series he assigns the rating of 7 to a weight of 30 grams (i.e., 30 appears to be of average or neutral heaviness). Then he will give the weight of 28 grams a lower rating than before, perhaps a 6 or a 5, indicating that in contrast to the heavy anchor (and the now heavier value at AL) this same weight is judged to be lighter than originally.

* Since there is some question whether the subject assigns a midrange response to an "average value" stimulus as defined by the midpoint of stimulus values, the median, the mean, or the geometric mean of the series, here we are using the term "average" roughly, referring to any of these measures.

Two questions can then be asked: (a) What anchor values can be expected to affect the value of AL? (b) Will only judgments of stimuli falling between the value of initial and anchored AL be affected by introduction of the anchor?

An answer to the first question will depend upon the statistic one utilizes in predicting AL. In Table 1 we have presented the AL values for a

Table 1. Effect upon AL of Introducing Anchors at Various Positions

	Series Presented	Arithmetic $\bar{x}$	Geometric $\bar{x}$	Range Midpoint	Median
A	5[a] . . . 26, 27, 28, 29, 30, 31, 32	26.000	25.49	18.5	28.50
B	26 26, 27, 28, 29, 30, 31, 32	28.625	28.54	29.0	28.50
C	27 26, 27, 28, 29, 30, 31, 32	28.750	28.68	29.0	28.50
D	28 26, 27, 28, 29, 30, 31, 32	28.875	28.81	29.0	28.50
D_1	28.9 26, 27, 28, 29, 30, 31, 32	28.990	28.94	29.0	28.95
E	26, 27, 28, 29, 30, 31, 32	29.000	28.93	29.0	29.00
F	29 26, 27, 28, 29, 30, 31, 32	29.000	28.94	29.0	29.00
G	30 26, 27, 28, 29, 30, 31, 32	29.125	29.06	29.0	29.50
H	31 26, 27, 28, 29, 30, 31, 32	29.250	29.18	29.0	29.50
I	32 26, 27, 28, 29, 30, 31, 32	29.375	29.29	29.0	29.50
J	26, 27, 28, 29, 30, 31, 32 . . . 53	32.000	31.29	39.5	29.50

[a] Underlined value indicates anchor introduced; series E is unanchored series.

series of weights with an anchor stimulus value (underlined) introduced at various positions within and beyond the original series. One may compare the effect of these different anchor values upon AL, as predicted in terms of the several statistics which have been used in calculating AL. First one may note that if AL is calculated to correspond to a mean of the stimulus series of values, one can expect some degree of contrast effects in judgment (i.e., a shift toward anchor of AL) however minimally the anchor is removed from the original value of AL. That is, an effective anchor need not have a value beyond the range of original stimuli to produce an effect. Given an arithmetic mean, the amount of predicted shift will be a simple function of the distance between original AL and anchor; with each additional gram weight of anchor value AL shifts upward by 0.125 gram. The geometric mean takes into account a psychophysical function in judgment. In calculating geometric mean values, shift is again a function of distance between original AL and anchor value, but here the "pull" of the anchor decreases as the stimulus value of the anchor increases, and a low anchor will thus be predicted to have a greater effect upon judgment than a high anchor.

If AL is calculated as a median value, the anchor will modify AL only insofar as it produces a median shift in the frequency distribution of values, and all variations in anchor value on a given side of the median, whether within or beyond the series, are equivalent; distance from AL in one direction is irrelevant. Finally, if AL is calculated as the midpoint of the range, an anchor can be expected to have *no* effect upon AL unless it lies beyond the original series in value and extends the range. If it does extend the range it has a "strong arithmetic mean effect"; in this instance each additional gram weight of anchor value beyond the initial range shifts AL upward by 0.50 gram. Taking into account, as Parducci (1963) does, both median and midpoint, one might say that although judgment is affected by adding more stimuli within a given range of value, the addition of a single anchor within the series is of little importance in this regard. The anchor's main effect is not upon perceived frequencies but upon the perceived range of stimulus values, and it will be extra-range anchors which are critical here. It is therefore not distance from AL per se that is predictive of a contrast effect in anchoring but distance of the anchor from the end of the stimulus series, insofar as this distance modifies the parameters of the array being judged.

This theoretical difference requires some explanation. Having calculated AL for a stimulus series, one will at the least predict which stimulus values will be judged on the positive side of the response scale and which stimuli will be judged negatively on the scale. Beyond this, Helson has suggested a modification of the Weber-Fechner law that will hopefully improve our ability to predict the exact response assigned to any stimulus in the series, i.e., the distribution of responses into the various categories on either side of the neutral rating. Such a prediction would be based both on the value of a stimulus being judged in terms of its distance from the absolute lower threshold and also on its distance from the value of AL. In making these predictions, the implication in Helson's own writing is that the value of AL functions as a point of reference or as a standard in the subject's judgment of a given stimulus. Thus, Helson (1964) observes:

Each class of stimuli is judged with respect to internal norms which can be objectively and quantitatively specified. Judgments are relative to prevailing *norms* or adaptation levels. [Italics ours.] (p. 26)

It is important to notice, however, that AL is not a standard for the subject in the sense of a clear-cut value in relation to which incoming stimulus values are judged. A "neutral" response is not directly assigned to particular stimuli as if this were a perceivable characteristic of the stimuli themselves: the response has meaning only in reference to what one judges to be the limits of the series. One does not know what stimulus to call "neutral" apart from its middling position within a definite range of stimulus values. As we have seen, it is the extreme values in the series which are most reliably responded to, and the phenomenon of mid-range variability suggests that the centering of one's response scale is constantly being derived from the distribution of incoming stimulus values one must place on the scale. To put this another way, the neutral category response requires more information than either response at the extremes of the scale. To assign a stimulus the highest rating on one's scale is merely to judge that it is more extreme in value than any other stimulus presented, regardless of the distribution or range of these other stimuli. Similarly, to assign a stimulus the lowest rating on one's scale is simply to judge it as "lowest of all." But to judge a stimulus as middling means to assign it a position relative to the range and distribution of both higher and lower values at once. If AL is viewed thus as a dependent, rather than an independent variable in judgment, it is understandable why Parducci, unlike Helson, stresses the particular function of the stimulus range (i.e., of endpoint stimulus values) in predicting AL.

In answer to our second question, we have indicated that Helson's equation provides for the predicted judgment of any stimulus value in a series, and insofar as an anchor affects the value of AL it will affect the judgment of any given stimulus.

. . . the response to any stimulus with respect to any attribute depends upon the distance of the stimulus from AL. . . . The magnitude of the perceived difference depends upon both the stimuli being judged and the value of AL. . . . [Helson's equation yields] a negatively accelerated curve resembling a logarithmic function and hence requires increasing increments of stimulation for equal differences in judgment. (Helson, 1959, pp. 585–586)

We can, of course, assume that a high anchor which raises the value of AL will correspondingly lower the judged value of stimuli falling between the original value and this raised value of AL (contrast effect). It has also been observed (Postman and Miller, 1945) that when one introduces an anchor value some distance above a range of series stimulus values it is the judgment of the stimuli nearest to the position of the anchor (i.e., the highest values in the series) which shows the greatest amount of contrast, while the ratings of stimuli lower in the series may remain unaffected by the anchor. Then as increasingly remote anchor values are introduced, contrast effects in judgment are seen to extend further and further down the series. This has been termed the "rubber-band effect." However, it has also been observed (e.g., by Sherif, Taub, and Hovland, 1958), and can be predicted within the framework of adaptation-level theories (Parducci and Marshall, 1962), that with the introduction of an anchor value which is at (or only slightly above) the range of series stimulus values, judgment of stimuli toward the anchored end of the series will shift toward the position of the anchor, i.e., will show assimilation toward the anchor. These several findings present a complicated picture. The direction and degree of response displacement to be predicted for a given stimulus, as a result of introducing an anchor, appear to be a function of at least three variables: (1) the distance of this judged stimulus from AL, (2) its distance from the anchored end of the stimulus series, and (3) its distance from the anchor value itself (which is partly a matter of the distance between the anchored end of the series and the position of the anchor). The problem for adaptation-level theories of judgment, insofar as they focus upon the role of scale centering in the response to a given stimulus, is to develop, within the AL formula itself, a formulation of AL which accounts for observed effects upon judgment of anchors introduced. That is, insofar as the effect of an anchor upon judgment can be adequately explained in terms of its predicted effect upon AL, rather than in terms of a direct effect upon stimulus judgment independent of any effect on AL, the term "anchor" can be eliminated as a special, unique factor in judgment.

Distance Theories of Anchoring. Conversely, distance theories of anchoring focus not upon the relation between the judgment of a stimulus and AL but directly upon the difference in value between judged stimulus and anchor. According to Sherif and Hovland (1961) and others, the condition necessary for obtaining assimilation in judgment is a short distance between stimulus and anchor, and for contrast is a large distance. Actually, this hypothesis pertains to the distance between *any* two stimuli. What characterizes the anchoring condition specifically is that in underestimating or overestimating such an inter-stimulus distance, the judgment of one of the stimuli (the anchored value) will remain stable while the judgment of the other stimulus is subject to the displacement. In a classical study by Hovland, Harvey, and Sherif (1957), the position of one's own attitude toward a social object was assumed by the authors to constitute an internal anchor in judging the position of other attitudes as series stimuli. Three groups of subjects were obtained on the basis of their attitudes toward prohibition: a wet group, a dry group, and an unselected group. Each subject rated himself on a nine-point dry-wet scale by checking the position on this scale he felt most nearly represented his own. Each of the nine scale points was illustrated by an attitude statement. Prior to the study, impartial judges sorted a large pool of communications expressing a range of attitudes toward prohibition, and from these the experimenters selected eight as representing distinct positions on the dry-wet continuum. They themselves added a ninth communication, very wet, and thus had available a scaled series of nine communication attitudes. One of these communications which expressed a moderately wet attitude (point 6) was then rated by the subjects on their own dry-wet scale, the scale on which they had indicated their own position. The results of this stimulus judgment by the subjects, although not reported in terms of statistical significance, were summarized by the authors as supporting their distance hypothesis of anchoring:

> The expectation is fulfilled that those at the wet end judge that the communication advocated a drier position than it did and those at the dry end judge that it was advocating a wetter position than it did. Those nearer the position of the communication reported it more objectively. The evidence concerning assimilation deviates somewhat from the theoretical curve. There were too few *S*s with intermediate positions to enable us to determine these positions adequately. (p. 248)

As we have mentioned, Sherif, Taub, and Hovland (1958) have also demonstrated assimilation and contrast effects with other than internal anchoring. In the judgment of weights, an anchor stimulus introduced at, or slightly beyond, the range of original stimulus values resulted in overuse of ratings nearest to the position of the anchor (assimilation), whereas the introduction of an anchor more distant from the stimulus range in value resulted in a piling up of ratings in categories further removed from the anchor position (contrast). One might note here the difference in anchoring effect criterion employed in these two studies. In the prohibition study a *particular stimulus* was selected (the moderately wet communication), and its value, established by impartial judges, was compared to the value assigned it by subjects under condition of (internal) anchoring. In judging weights, the authors examined the relative frequency of usage or *response distribution* for the scalar values available for judgment and compared this distribution under nonanchored and anchored conditions. We can indirectly infer that there are stimuli which are being assigned a changed rating under the anchored condition, although we are not examining the change in judgment for any particular stimulus.

Helen Peak (1958) has provided a theoretical model based on Hullian learning theory to account for assimilation and contrast effects as a function of interstimulus distance. Using her model, we can compare the judgment of stimuli presented simultaneously (condition of multiple input) to the "true" ratings of these stimuli when they are presented singly. We shall consider the judgment of just two stimuli, where one is a stimulus in a judgment series and the other is the anchor value introduced along with it.

First, assimilation can be explained in the following fashion: A stimulus is surrounded by a gradient of generalization along whatever attribute is being judged. Presentation in training trials of a given stimulus input value to which the subject responds establishes not only a high probability of the subject's responding to this value but also tendencies for his responding to other values along the dimension; these probabilities decrease with distance (in *j*nd units) from the input value. We might say that there is a gradient of activation potential surrounding any input value. Moreover, it is assumed that a stimulus value falling between the value of two input stimuli may have probabilities of response from both input sources at once. When the two input sources are optimally near each other in value and when both are presented simultaneously, it can be shown that the combined probability of responding may be higher at some point between them (and the subject will respond here) than for either input point. This would account for the phenomenon of *assimilation.* To illustrate, a subject who is given a 50-gram weight singly and has a strong tendency to rate it as "3" and a moderate tendency to rate it "2" or "4" will rate it "3." He is given, again singly, a 52-gram weight, and responds with his strongest tendency to rate it "5" rather than "4" or "6." Now he is given this 52-gram weight to judge again while the 50-gram weight is simultaneously presented as an anchor stimulus. The merely moderate tendencies to respond "4" to each of these stimuli presented singly now summate with the two sources of input combined and result in a higher probability here than for the previous response of "5." The subject then "underestimates" the value of the 52-gram stimulus and rates it "4," in the direction of the anchor.

To explain contrast at greater input distances, Peak first makes the assumption that the psychological distance between two stimuli on a dimension can be defined in terms of the number of other psychologically discriminable events which lie between them on this dimension. If two adjacent stimulus points have the same combined probability of response, furthermore, they may be considered to be one indiscriminable event. So, conversely, Peak defines the number of perceived events between input points as a direct function of the amount (sum) of difference found between the combined probability of each intervening stimulus point and that of its neighbor. Defining a hypothetical gradient of response probabilities around each of two input stimuli, Peak calculates that the differentiation (of probabilities) among the intervening stimuli will increase with increasing distance between the two stimuli, but not at a linear rate. At a distance between inputs where they no longer provide combined probabilities for the intervening points, increasing differentiation is a more-or-less simple function of scalar distance, and judgments will be "objective." But up to this point, as distance between the input stimuli is increased, it can be calculated that differentiation among intervening activation points will increase at a relatively faster rate, producing the overestimation of distance which we call contrast. In this area, two stimuli presented simultaneously would be judged farther apart than if the same two were presented singly.

On the basis of this model, once can specify the particular scalar distances at which assimilation and contrast should occur only if one knows how far the stimulus generalization gradient extends around any given input and what the exact response probabilities are for any point along the gradient. Although one might possibly deduce this information from the empirical findings in a given instance, one must also be able to apply it in predicting the results to be obtained with new data.

As we see, the distance hypothesis of anchoring tends to take as a model a judgment situation in which there is a single distance to be considered, that between anchor and a stimulus being judged. Even when several stimuli are being judged, each is seen in terms of its distance from the anchor. Centering theories, on the other hand, assume a much more complex field of distance relationships within which a given stimulus is judged; the field consists of the relation between the value of any given stimulus and all other stimuli presented, of which the anchor is only one. Whether a paradigm such as Peak's would result in predictions similar to those of adaptation-level theories if it were applied to a more complex set of distance relationships remains to be explored.

PROBLEMS IN THE STUDY OF ANCHORING: AN OVERVIEW

The attempt to evaluate one theory of anchoring against another is extremely difficult and may even be a premature concern at this stage in our understanding. The reason is that we have not yet reached a point where we agree on everything but the interpretation of our findngs.

Rather, there are disparities among anchoring studies all along the line, from the materials we present for judgment to the way we define the presence of an anchor to the way we measure its effect upon judgment. Let us return here to the questions we asked at the beginning of this chapter and see how well we are able to answer them.

1. In what kinds of judgment tasks are anchoring effects found? Anchoring effects (both in regard to random and to constant errors of judgment, i.e., to general variability and to displacements in a given direction) are found in the task of making absolute judgments. They are most consistently found when the subject must rate his stimuli on an equal-interval judgment scale. It is not clear whether, or in what instances, anchoring effects occur in the making of magnitude estimations, a ratio level of scaling. As Stevens, Attneave, and others have suggested, we may better understand anchoring as well as other judgment phenomena if we consider the kind of material we present to the subject and the sort of response we call upon him to make *in relation to each other*. Thus, if in some experiments one finds anchoring effects for magnitude estimations and in other experiments one does not, the reason *may* be that in the former case the subject is dealing with stimuli which he is unable to conceive of in terms of magnitude units and in effect is not judging at the level of scaling ostensibly provided him. Similarly, one may ask what there is about an attribute to be judged that absolute judgments in general, in contrast to direct comparisons among the stimuli presented, allow for anchoring to occur.

2. Can anchoring effects be considered distortions of judgment? This question is partly related to the first question. The issue has been periodically raised as to whether contrast and assimilation effects in scalar ratings, as a function of introducing an extreme anchor, can be seen as a distortion in perceived magnitudes at the "psychological level" or whether they do not simply reflect an adaptation to changed conditions at the "response level," i.e., in use of scale values provided. The McGarvey study (1943) is illustrative of this problem. If a subject is allowed to rate six lower-class occupations on a ten-point (equal-interval) scale of socio-economic status, the occupation of cashier may be rated near the top of the scale, e.g., "3." This position, in relation to those of street cleaner, ditch digger, and so on, is fairly high. If, however, the occupation of doctor is then added to the series, the rating of cashier may fall considerably, e.g., to "8," whether or not the subject is told explicitly that doctor represents a "1" occupation. Does this mean that cashier is now seen to be a lower class of occupation than it was initially, or does it mean that the perceived position of cashier on the status continuum is simply referred to a new response scale? If we judge a cat to be

"large" when judged in a series of mice stimuli and then "small" when judged in a series of dog stimuli, do we perceive a change in the cat's "own" absolute size, a perceptual nonidentity?

Several answers have been given to this question. Adaptation-level theorists such as Helson view the rating response as indicative of the subject's perception (provided that enough response categories exist to allow him to represent perceived stimulus values). A given magnitude input does not, according to these theorists, have a constant or absolute psychological value for the subject apart from the stimulus context in which it occurs. A given brightness of light is not recognized to be the same light when it is presented first among a brighter series and then among a dimmer series; an extreme anchor, then, literally changes the perception of stimuli which are judged in contrast to it. Stevens, as we have seen, as well as Galanter and others, tends to regard equal-interval ratings as less tied to perception than ratio scaling, at least for prothetic stimulus dimensions (see p. 10). Galanter (1962) writes:

> The category scale value for a particular stimulus is not as intimately associated with the stimulus as is the magnitude value. In consequence, many psychophysicists have come to believe that the magnitude scale reveals more about the sensory effects of stimuli, and therefore more about the bases of the judgmental process of people when they are called upon to act with respect to the magnitudes of stimuli in their environment. (p. 153)

From this viewpoint, a shift in scalar rating of a stimulus consequent to introducing an anchor is indicative of little more than the way we utilize our response scales, and does not imply that any change has occurred in the perceived value of the stimulus itself. On the other hand, anchoring displacements in magnitude judgments would, apparently, entail such a perceptual modification. One may take a third position on this matter; namely, that every ordinal judgment at every level of measurement is by its very nature a relative affair, and that no judgment is more "purely perceptual" than any other. If scalar ratings show anchoring effects, it is not because such judgments are less "intimately associated with the stimulus" but because the stimulus in this case is perceived in relation to inconsistent referents. Conversely, a given length of line will be consistently perceived as "a magnitude of 5" regardless of the range and distribution of other line lengths in a series (will fail to show anchoring shift), not because this magnitude is any more directly or absolutely perceived as a sensory property of the stimulus-in-itself, but because it is perceived in relation to a consistent referent in the subject's mind, a base magnitude unit. The line is not judged to be simply 5, but 5 *inches,* or 5 *millimeters,* etc., which is to say it is perceived as equivalent to five inch-units, or five millimeter-units of length. The problem here is not whether one can judge the line independently of any referent but whether one can keep in mind what is to constitute the base unit in the absence of such a standard presented perceptually as an actual stimulus. The problem may be also, as Restle (1961) has suggested, whether one can perceive the stimulus material to be judged as "breakable into discrete component units." It is here that Stevens' neurological speculation makes at least intuitive sense: our awareness of increasing magnitudes such as loudness or brightness of light is like a homogeneous piling up of excitation in one place, so that it is difficult for us to conceive of a very bright light or a very loud noise as if it were "really" composed of a certain number of minimal brightness units or loudness units. On the other hand, numerousness of dots, length of lines or visual area, duration of noise, or rate of repetition are continua for which a unit in one place (or time) can be added to a unit in a different place (or time). These dimensions seem to be extensive rather than intensive; we can indeed conceive of a 5-inch line as equivalent to five 1-inch lines laid end to end.

In summary, part of the perception-versus-response issue is resolved for those who view the perception itself to be relationally determined. The only question that then remains is whether the subject is allowed to make responses which represent the relationships he perceives. For example, if we provide him with a five-point (equal-interval) rating scale to judge a stimulus series consisting of 1-, 2-, 3-, 4-, and 5-gram weights, and then we introduce a 10-gram anchor, we cannot simply add one more point to the scale, making it a six-point scale, and expect him to represent the stimulus relationships perceived. In this instance the only way the subject can represent the relatively large gap in the series between 5 and 10 grams is to mass his series stimuli together at the lower end of the response scale, say from point 1 to point 3, assigning the anchor value to point 6. In this case one may well question whether the assignment of 1- and 2-gram weights to the common response category of 1 on the rating scale reflects the subject's perceptual inability to discriminate between them as a function of introducing the remote anchor value.

It is not simply necessary to *allow* the subject to extend his rating scale to represent the interstimulus intervals involved when an anchor is added to the series. The instructions to "use as large or small a number as you want in rating each stimulus" may not be adequate to modify the response scale for a subject whose ratings of the unanchored series have been obtained over many trials before the anchor is introduced. This initial replication is common in obtaining judgments of psychophysical stimuli. In overcoming a possible set disposition of the subject to regard category 1 as equivalent to "lightest" and category 5 as equivalent to "heaviest" in the above instance, it may be necessary, when the remote anchor is introduced, to provide explicitly an extended scale for which, say, category 10 is now to be considered equivalent to "heaviest." Alternatively, one may simply provide finer intervals between 1 and 5 on the initial scale (e.g., 1, 1½, 2, 2½, etc.). The disadvantage of this technique, particularly when the initial series has been replicated in training, is that the subject is confronted with a conflict-of-response situation. He may show lack of reliable discriminations in his judgments of the series stimuli simply because he is confused; the weight he has called "2" must now be called "1½," "5" must be called "3," "4" becomes "2½," and so on.

These are some of the practical problems which face the researcher in dealing with perception-versus-response discrepancies once he has resolved the distinction theoretically.

3. What is the proper reference point to use in defining a shift in judgment as either contrast or assimilation? This question relates in part to the issue of whether anchoring is to be seen as a judgment distortion. More broadly the question involves the measurement criterion one should use to define an anchoring effect. In the judgment of psychophysical stimuli, for example, we may compare the subject's response to a given stimulus under condition of anchoring with his response to this stimulus under nonanchored condition. A shift toward the value of the anchor will be called assimilation; a shift away from the anchor value will be called contrast. One might note here that we are defining contrast and assimilation in relation to the anchor value because it is assumed that it is in reaction to the anchor value that the shift occurs. At the same time one can observe that the shift downward in the judgment of stimuli high in the series (with a high anchor) is simultaneously a shift in the judgment of these stimuli *toward* the ratings of stimuli low in the series. A low stimulus continues to be rated "2"; a higher stimulus, previously rated "4," is now rated "3"; we could thus say that this higher stimulus assimilates toward the lower stimulus at the same time that it contrasts away from the anchor!

In the judgment of social or clinical materials, it is undesirable to compare the unanchored-versus-anchored judgment of a stimulus by the same subject, since a memory factor may dispose the subject to be consistent in his response in spite of any anchoring effect. We may not recognize a weight of 5 grams given under anchored and unanchored conditions to be the identical stimulus *object*. The item "He threw his soup at the waiter" is more likely to be recognized as the stimulus we have already judged to be 10 on an aggression scale, even though we might otherwise now judge it as 5 in the context of a high anchor. One way to solve this problem is to use different subjects for obtaining anchored and unanchored judgments and to compare the two as before to define any anchoring effect. In this case, of course, we must be able to say that our two groups of subjects come from the same population and differ only in respect to the presence or absence of anchoring.

The question of whether the anchored response is a *distortion* of judgment is likely to arise with such material. In the ratings of stimulus dimensions such as size, weight, and so on, "the relative nature of absolute ratings" has become such a striking and familiar phenomenon to us that it hardly occurs to us to consider the judgments obtained in any particular stimulus distribution to be more valid or normative than the ratings obtained in another possible distribution. We know that the same hunk of lead will be judged "heavy" in one context and "light" in another. On the other hand, when we obtain an unanchored value for a social stimulus, we usually tend to equate this with the "true" psychological value of the stimulus, rather than with its value under one possible stimulus distribution. Why? One reason, as we shall see in the studies to be described in Chapter 6, is that we think we can sample a complete range of stimulus values for psychological attributes. Our range of possible values seems to be finite here, and we can then take this entire range as our normative distribution. At least subjectively it appears that the range of our size dimension, for example, is rather indeterminate. For example, we are not very clear or consistent about either the highest or the lowest possible pitch of a note. In addition, the extent of such a physical range seems tremendous to us, and beyond practicality to present. We cannot, for example, in our unanchored condition, present a 3-inch square in the context of an atom on the one hand and the universe (?) on the other.

There are some (metathetic) physical dimensions, such as the angle tilt of a line, for which such a generalization does not apply. At any rate, it does not seem to apply to our psychological dimensions, even those which appear to refer to magnitudes of an attribute. Here we seem to have fairly absolute extreme end anchors, particularly for the high end of our dimensions. There is at least some degree of agreement among us and self-consistency within us as to what we would call, for example, minimally pathological and maximally pathological behavior, or very extreme and very mild aggressiveness. (Our disagreement here is more likely to stem from the difficulty of keeping our dimensions "pure." For example, in a study to be described in the next chapter, an effort was made to construct a dimension of overt aggressiveness, eliminating examples of passively hostile behaviors.) There seems, then, to be some justification for our tendency to consider unanchored social judgments as normative and shifts with anchoring as judgment distortion, on the basis of the full range of values in which the unanchored judgment is obtained. Recalling our earlier discussion of whether a stimulus is ever judged in the total absence of anchors, what we are calling an unanchored social judgment is really one in which the stimulus is presented with both extreme anchors included in the series, whereas an "anchored" judgment is one in which the stimulus is presented in an asymmetrical distribution of values with only one of the extreme anchors included.

Distortion of judgment as the result of anchoring is not always defined on these grounds. In the Hovland study of prohibition attitudes, for example, where internal anchors are presumably involved, it is assumed that an unanchored judgment can be made by a judge having no *ego-involvement* in the issue, and thus no position of his own on the attitude scale. These judges are considered to give true, unbiased ratings of the stimulus values of the communications. The subjects, themselves internally anchored on the scale, show a disagreement with these judges in their ratings of the communications, a disagreement which is then definable as a judgment distortion. Again, a shift from unanchored to anchored rating of the communication stimulus toward the position of the anchor is termed assimilation, whereas a shift away from the position of the anchor is termed contrast.

As we understand the discussion of Sherif and Hovland (1961), the distortion observed here is seen to involve some kind of motivational factor: there is internal anchoring when a subject is ego-involved and himself feels strongly about the material he is judging. When this is true of the subject, then wherever his own position falls on the scale he will overestimate the similarity to his attitude of a stimulus near to his own position and overestimate the difference from his attitude of a stimulus at some distance from his own position. One might point out, however, that *intensity* of feeling, or saliency of the issue to the judge, i.e., ego-involvement, is synonymous with *extremity* of self-rating on a scale. Presumably the unbiased judges in this study who were used to obtain the nonanchored values of communication stimuli would, if also asked to give self-ratings of their own position toward prohibition, rate themselves around the middle of the scale. In this case, assimilation and contrast effects occur specifically for judges whose own positions in fact lie toward either extreme end of the scale, not for judges who are more neutral. Whereas ego-involvement presumably differentiates moderate and extreme positions, we can more parsimoniously include the instance of internal anchoring within a general formulation if we focus directly on the scalar position of the anchor in relation to the position of the series stimuli judged. That is, the observable shifts brought on by internal and by external anchoring appear to be the same, whether or not we invoke in the former case a motivational factor to explain the shift here, and whether or not we wish to consider here the nonanchored judgment as less biased or distorted in some absolute normative sense. What we are suggesting is that, in relation to any "nonanchored" situation of judgment in which both extremes of a stimulus distribution are equally salient to the judge, a shift in responses occurs when there is *asymmetrical end anchoring* of the scale, whether such an anchor is introduced by the experimenter as an additional external stimulus or whether it is "brought along into the situation" by the subject himself as an internal stimulus. A recent article by Upshaw (1962) has examined the effect of own attitude position as an anchor like any other stimulus. The function of own attitude in making scalar judgments of objective stimulus values will be discussed further in the next chapter.

Thus far we have considered one broad criterion of defining an anchoring effect, a shift in the scalar positioning *of a given* judged stimulus from that under a nonanchored condition to that under an anchored condition of judgment. Now it has also been implied in the Hovland, Harvey, and Sherif study that such a shift represents an increased or decreased distance *between* this stimulus and the position of the anchor. "The *S*s . . . perceive the communication as further removed from their own stand *than it is*" (p. 251; italics ours). Actually, in this study we do not have any measure of a difference in perceived subject-to-communication distance between unanchored and anchored conditions. We can assess the distance between a subject's rating of communication and of self, but all we have from the unbiased judges is their rating of the communication and not their rating of the subject's position on the scale. We assume that subjects and judges would agree in their rating of the subjects' attitudes and disagree only in their rating of the communications. It is conceivable, for example, that whereas a subject rates himself 8 and a communication 7, the judges who rate this communication only 6 might also rate the subject's attitude as only 7, indicating no shift in perceived subject-to-communication (anchor-to-stimulus) distance. Because one can expect less variability in the judgments of an extreme value, quite often a judgment of the anchor value is not obtained in both conditions to be compared. Sometimes, as we recall, the anchor value is simply defined by the experimenter and no judgment of it is called for at all (see p. 18). To assess both anchor and stimulus values does allow us to speak of assimilation and contrast in terms of changes in distance from anchor and thus is an additional legitimate measure of anchoring effects. Hopefully we will find that it is the judgment of the stimulus which shifts in relation to the introduced anchor. If both values shift in the same direction, or if the value of the anchor shifts toward the stimulus series as much as the stimuli shift toward the anchor, what we imply when we speak of "an anchoring effect upon judgment" must itself be modified.

There is nothing magical in comparing an anchored judgment to a nonanchored judgment. In the experiments by Campbell and his co-workers, for example, the authors measure the anchoring effect by comparing the judgment of a moderate stimulus under high-anchor condition to its judgment under low-anchor condition. Any significant difference between these judgments of the given stimulus is defined as an anchoring effect, and the direction of the difference tells us the direction of the effect. Thus, if a stimulus is judged lower under high-anchor context than under low-anchor context, the effect is one of contrast; if it is judged lower under low-anchor context the effect is one of assimilation toward the presented anchor. The only limitation in using this criterion is that we do not know whether both or only one anchor is producing the difference between the two judgments. Only information about the judgment under nonanchored condition can tell us this.

Finally, when one is observing anchoring effects over a series of judgment trials one may wish to measure the trend in anchoring tendency across these trials. However the stimulus is judged on the first anchored condition, if it is judged nearer to the contextual anchor on the next trial we can say that there is a trend here in the direction of assimilation; if it is judged to be progressively more distant from the presented anchor we can speak of a trend toward contrast. This is a useful criterion because the initial anchor trial may serve to "channelize" judgment of a critical stimulus, obscuring the relatively smaller effects of subsequent anchors. For example, in some of Campbell's studies, as well as in our own, the subject reacts with a strong contrast effect to the first anchor context with which he is presented; if he is given a high anchor he is likely to judge the critical moderate stimulus quite near to the low end of the scale. Similarly, the initially low-anchored subject will judge the moderate stimulus to be quite high on the scale. Throughout subsequent trials, subjects in the first group will continue to judge equivalent moderate stimuli generally in the low range of the scale, whereas subjects in the second group will continue to respond generally in the high range. Within these "channels," however, one can observe significant ups and downs of judgment as anchors are alternated on successive trials. In effect, this criterion allows us to discount primacy and measure "weak" anchoring tendencies.

It should be evident from this discussion that there is not necessarily a "true" measurement criterion of anchoring effects, but rather that one's approach must take into account the particular limitations and opportunities presented by a given experimental condition. Moreover, we prefer neither to consider any unanchored condition of judgment as giving us more valid or normative responses to the stimuli nor thus to consider an anchoring shift as a judgment distortion. Since it would appear that any judgment of a stimulus, "unanchored" as well as "anchored," is made in reference to one context or another, we must at least take the question of validity back a step further and ask on what grounds are we justified in considering one context to be better, in some sense, than another. At the same time it should also be clear that at least some of the difficulty we have in reconciling various theories of anchoring is related to the difficulty we have in comparing the studies which stem from these different theoretical orientations, particularly insofar as they employ different criteria as measures of anchoring.

One further complication here should be noted. Many of the adaptation-level experiments have focused on the specific question of how the introduction of an anchor affects AL. The question asked here is: What is the mean stimulus value of stimuli placed in the neutral (AL) response category by the subject? If an average weight of 10 grams is judged at AL for an unanchored series, while an average weight of 12 grams is judged at AL under high-anchor condition, we can infer that stimuli averaging 10 grams are being rated lower on the scale than AL on the anchored trials. Contrast here therefore refers to a shift in judgment of average stimulus values, but not to a shift in judgment for any particular stimulus in the series. Nor are theorists here usually concerned with judgment categories other than AL, the neutral rating. In the studies of Campbell and his co-workers, as well as in the studies we have conducted, what has been measured is the effect of anchoring upon the judgment of a particular stimulus value. We do not ask what is the average stimulus value that is placed in the middle of the response scale under different anchoring conditions, but rather what is the average response scale placement assigned to a given stimulus of moderate stimulus value under different anchoring conditions. With this approach it is the shift in AL which is inferred. As in the first approach we do not directly examine the effect of the anchor upon the judgment of a whole array of stimulus values or upon the use of all the responses on the rating scale.

The first approach therefore focuses on changes in average stimulus value for a particular (AL) response category, whereas the second approach focuses on changes in average response rating applied to a particular stimulus value. The studies of Sherif and Hovland, and of those concerned with the "rubber-band effect," take a third approach, which focuses upon the response scale and examines the effect of anchoring upon the relative frequency with which the different responses are used. Under nonanchored conditions, this distribution of responses tends to be normal for a rectilinear distribution of stimulus values; responses around the middle of the scale are overused, and the more extreme responses are underused. Assimilation is then observed to be an increase in the use of response categories nearest the position of the anchor, and contrast is shown in a decreased use of these nearest response categories (and *ipso facto* a relative increase in the use of categories further removed from the anchor position). One infers here that if, say, the highest rating is underused (contrast) in relation to its frequency of use under nonanchored condition, then at least some stimulus values previously rated in this category are now being assigned lower ratings.

It is evident that because of these differing approaches to the examination of anchoring effects, comparing one finding of anchoring with another is difficult. The problem may be compounded if, as suggested, shift in judgment is a function of distance from the anchor. If judgments of stimuli near to an anchor can be expected to assimilate toward it, while judgments of more distant stimuli can be expected to contrast, the judgments one analyzes will determine whether one gets contrast or assimilation. Such problems need further consideration.

4. How is the presence of an anchor to be defined? Simply in terms of manipulations by the experimenter, the presence of an anchor usually seems to be defined in one of two ways. Either a stimulus of any value is added to an ongoing series being judged and is called an anchor because its response value is explicitly designated for the subject; or else the most extreme stimulus value of those presented the subject is considered to be an (end) anchor. Its response value may or may not be designated for the subject, and it may or may not be part of the original series given the subject. It is this latter definition which seems to involve some inconsistency and confusion. For example, in the judgment of psychophysical dimensions we often say that the subject originally receives an *un*-anchored series of values to be judged and then receives an anchor stimulus when a value beyond the range of this original series is added to it. On the other hand, if we speak of the most extreme stimuli in any series as constituting natural anchors, in the above case we should really talk about a change in the value of one of the end anchors, or the introduction of a more extreme anchor value, rather than about the introduction of an anchor in contrast to total absence of anchoring. When social stimuli are used, presence or absence of an end anchor is defined in a

more absolute sense in reference to the assumed "complete range" of the dimension. Thus, whether it is included in the initial stimulus series a subject receives or whether it is introduced only in a subsequent series, we may say that the subject was or was not presented with a stimulus representing an extreme of the dimension being judged, i.e., an end anchor. There is some evidence (Miller and Bieri, 1964) that this distinction between psychophysical and social or psychological dimensions is not simply arbitrary on the experimenter's part. In sampling different ranges of stimuli to be judged, Miller and Bieri found that for behavioral dimensions, but not as clearly for psychophysical dimensions, information transmission increases from a condition of no anchor to one anchor to two anchors present. Anchor is here defined as an extreme stimulus on the attribute dimension, and not simply as whatever stimulus is most extreme in the series presented. That is to say, in terms of the effect of an anchor in increasing reliability of judgments, the end stimuli in a series do not function as anchors for these behavioral dimensions unless they also happen to represent the ends of the attribute dimension.

Again in terms of manipulations by the experimenter, we find that in cases where it is said that an anchor was introduced, it may be that the anchor was shown initially but removed before judgment began, or that it was shown intermittently through the series, or finally that it was shown systematically before the presentation of each series stimulus to be judged. It is not unusual in contemporary journal reports of anchoring experiments for no mention at all to be made of the method by which the anchor is introduced. As Parducci and Marshall (1962) have pointed out, when an anchored value is either continuously present or repeatedly presented before the judgment of each series stimulus, the effects we observe may well be treated as classical phenomena of comparative judgment, even though the subject is nominally making an absolute judgment of each series stimulus. Whether or not the repeated stimulus is anchored in the sense of being given a designated or understood value on the response scale, it can here function as a standard input in relation to which the values of other stimuli can be directly compared.

All this empirical variability in the conditions under which the experimenter defines an anchor to be present seems to imply that we really lack any basic agreement in our use of the term. But we do not take such a pessimistic view. Each experimenter makes the assumption that this procedure is adequate and appropriate to determine if an anchor is established psychologically for the subject. That is, implicit throughout our "operational definitions" is the prior assumption that an anchor is a psychological variable: a stimulus, to result in increased reliability or contrast or assimilation in the judgment of other stimuli, must have for the subject a fixed, i.e., anchored, value on his response scale. For our part we do as little or as much as we consider necessary to allow us to assume that he does perceive such a fixed value.

At the same time there is a danger of our being caught in a circular definition of anchoring unless we can demonstrate the presence of anchoring for the subject independently of its subsequent effects upon judgment. We cannot, for example, predict that an anchor will result in a contrast effect and then, having presented a stimulus which does result in a contrast effect, turn around and use this as evidence to define the stimulus as an anchor. Furthermore, the assumption of a one-to-one correspondence between a manipulation by the experimenter and a psychological process in the subject is itself questionable. We might make a distinction here between the possibility for anchoring which we provide by our manipulations and the success which these manipulations actually have as far as the subject is concerned.

In this regard, the presence of an anchor for the subject may be a matter of degree rather than an on-or-off affair. It is relevant here that the human subject is capable of carrying on symbolic or imaginative processes. We may tell the subject that he will be asked to judge a series of lights on a five-point scale of increasing brightness. When we begin to anchor his judgment scale we might simply tell him that response "1" is to correspond to a stimulus that is "very dim" and "5" a stimulus that is "very bright," although it is likely that different subjects will not imagine the same anchors in association with these verbal labels. We may hope to increase the degree of anchoring by showing the subject sample stimuli of a "very dim" and a "very bright" light before the series begins, or we may continue to present these samples in conjunction with each series stimulus to be judged. However, clarity or fixity of stimulus-response association (anchoring) is not necessarily a simple function of the frequency of presenting sample stimuli across stimulus domains. There may be minimal ambiguity for a subject in no more than verbally defining a scale of grayness as ranging "from black to white."

5. What difference does it make what particular stimulus dimension is being judged as far as the anchoring effects obtained? First, we may refer to Stevens' distinction between metathetic and prothetic dimensions. Insofar as scalar ratings of stimuli depart from their magnitude estimations, one must take into account the psychophysical function, as measured by the latter, in predicting stimulus discriminability for rating judgments. Thus an extreme high anchor on a magnitude dimension such as weight cannot be expected to increase reliability of judgments for stimuli in its vicinity beyond the limitations of physical discriminability; there will be decreasing discriminability with increasing magnitudes in any

case. Stimulus magnitudes to be rated on an equal-interval scale are therefore usually selected to preserve equal discriminability, increasing the interstimulus interval as the physical magnitudes increase in value. Second, it has been suggested that for psychophysical dimensions the ends of the series of stimulus values selected for judgment function as natural anchors for judgment and that the effect of a remote anchor varies with its distance beyond the series range. For social or psychological dimensions, on the other hand, the extremes of the dimension itself may serve as effective anchors while the ends of a limited stimulus distribution within this range do not function as natural anchors. Third, there is some evidence that alternating high and low anchors over a series of judgment trials produces some differences between psychophysical dimensions and social dimensions. The following chapter will present some experiments designed to study such anchoring effects in the judgment of clinical and social stimuli.

chapter 6 EMPIRICAL AND CONCEPTUAL ANALYSES OF ANCHORING

The research literature which has developed on the nature of the judgmental process spans many fields of psychological inquiry. Since the study of judgmental phenomena bears upon such diverse realms as psychophysics, social attitudes, personality functioning, and the behavior of the clinician, any potentially integrating concepts warrant close examination. One such concept is represented in the notion of *frame of reference.* Whether construed as a normative standard, previous experience, available information, or a stimulus context, this concept has provided an orienting framework for judgment research, particularly in social psychology. The wide application of this concept, however, has not been accompanied by a systematic investigation of its properties. The aim of the present chapter is to examine the research evidence which centers on a more explicit formulation of this frame of reference notion, namely, in the work on anchoring effects in judgment.

An important goal of judgment research is the development of general laws or principles that may apply to judgments made in varying contexts. Sherif and Cantril (1945) have suggested that judgments made in the experimental laboratory and judgments made in complex social situations follow similar laws. Perhaps the major systematic development which has aided this extension of judgment research to diverse fields has been Helson's adaptation-level theory (1964), discussed in Chapter 5. A major assumption of this approach is that the judgment of a stimulus is made in comparison to some normative level of previous experience.

Seen in this light, adaptation-level theory is one way of formulating the notion of frame of reference in social psychology.

Broadly conceptualized, the idea of a frame of reference can be employed to interpret the findings of a number of social psychological studies. For example, Sherif (1936) investigated judgments of the extent of movement of a stationary point of light in a completely darkened room. Not only did he experimentally produce the autokinetic phenomenon, but he observed that under conditions in which there was no objective basis for gauging movement, "there develops a subjectively established standard or norm . . . which serves as a reference point with which each successive experienced movement is compared" (Sherif, 1936). Thus it was found that individuals established an internal reference point which was preserved in subsequent experiments. When an individual experienced the autokinetic phenomenon in a group situation, a common norm or group consensus developed which persisted when the individual later was placed in a solitary setting. Sherif concluded that such standards or norms arose in unstructured situations where ambiguity concerning judgment existed.

The setting of one's level of aspiration was considered by Chapman and Volkmann (1939) to represent a special case of the frame of reference effect, insofar as the prediction of one's performance in a task with which one has had no prior experience should depend on some provided frame of reference. Their subjects estimated the performance expected on a test of literary acquaintance after they were supplied with fictitious scores attained by groups varying in prestige from authors and literary critics to other students to WPA workers. They have found that estimates of performance varied, as expected, in conjunction with the data provided, with estimated scores higher than the low prestige group, lower than the high prestige group, and comparable to a group composed of individuals of similar status. However, these findings were not reproduced when the subjects were provided with information concerning their own previous day's performance on a problem-solving test. Presumably the indeterminateness of the situation was reduced, thus shifting the individual's anchoring point to his own actual performance.

Hyman (1942) has shown that an individual's judgment of his own position or status will change depending upon which *reference group* he uses as a judgmental comparison. By experimentally providing three different reference groups to be used as a basis for judgment he was able to demonstrate shifts in various dimensions of status (economic, intellectual, cultural, social and attractiveness). In a theoretical discussion of social comparison processes, Festinger (1954) has offered some hypotheses concerning opinion influence in social groups. He suggests that in situations where the criterion of evaluation is unambiguous and clearly ordered, as in the evaluation of abilities which can be objectively measured, an "objective reality" for evaluation is available. Dependence upon the opinions of others is therefore reduced to a minimum. However, to the extent that objective, physical bases for evaluation are not available, subjective judgments depend upon comparisons with others—i.e., upon the establishing of a "social reality." While Festinger postulates certain conditions for predicting how "social reality" emerges, it is noteworthy in this discussion that his hypotheses are further elaborations of the factors noted above, namely, the role of ambiguity and the importance of reference points for the resolution of this ambiguity. Similarly, Asch (1938, 1940) has hypothesized that prestige influence, authoritative standards, and suggestions operate to restructure the meaning of material susceptible of more than one interpretation. Assuming that judgment follows Gestalt principles of perceptual organization, he argues that acceptance of an authoritative suggestion does not merely reflect a tendency to yield. Rather, he feels that beliefs are organized into interdependent patterns, and in an effort to integrate new and ambiguous material into this pattern, the individual uses the suggestion to provide a context of judgment. Lewis (1941), in a study of prestige suggestions in the field of political judgment, concluded that subjects maintained stable rankings of political slogans under the influence of both conflicting and agreeing standards. However, when a suggestion did prove effective, it usually operated to redefine an ambiguous situation so that the slogans acquired a new meaning in response to the changed judgmental context.

Although the concept of frame of reference has been invoked widely as an explanatory variable in social psychological research, it remains a general concept lacking specific systematic development. Fortunately, the study of anchoring effects offers a major avenue through which the more specific delineation of the frame of reference notion can be approached. Since this chapter centers on the role of anchoring effects as frame of reference phenomena, we shall present a review of the major empirical findings in this area.

ANCHORING

We have noted in the previous chapter some of the various forms which the study of anchoring effects may take. For example, studying the influence of extreme stimuli on the judgments of stimuli which are some distance from these extreme (anchoring) stimuli is a rather typical approach. In psychophysics, we may investigate how experience in judging very loud tones influences the judgment of more moderate tones. In social psychology, the analogous situation may involve the judgment of moderate attitudinal statements after experience in judging very extreme statements. Of course a question immediately arises as to whether the judgment of relatively simple, unidimensional sensory stimuli is comparable to the judgment of more complex, multidimensional clinical and social stimuli. Can we isolate general principles or laws of judgment that extend across different stimulus materials, involving different types of anchors and conditions, such as saliency of anchor and number of judgment categories, which are varied? At least four such principles can be tentatively advanced at this point.

1. Extension of Subjective Scale after Introduction of Extreme Anchor

Early experimentalists investigating the effects of anchoring typically asked subjects to make an absolute judgment in determining the response category for a stimulus. An absolute judgment is one in which a subject makes a judgment in absolute magnitudes upon each single presentation of the stimulus in a stimulus series (Wever and Zener, 1928). Since the term absolute may evoke questions concerning the fact that the judgment of the fifth stimulus in a series may, for example, be made relative to the previously presented stimuli, a note should be added concerning this point. As Volkmann (1932) has observed, absolute judgment and absolute method are misnomers if one considers absolute as opposed to relative. He noted that absolute judgments are not independent of similar judgments made for preceding stimuli and are, accordingly, relative to other absolute judgments. However, absolute has a proper meaning if it is opposed to comparative: an absolute judgment need not involve a comparison of the given stimulus with some given preceding stimulus. In an early study, Volkmann (1936) asked subjects to judge the inclination of a line of light in a dark box. The six inclined lines of light which were presented varied from 40 to 50 degrees above the horizontal and were judged in terms of six absolute categories. After making these judgments the subjects were instructed that the horizontal was to define their category "one." This horizontal line may be considered a designated anchor even though it was presented as one of the stimulus inclinations. Volkmann found that the introduction of this anchor produced an extension of the scale in the direction of the horizontal. The extension of the scale was not complete because the scale of judgment did not actually reach the horizontal. The nature of the anchoring effects produced seemed to include the following two major effects.

First, after a surprisingly short time, the distribution of judgments of each subject indicated that his subjective scale was "stimulus-anchored." This meant that the stimulus range was adequate for the number of categories in which the subject was instructed to judge. Second, after the introduction of an anchor, the subject's subjective scale extended toward the anchoring value. Since the number of stimuli remained unchanged, the scale extended past the previously judged stimuli, with the result that the previously judged stimuli fell in higher categories of the scale. The subjective extension of the scale of judgment in response to an extreme stimulus has been replicated using different physical stimulus modalities. Rogers (1941) demonstrated similar effects with inclined lines and with judgments of the heaviness or lightness of weights. Similarly, Postman and Miller (1945) presented subjects with noises of different lengths and asked subjects to judge the duration of each noise on a five-point scale. In all cases, introduction of an anchor produced extension of the scale toward the new anchoring values.

2. Extension of the Scale under Conditions of Judgments of Affective Stimuli

When an individual is asked to judge the brightness of a color or the heaviness of a weight, he is essentially asked to order the physical stimuli along some continuum of brightness or heaviness. Is the same extension of the scale in the direction of an anchor found when the subject is asked to judge in relation to his affective reaction? Using a scale of eleven categories, with the low numbers representing low affective values and the high numbers representing high affective values, Hunt and Volkmann (1937) asked subjects to judge the pleasantness of colors. They then anchored category 11 with the statement that "eleven means a pleasantness equal to that of the most pleasant color you have ever seen," and asked the subjects to rejudge the stimuli. The perceptual scale was then extended to include this anchoring value, and judgments of the original stimuli were being displaced toward the lower end of the scale. Stimuli were thus judged less pleasant when considered in reference to "the most pleasant color you have ever seen." Hunt (1941) sought further proof of the generality of this principle by extending the study of anchoring effects beyond the psychophysical and affective judgments. He asked subjects to judge the esthetic value of carvings and paintings, the ethical nature of various crimes, as well as the degree of intelligence represented in children's photographs. In each of these experiments he demonstrated similar effects of anchoring, although not all the results were statistically reliable. McGarvey (1943) varied the stimulus material still further in two experiments in which judgments were made of the social prestige accorded to a range of occupations and of the social desirability (in the opinion of the subject) of a range of social behavior. In the first experiment subjects were provided with an occupation to define the topmost category of their scale after they had made their initial judgments. Subsequent judgments revealed that, as in the previous studies, the subjects' subjective scales extended in the direction of the anchoring value. When the subject was told that category 6, previously defined by the occupation of "machinist," was to be defined by "doctor" or "opera singer," his stimulus range was then covered by a smaller and smaller portion of the judgment scale. Subjects were no longer able to use the higher categories since no items in the stimulus series then satisfied their changed criteria for a six or a five. Thus the categories at the lower end of the scale necessarily became wider as the subject assigned more occupations to them. Similar tendencies were observed in the ratings of the desirability of social behaviors.

3. Extension of the Subjective Scale Regardless of Saliency of Anchor

Is the anchoring effect produced dependent upon the specification of the stimulus which is to serve as the anchor? In the study by Volkmann (1936) mentioned above, the anchor provided consisted of a definite, reproducible value designated by instruction, although not presented as a stimulus in the series. Similarly, McGarvey (1943) specified the occupation which was to define the topmost category. However, in a second experiment by Volkmann (1936) the anchor was not made salient insofar as the subjects were instructed to "select a value of inclination greater than any which they had hitherto seen in the experiment, to hold this inclination clearly in mind and let it define their category one" (p. 742). In the judgment of pleasantness of colors by Hunt and Volkmann (1937) subjects were not provided with the "most pleasant" color. Rather, they were asked to "think of the most pleasant color you can, . . . hold the pleasantness of this color in mind, . . . and let its pleasantness define the step 11 on your scale" (pp. 90–91). Despite the fact that similar findings were obtained under conditions of saliency and nonsaliency of anchor, Postman and Miller (1945) sought to extend these findings one step further by not making the anchor salient and by not instructing the subject to consider the extreme stimulus (unspecified) as defining the end category. The results of these experiments confirmed the findings of Volkmann, Hunt, Rogers, and McGarvey. In a more recent experiment, Fillenbaum (1961) studied the effect of a remote anchor upon judgment with a salient within-series stimulus object. He found not only that the range of stimulus objects affected judgments, but also that even with a salient within-series anchor, judgment was not absolute.

4. Extension of the Scale and Broadening of Categories as a Function of Perceptual Distortion or Response Category Limitations

An examination of this early psychophysical literature suggests the possibility of two alternative interpretations of the anchoring phenomena. The widening of categories at one end of the scale may reflect judgmental distortion; that is, a loss of discrimination among stimuli when the extreme anchor is introduced. On the other hand, Campbell, Lewis, and Hunt (1958) have argued that the interpretation of these studies is ambiguous because of the use of a restricted number of response categories, as well as of situationally relative language, often arbitrarily defined in terms of the experiment. They suggest that with a limited number of response categories an extreme anchor forces the subject to redefine his existing categories in order to accommodate this extreme stimulus. This process may be independent of any actual judgmental distortion. Furthermore, they argue that having learned a previous "set" for judging, the subjects may feel that they are employing incorrect category definitions after the anchor is presented. This, together with the fact that category labels such as "very heavy" or "very light" can be understood only in relational contexts, may create shifts in judgment without any necessary perceptual distortion.

Campbell et al. asked subjects to judge the pitch of notes in terms of a piano keyboard and thereby provided an extensive number of categories. A common medium note was repeated within each of two alternating high and low contexts. Despite the extensive number of categories available, shifts in judgments reflecting typical contrast effects were obtained. These results obviously could not be attributed to response category restriction. However, the fact that a loss of discrimination in the lower categories was not obtained did demonstrate some effect of a restriction of response categories. In a later study, Krantz and Campbell (1961) distinguished between "perceptual" shifts (to be measured in terms of judgments in inches) and "semantic" shifts (to be measured in terms of an experimenter-defined response language where the value 100 was to be considered average). Their choice of the latter form of rating was dictated by their desire to eliminate the effects of vocabulary exhaustion, such as occurs when all of a restricted number of ratings have been employed prior to a shift of context. For both response languages, significant anchoring tendencies in the form of initial contrast effects were obtained, although the effect of rating judgments was significantly greater than the effect of estimations in inches. Thus, although the anchoring effect produced was greater under conditions of an experimenter-defined response language, one cannot discount the finding that a significant effect of "perceptual" distortion was found as well.

Fillenbaum (1963) asked subjects to rate a series of rectangles on a slimness-broadness dimension and required some subjects to use a fixed, arbitrary five-category scale and required others to make their ratings by estimating the ratio of height to base. With categorical instructions the usual anchoring effects were obtained, while with ratio instructions there was no systematic effect. He concluded that at least some context effects in judgment may be attributable to semantic effects of the situationally relative and arbitrarily limited language with which the subject is required to express his judgments. However, although anchoring tendencies may be enhanced by category restriction and by situationally relative language, these factors have not been shown to account completely for these effects.

ANCHORING PHENOMENA IN CLINICAL AND SOCIAL JUDGMENT: ASSIMILATION TENDENCIES

Although the general anchoring phenomena noted above have been observed in a variety of situations, the direction of the displacement of stimuli *away* from the anchor and toward the opposite end of the scale has not always been uniform. As we described in Chapter 5, two characteristic anchoring phenomena, namely, *contrast* and *assimilation*, have been identified. Both effects have been considered as distortions of perception which affect one's judgment of stimuli. Contrast has generally been considered a tendency to judge subsequent stimuli at a greater distance from previous stimuli (or anchor stimuli) than they actually are, while assimilation reflects a tendency to judge subsequent stimuli as more like previous stimuli (or anchor stimuli) than they actually are.

Various theoretical formulations, outlined in Chapter 5, have been advanced to explain these effects. It should be re-emphasized that early studies of anchoring, especially in psychophysics, yielded contrast effects primarily. Consistent with these empirical findings, the theoretical conceptualizations which were developed in Helson's adaptation-level theory and Volkmann's "rubber-band effect" sought to provide a theoretical basis, or rationale, for these data. Only more recently, however, have assimilation tendencies been observed. Although there has been a corresponding emergence of theories which attempt to explain these phenomena in terms of distance factors, the nature of assimilation effects is not clearly understood. Can we specify some of the conditions which appear to facilitate these phenomena? It is in an attempt to answer this question that our attention will now be directed.

Alternation of Context Anchors

In the early psychophysical research, most studies centered upon the presentation of an anchor at one or both ends of the series of stimuli being judged. Little systematic attention was given to the possible effects of variations in the *method* of stimulus presentation, particularly in regard to the potential significance of a shift in anchor from one end of the series to the other. In the research of Segall (1959), for example, subjects were asked to judge neutral statements in an anchor context in which only anti-fraternity items were presented. He obtained the expected contrast effect. Subjects then judged another set of neutral items which were presented in an all pro-fraternity context. It was after this shift from one anchor context to the other that some assimilation tendency was noted, contrary to the prediction. However, the basis for these assimilation findings was not further explored. In the study by Campbell, Lewis, and Hunt (1958) mentioned earlier, subjects were required to judge the pitch of notes in terms of a piano keyboard reference system. They employed a three-phase design in which the alternation of a high and then a low anchor context (or vice versa) was separated by a transitional context. In other words, the low-high group first heard notes varying in a relatively low context and later were shifted gradually by means of transitional moderate notes to a high context. The high-low group received the reverse treatment. The predicted contrast effect in the judgments of a common note repeated in both contexts was obtained. However, they also reported that in addition to the typical contrast effects a small, "but possibly significant," number of subjects seemed to respond to the shift in context with an assimilation error. In a similar design in which subjects judged in shifting contexts the lengths of lines projected on a screen, Krantz and Campbell (1961) demonstrated the same reversible perceptual-contrast effect for judgments made in inches. With responses in ratings, however, they found that the judgments which showed contrast to the initial anchor context tended to be maintained despite the change of context, and moved only to a slight degree from the new opposite anchor.

In a similar investigation using alternating anchors with a transition group, Campbell, Hunt, and Lewis (1957) found contrast in the initial phase but definitely no contrast in the final phase. Their subjects were required to judge the degree of disturbance manifested in responses of schizophrenics to items in a vocabulary test. When stimuli of moderate scale position were judged in conjunction with extreme items indicating very high disturbance, they were judged as less severe than under conditions where the same stimuli were presented with extreme items indicating very little disturbance. However, judgments retained a level of consistency under reversed anchor which indicated some assimilation. That is, the subjects judged the moderate stimuli as similar to the context in which they were presented. It was also observed that the shift in context had the significant effect of reducing discrimination among items judged in the third (last) phase.

It would appear then that one approach to the study of assimilation phenomena may lie in an experimental design involving an alternation of context anchors. Bieri, Orcutt, and Leaman (1963) attempted to establish the presence of assimilation tendencies by studying serial judgments of clinical stimuli using an alternation of stimulus contexts. Because of the importance of this research in explicating the nature of assimilation phenomena, this study will be presented in considerable detail.

A STUDY OF ANCHORING IN SEQUENTIAL CLINICAL JUDGMENTS

Bieri et al. (1963) required subjects to judge the degree of maladjustment displayed in brief "cases" consisting of descriptions of either aggressive behavior or dependency behavior of an adult male. Based on ratings made by independent judges, these cases were considered to represent either high pathology, moderate pathology, or low pathology. In order to investigate serial effects in anchoring, these cases were presented in four sequential phases, with three cases presented at each phase. The use of transitional phases, as employed by Campbell, was eliminated in order to permit greater opportunity for assimilation effects to be assessed. It was reasoned that if an assimilation effect was to be identified it was necessary to use a *succession* of alternated contexts. A sequence of nonalternated contexts as used by Levy (1961), or a single alternated anchor sequence, with a shift from one extreme context to only one other extreme context, as used by Campbell et al. (1957, 1958), can demonstrate only a dissipation of the initial contrast effect. However, in order to demonstrate assimilation, that is, a tendency for judgments to shift *toward* the anchor stimulus, it was considered desirable that the alternated series be continued beyond two shifts of contexts.

The three stimuli in each context consisted of two cases at one extreme of pathology followed by the third moderate or middle case. The two extreme cases provided the context or anchor condition within which the middle case was judged. The anchor conditions were alternated from each phase to the next, with half the subjects receiving high anchor conditions initially. Half the subjects received all aggression cases on the first two phases and all dependency cases on the last two phases, whereas the other half received the reverse order of behaviors. Systematic variation of the phase and anchor context in which each middle case was presented provided an additional condition. This 2 x 2 x 2 factorial design, then, included the following three conditions: order of anchor alternation; order of behavior (aggression or dependency); and order of middle case. Each case was judged on a twenty-category scale range from low pathology to extreme pathology.

A total of 176 graduate social work students were assigned randomly to the following eight experimental groups outlined in Table 1 (N = 22 in each group).

Table 1. Order of Case Judgments for the Eight Experimental Groups (Bieri, Orcutt, and Leaman, 1963)

Experimental Group	Phase 1	Phase 2	Phase 3	Phase 4
	Aggression		Dependency	
I	HHM_1	LLM_2	HHM_3	LLM_4
II	LLM_1	HHM_2	LLM_3	HHM_4
III	HHM_2	LLM_1	HHM_4	LLM_3
IV	LLM_2	HHM_1	LLM_4	HHM_3
	Dependency		Aggression	
V	HHM_3	LLM_4	HHM_1	LLM_2
VI	LLM_3	HHM_4	LLM_1	HHM_2
VII	HHM_4	LLM_3	HHM_2	LLM_1
VIII	LLM_4	HHM_3	LLM_2	HHM_1

H = High case — M_1 and M_2 = Middle aggression cases
L = Low case — M_3 and M_4 = Middle dependency cases
(By permission, American Psychological Association)

Criteria of Anchoring

In order to establish whether anchoring effects have been obtained, it is necessary to consider a variety of possible criteria which may be used to measure the presence of anchoring effects. At least four such criteria may be employed to assess these anchoring tendencies.

Criterion 1. An anchoring effect is defined as a significant difference between judgments of a given moderate stimulus under high versus low anchor conditions for the same judgment phase.

Criterion 2. An anchoring effect is the significant deviation of an anchored judgment of a moderate stimulus in a given phase from the judgment of this same stimulus obtained under nonanchored conditions.

Examining the direction of the deviation in this way provides evidence of whether the effect obtained is to be termed contrast or assimilation.

Criterion 3. An anchoring effect is the significant difference between judgments of equivalent moderate stimuli by the same group of subjects from one anchor context to the next.

Criterion 4. An anchoring effect is the degree of difference in rating among the stimuli presented in a given phase.

In applying these criteria to the analysis of the findings, answers were sought to three basic questions. The first of these was: Will anchoring effects be observed in judgments of these clinical stimuli? Considering criterion 1, it was found that there were significant differences in the judgment of the middle cases as a function of anchor conditions, both for aggression and dependency behaviors, on all phases except the third. Table 2 summarizes the orthogonal comparisons of the middle case judgments at each phase.

Table 2. Orthogonal Comparisons of Middle-Case Judgments on Each of Four Phases

(Bieri, Orcutt, and Leaman, 1963)

Source	df	Phase 1 F	Phase 2 F	Phase 3 F	Phase 4 F
H-L A	1	15.58 [a]	28.71 [a]	2.09	63.63 [a]
H-L D	1	14.45 [a]	28.71 [a]	3.13	35.54 [a]
M_1-M_2	1	...	...	...	...
M_3-M_4	1	3.47	13.57 [a]	4.70 [b]	2.89
A-D	1	2.27	...	1.23	...
Residual	2	...	1.11	1.70	2.67
Within	168				
Total	175				

[a] $p < .01$ [b] $p < .05$

(By permission, American Psychological Association)

Although there were no significant differences in the judgments of the two middle aggression cases (M_1-M_2) on any of the four phases when anchor conditions were combined, less equivalence was found for the two middle dependency cases (M_3-M_4) on phases two and three.

Having observed that anchoring tendencies can be obtained with clinical stimuli of this type, the question arose as to the *direction* of these anchoring tendencies. That is, what tendencies toward assimilation or contrast were observed? Specifically, the second question asked was: Will the use of alternated anchors increase the likelihood of assimilation effects? If we consider criterion 2, the most stringent of the various criteria employed, we can determine the direction and extent of the deviation of the anchored middle case from its judgment under nonanchored conditions. (Judgments had also been obtained from three groups of graduate students who received exclusively either high, middle, or low pathology cases. This yielded a mean scale value for each high, middle, or low pathology case under nonanchored conditions which could be compared with each case's mean value as judged under anchored conditions.) This analysis was applied to each of the eight experimental groups, with the result that strikingly similar trends, differing only in degree, were found for all groups. In phase 1, all groups deviated in their judgments from the nonanchored values in the direction of *contrast* from their respective anchor cases. (Two of these mean differences are significant, $p < .05$.) In phase 2, where the anchor cases were now at the opposite end of the scale from the initial phase, all groups showed an *assimilation* effect, with four of these differences reaching significance. In phase 3, when there was a shift in the behavioral dimension of judgment, all groups indicated a convergence of middle-case judgments toward their nonanchored values. Although five of these groups displayed some degree of assimilation, only one deviated significantly. Finally, in phase 4, all eight groups shifted away from the nonanchored judgment and toward the anchor (assimilation), with a statistically significant level attained by five groups.

Having identified an assimilation effect within phases 2, 3, and 4, we may next ask a third question: Will the effects observed tend to weaken over a series of judgment trials? In other words, as the anchoring task is extended is there evidence of a continued assimilation trend? Criteria 3 and 4 bear upon this question. Considering criterion 3, it is possible to compare the shifts in judgments by the same group of judges from one anchor context to the next. These shifts can be graphically observed in Figure 1. Analysis of the sequential trends represented in Figure 1 indicates no significant differences in the middle-case judgments between phases 1 and 2 for either the initially low or high anchor combined groups. Between phases 2 and 3, however, both curves deviate significantly ($p < .05$) from the phase 2 anchor *toward* the anchor presented in phase 3. Between phases 3 and 4, the curves again deviate significantly *toward* the anchor in phase 4.

Further support for the assimilation trend is found when analyses derived from criterion 4 are performed. If the degree of scalar discrimination between judgment of the middle case and the most extreme anchor judgment decreases from phase to phase, then additional evidence is available to indicate an assimilation effect. It was found that the degree

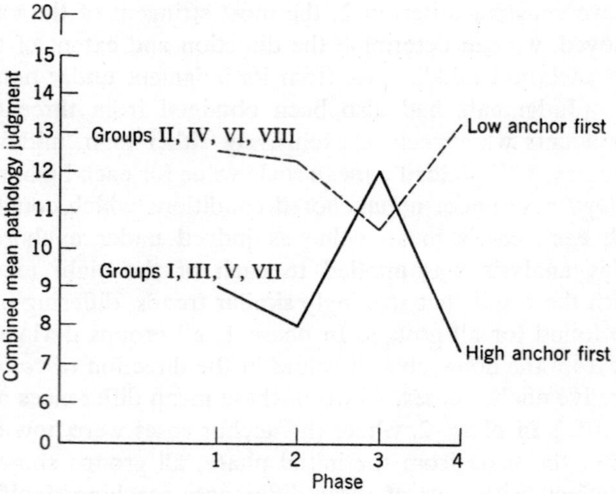

Figure 1. Combined means of middle-case judgments of four groups with initial high anchor and of four groups with initial low anchor. (Bieri, Orcutt, and Leaman, 1963. Reprinted by permission of the American Psychological Association.)

of scalar discrimination did, indeed, drop significantly from phase 1 to phase 2 ($p < .01$), rose when new behavioral material was presented in phase 3 ($p < .05$), and dropped again from phase 3 to phase 4 ($p < .01$). There was a significant loss in discrimination between phases 1 and 3, as well as between phases 2 and 4. It should be noted that since the judgments of the most extreme anchor were made progressively nearer the extreme ends of the scale across successive phases, the loss of discrimination described above can be attributed to a shift of the middle cases *toward* these extreme anchors (assimilation).

These results indicate, then, that systematic distortions in moderate stimulus judgments can be obtained as a function of sequential judgments under conditions of alternating context anchoring. These anchoring tendencies are initially contrast effects followed by assimilation effects. The question arises as to whether the existing theories of anchoring described in the previous chapter can adequately account for these effects, particularly the assimilation tendencies. The centering theories of both Helson and Volkmann would predict the initial contrast effects obtained, but the trends in the judgments *toward* the anchor stiumuli are not as easily reconciled with these two approaches. While neither formulation deals specifically with sequential effects, both would predict, it would seem, that over a series of high and low anchors the subjective center of the scale would shift in response to the extreme anchors presented, with the middle case judgment shifting downward and upward in a contrary direction. A series of alternating contrast effects, dissipating in degree and gradually approaching the scalar midpoint, would presumably result. In any case, differences in middle-case judgments between subjects receiving the high-low-high-low anchor sequence and those receiving the low-high-low-high sequence should be greater in phase 1 than in phase 4, since by the final phase these two groups have received identical anchor conditions.

The distance formulations offer little additional clarification of these results. Despite the fact that the distance theories incorporate assimilation effects in their predictions, the specification of that distance between the anchor stimulus and the moderate stimulus which will favor contrast (optimally far), accuracy, or assimilation (optimally near) is not clear. In addition to this limitation, it is difficult to interpret a contrast effect on one trial and an assimilation effect on another when the objective distance between anchor and moderate stimulus has remained unchanged.

Any systematic account of the marked assimilation trends produced in this study would have to incorporate the notion that these effects appear to depend upon both *serial* effects in judgment and alternation of anchors. That is, we noted in the earlier research of Campbell, Lewis, and Hunt (1958) that one alternation of anchor context *decreased* contrast and produced some assimilation. In the study we have just presented, pronounced assimilation was still being manifested on the fourth alternation phase. It is possible to hypothesize that such serial alternation of anchors tends to *decrease* the overall discriminability of the stimuli, so that the extreme anchor stimuli exert a polarizing influence on the moderate or ambiguous stimulus. In effect, we would hypothesize that any judgment condition which would tend to increase the *relative strength* or *saliency* of the anchor stimuli in relation to the moderate stimulus would increase the likelihood of such assimilation trends. In an alternated anchor task, the moderate stimulus is more salient on the first phase because it serves to define the opposite end of the scale in the absence of an anchor stimulus at that end. However, by the second phase the new anchor stimulus *does* define the initially unanchored end of the scale, and thus the moderate stimulus becomes more ambiguous in relation to the anchor stimulus. Furthermore, these moderate stimuli may assume decreased clarity as a result of their being displaced first in one direction and then another. Additional evidence for this *relative saliency* hypothesis of assimilation comes from a recent study (Bieri, Atkins, Kujala, and Meyers, 1965) in which two conditions of alternated contexts were used. In one condition, all three stimuli were presented simultaneously, whereas in the second condition the subject received on each phase one extreme stimulus, then the second (equivalent) extreme stimulus, and then the moderate stimulus. We would expect in the former condition of simultaneous presentation where *direct* comparison of the moderate stimulus with the extreme anchor stimuli is possible, that contrast effects would be greater and that assimilation trends on subsequent phases would be fewer than in the single stimulus mode of presentation. In this latter mode, the moderate stimulus is relatively less salient or clear because of the lack of a direct comparative referent. The results of this study supported these expectations concerning the relative strength of assimilation tendencies. It should be mentioned than an additional serial phenomenon contributing to loss of discrimination and thus to assimilation may be a loss of vigilance or a dissipation effect, as reported by Levy (1961).

Finally, we would expect that any additional factors which contribute to the greater relative saliency of end stimuli would contribute to assimilation trends in sequential judgment. We shall next consider the operation of some motivational or affective variables in social judgments which may contribute to such effects.

Own Attitude as Internal Anchors

Although an alternation of context anchors can provide conditions suitable for the study of assimilation trends in clinical judgment situations, the application of such an approach to some types of social judgment is more complex. For one thing, the nature of social attitudes necessitates the study of additional factors which impinge on the judgment process. In particular, social judgments arouse affective predispositions of the judges in terms of their own attitudes toward the issue in question. This factor takes on added significance when we realize that one's own attitude may serve as an *internal anchor* in the judgment of social stimuli. As we noted in Chapter 5, the distance formulation of Sherif and Hovland has drawn attention to the role of one's own attitude as an internal anchor. For example, in the area of social judgments, Sherif and Hovland (1961) applied the distance hypothesis to the evaluation of statements or communications at varying distances from one's own position. They wrote:

> When the position in communication is susceptible to alternative interpretations, displacements of the position advocated will vary as a function of its distance from the subject's stand. The greater the discrepancy between the subject's own stand and the position advocated, the greater the displacement away from the subject's position ("contrast effect"). When only a small

discrepancy in positions exists, there will be a tendency for displacement toward his own stand ("assimilation effect"). (p. 149)

Thus, as described earlier, Hovland, Harvey, and Sherif (1957) classified subjects on the basis of their initial attitudes toward the prohibition issue and exposed them to three communications, one advocating a strong wet position, one advocating a strong dry position, and one advocating a moderately wet position. Systematic variations in the evaluation of the moderately wet communication were found as a function of differences in own-attitude positions. Subjects whose own positions were moderate, and thus closest to the communication, judged the communication fairly accurately. Those whose positions were not far from the communication tended to judge it as more like their own than it actually was (assimilation). However, those farthest from the communication, i.e., those who held more extreme positions, tended to judge it as more distant from their own position than it actually was (contrast). Although the exact determination of assimilation and contrast ranges has not been specified, the effects of own attitude as an internal anchor are striking.

Sherif and Hovland (1961) pointed out that anchoring phenomena associated with "motivationally neutral" stimulus materials, such as physical stimuli, do not adequately encompass the effects of internalized anchors as they operate in the judgment of social and attitudinal stimuli. Interestingly, in his experimental work undertaken to prove the generality of findings from the psychophysical laboratory, Hunt (1941) at an early point noted that certain differences attributable to variations in stimulus materials did manifest themselves. He found that with certain tasks such as judging the ethical nature of social behavior, the subject, after being given an anchoring value at one end of the scale, spontaneously added an anchoring value of his own at the opposite end of the scale. Hunt referred to this as a "double anchoring effect." In his study of the effects of own position and experience on the judgment of controversial statements described earlier, Segall (1959) attempted to experimentally vary three components of Helson's adaptation-level formulation, namely, background, residual, and focal stimuli. Manipulation of the order of occurrence of statements to be judged was considered an empirical translation of variation in background and provided a context for the judgment of focal stimuli. Variations in judges' attitudes represented variations in residuals; judges were classified on the basis of the favorableness of their own attitudes toward college fraternities and were required to make judgments of the favorableness or unfavorableness of statements toward fraternities. One group judged these statements under conditions where the favorable items, that is, pro-fraternity items, appeared first in the series, while another matched group judged under reverse conditions. In addition, two types of judgments were studied: absolute judgments, where each item was judged singly and placed in an appropriate category from one to seven, and relative judgments, where one's own position represented category four and all items were to be judged relative to this category. Analysis of the results indicated that in the absolute judgment condition the context in which the neutral items were judged proved to be a significant determinant, while own position did not. However, under the relative judgment condition, own position had a significant effect, but context did not. Segall's findings thus suggest that the saliency of the anchor in question may be an important consideration.

Although the effects of variations both in the order of presentation of stimuli and in the designation of extreme anchors upon judgments of opinion statements have been studied further (Rambo, 1961; Weiss, 1961), the specific nature of own-attitude effects remains undefined. Manis (1961) has found that in making predictions of the communicator's position toward fraternities, subjects tended to displace the communicator's position toward their own position when responding to messages with which they agreed or which deviated moderately from their own positions. Subjects who favored fraternities felt that the neutral communicators were more pro-fraternity than did subjects who opposed them (assimilation). When the subjects responded to statements that were definitely opposed to their own stands, no consistent displacement trends were obtained. Manis suggested that these distortions arose from the subject's efforts to maintain attitudinal consistency when confronted with a high prestige communicator whose position generated a certain amount of pressure toward change.

In the early research on the construction of attitude scales, it was assumed that own-attitude effects were negligible. Thurstone (1929), whose equal-appearing intervals method required subjects to sort items into a number of categories from which final scale values were determined, assumed that ratings were independent of the attitudes of the judges. In the first test of this assumption, Hinckley (1932) had white judges with pro-Negro and anti-Negro attitudes, as well as judges who were themselves Negro, sort 114 statements on the social position of Negroes. He found that the average scale values for judges in the two white groups were highly positively correlated and that scale values for anti-Negro and Negro judges were also closely related. However, Hovland and Sherif (1952) undertook to replicate this experiment on the assumption that highly ego-involving attitudes would be expected to manifest some systematic variations in the placement of items. They specifically sought to investigate the effects of Hinckley's elimination of judges who, presumably through poor discrimination and carelessness, placed thirty or more of the statements in any one category. As they suspected, the concentration of items in a few categories reflected highly ego-involved attitudes on the part of the judges. They found that strongly pro-Negro white judges and Negro judges showed a marked tendency to displace neutral items toward the unfavorable end of the scale. In this way, judges' own attitudes had, in fact, caused systematic errors in judgment. However, a recent replication by Hinckley (1963) of his original study indicated that even when the judgments of all raters were included the scale constructed was not influenced by the attitudes of the subjects used in its construction.

Upshaw (1962) attempted to assess four theoretical interpretations of the relationship between judges' attitudes and equal-appearing intervals scale values. Three of the theoretical interpretations, perceptual vigilance, the assimilation-contrast model, and adaptation level, all yielded different predictions of the role of own attitude in judgment, while the fourth, the variable series model, assumed that the stimulus range was the major determinant of the particular values assigned to items in a series. According to this model, own attitude is an extraneous variable which acquires importance only when the item series is such that the positions of some judges are outside the series. Under such conditions the judge would subjectively augment the range to include his own attitude as an anchor at the aborted end. Thus the scales adopted by in-range judges would presumably be narrower than those of out-of-range judges and would lead to relatively finer (and more accurate) discriminations among the items. By manipulating the item series as well as judges' attitudes, Upshaw found support for the variable series model although he also found a positive relationship between own position and scale values assigned to extremely pro and moderately pro items.

Despite Hinckley's (1963) evidence that rating may be independent of the judges' attitudes, there appears to be a substantial amount of support indicating that judgments *are* influenced by raters' attitudes which function as internal anchors (Zavalloni and Cook, 1965). Yet, as we have seen, the empirical findings concerning the nature of this influence have not been consistent. Depending upon the model of social judgment employed, differential predictions can be made of the manner in which one's own attitude may affect scale ratings. For example, considering the Sherif and Hovland model we predict that over small distances any displacement of the items being judged will be in the direction of assimilation to one's own position. However, considering adaptation-level theory, we must predict that judgments of stimuli are not sensitive to the distance between the stimuli being judged and one's own attitude. Rather, own-attitude, a residual factor, may be pooled with a congruent background set of stimuli to actually enhance a contrast effect. Clearly, a more precise delineation of the various factors impinging on this internal anchor must be considered. Among these factors it appears that the following variables, or conditions, are important.

Extremity of Own Attitude. Will extreme attitudes operate as more effective internal anchors than more moderate attitudes? The effect of extremity of own attitude upon scalar judgments presents a multifaceted problem. Sherif and Hovland (1961) indicated that extreme judges tended to show greater contrast effects in judgments. Items in the categories opposite to the judges' own positions along an attitudinal continuum tended to be piled into a few categories. Upshaw's findings (1962), on the other hand, suggest that this may be true only under conditions where the judges' attitudes are out-of-range. Moderate judges, according to the assimilation-contrast model, would be most susceptible to assimilation tendencies, insofar as the distance is minimal. Whether distance is the sole or major determinant of such displacement effects appears highly debatable, especially in light of the findings to be reported later in this chapter in the study by Atkins (1964).

Involvement of Own Attitude. It has been suggested (Sherif and Hovland, 1961) that ratings are biased most strongly by judges with extreme positions who also show strong ego-involvement. Again, these conditions presumably enhance contrast effects. Since moderate judges will by definition show less ego-involvement, it is suggested that this variable relates only indirectly to the production of assimilation. Although the assumption of greater contrast displacement as a function of greater involvement remains questionable (Zavalloni and Cook, 1965), consideration of this variable for both contrast and assimilation appears noteworthy. In Chapter 9 we shall suggest an approach to the study and clarification of this problem.

Latitude of Acceptance-Rejection. Sherif and Hovland (1961) have suggested that an individual's stand be thought of as a range or latitude of acceptance and rejection. Rather than denoting an individual's attitude in terms of one scale position they have recommended that one's attitude be specified in terms of the range of statements on an issue that an individual considers acceptable to him. They have attempted to demonstrate that extreme subjects characteristically have a very narrow latitude of acceptance and consequently reject more statements than do individuals with moderate positions. In effect, these extreme subjects would therefore be expected to show a very narrow assimilation range and a broad contrast range. Although it is conceptually meaningful, an empirical demonstration of the relationship between latitude of acceptance and assimilation-contrast effects is necessary. Evidence suggesting that assimilation tendencies can be noted for extreme subjects who have broad latitudes of acceptance has recently been reported (Atkins, Kujala, and Bieri, 1965).

Items Most Susceptible to Displacement Effects. In our earlier review of the anchoring effects observed with sensory stimuli, it was shown that midrange stimuli were most susceptible to displacement effects. Similarly, we have seen in the study reported above by Bieri, Orcutt, and Leaman (1963) that stimuli drawn from the midrange of a pathology continuum of aggressive and dependent behavior are subject to marked displacement effects. Although systematic shifts are most pronounced for these moderate stimuli relative to the extreme anchors, one may ask whether moderate (midrange) statements of attitude will be most responsive to the biasing effects of extreme own-attitude anchors. Sherif and Hovland (1961) as well as Zavalloni and Cook (1965) report that neutral attitudinal items do show greatest displacement effects, although contrary findings have also been noted (Prothro, 1955, 1957; Upshaw, 1962). To some extent, this inconsistency may result from the nature of the dimension on which the stimuli are being judged. Zavalloni and Cook (1965) suggested that when the dimension on which the stimuli are judged involves a qualitative shift at the midpoint (favorable-unfavorable, sweet-salty) less shift of midscale items is found than when the stimuli represent a continuous array lacking a clear midpoint (light-heavy, short-long).

DISCRIMINABILITY OF STIMULI

In our discussion of both sequential alternations of context anchors and internal (own-attitude) anchors we have attempted to outline some of the conditions which produce systematic assimilation phenomena. Before presenting an experimental study which combines both these factors in anchoring effects in social judgment, we shall discuss one additional factor. Sherif and Hovland (1961) have placed great importance upon the assignment of items to categories as a means of eliciting an individual's attitude toward some issue. They have written,

> An attitude toward an object, person, group or social issue is not directly observable but is inferred from a persistent and characteristic mode of reaction to that stimulus or stimulus class. It is inferred that the object of attitude is placed in a category or class favorable or unfavorable in some degree. . . . In short, one essential aspect of the attitudinal reaction is a

categorization process, whether or not the individual is aware that he is passing a judgment. (p. 5)

As we have observed, there are systematic differences in the categorization process attributable to one's own position. Another aspect of the categorization process, however, is the degree to which an individual is *able to discriminate* among stimuli. Two individuals with a similar attitude toward an issue may, nevertheless, articulate differently the various facets of the issue. One individual may discriminate characteristically only the extremes of an issue, while another may discriminate numerous intervals between the extremes. For example, in the study by Atkins (1964) to be described below, individuals obtained scores on a discriminability task ranging from four to eight perfect discriminations. Thus, on a fifteen-point attitude scale, some individuals reliably placed twenty-one items into only four different categories while some individuals used as many as eight categories reliably.

Berkowitz (1960) has attempted to demonstrate that the categorization process is closely related to assimilation and contrast tendencies. He has assumed that psychological distance can be equated with the number of discrete categories the subject can establish between the stimulus and the anchor. The greater the number of discriminations made, the greater the perceived distance, and therefore the greater the contrast tendencies. Individuals making fewer discriminations use broader categories which facilitate assimilation trends. In an experiment with Schilling, Berkowitz (1960) asked subjects to judge the overall "goodness" of eleven personality traits. The first seven traits, which were presented either in an all "good" condition or all "bad" condition, served as the anchor, and were followed by four neutral traits presented individually. The results showed a significant contrast effect, with the neutral traits being displaced away from the preceding seven stimuli. When the same eleven traits were described as referring to the same person, however, subjects tended to group the neutral traits together with the preceding seven traits. Presumably the grouping effect lessened the distance between anchor and neutral stimuli and diminished the contrast effect.

Interpreting self-other evaluations in this framework, Berkowitz considered one's self-concept as constituting an anchor, with perceptions of others dependent upon the perceived distance between self and others. Assimilation and contrast tendencies were interpreted to reflect varying degrees of perceived similarity between the self and others. In further experimentation he investigated the dynamics of the categorization process under stressful conditions. Reasoning from earlier evidence that the authoritarian's categorizations become broader under mild stress, he subjected two groups, one highly prejudiced and the other low in prejudice, to either a mildly stressful situation or a less stressful one. The subjects were required to evaluate the general goodness of eleven personality traits, the first seven of which served as anchor (either all good or all bad) and the remaining four of which were neutral. Although not all his findings were consistent with the predictions, he did obtain evidence to support the position that highly prejudiced subjects showed less contrast effects under greater stress conditions than under lower stress conditions. Moreover, he inferred that stress tended to narrow the categories established by low prejudiced subjects, resulting in a sharp differentiation between anchor stimuli and the more neutral traits. It should be noted that no direct evidence on discriminability is provided in these studies.

In a series of experiments, Holzman (1953) and Holzman and Klein (1954) have delineated "levelers" from "sharpeners," and suggested that individuals with a tendency to minimize stimulus differences may be more susceptible to time-error assimilation effects. Sharpening refers to a "propensity to maximize stimulus differences, an attunement to small gradients of differences between figure and ground," while leveling refers to a "propensity to minimize such differences and to fail to recognize gradual changes in the stimulus field" (Holzman, 1953). Levelers are expected to rely heavily upon anchors and strongly confirmed frames of reference to maintain an organization. Thus, they reasoned that in dealing with visual or auditory stimuli, the introduction of a stimulus between the standard and comparison which was more intense than the comparison would result in the subject's considering the second of the two compared stimuli as less bright than the first. This positive "time error" was expected to occur because the trace of the first stimulus assimilates to the persisting level or trace of the interpolated bright light. Their studies indicated that such time errors were found across a variety of sensory modalities, with levelers generally showing more significant assimilation tendencies than sharpeners. Not only did levelers show significantly greater time-error assimilation effects, but there was a marked tendency for the same individual to respond with the same degree of assimilation in a variety of tasks. In line with earlier findings in psychophysical research, both levelers and sharpeners were relatively accurate in their size rankings of squares when the stimuli were either the largest or smallest in the series. Levelers, however, tended to be significantly more inaccurate than sharpeners when judging stimuli in the middle of the series. Sharpeners, on the other hand, appeared to be more alert to differences and judged the embedded stimuli more accurately.

If such stylistic consistencies as leveling and sharpening can be assumed to exist, individual differences in anchoring tendencies may also be thought of as cognitive styles. Efforts to identify such stylistic types as assimilators and contrastors in anchoring tasks have not been reported with any great frequency. Recent evidence reported by Atkins, Meyers, and Kujala (1965) suggests that anchoring tendencies do not have strong consistency across physical and social stimulus realms. For example, judges who manifested more marked contrast tendencies in judging sizes of squares did not have more marked contrast tendencies in judging social stimuli. Another consideration, then, in our approach to the study of assimilation centers on individual differences in the discriminability of stimuli. If assimilation represents a minimization of the distance between the anchor and the stimulus being judged, individuals who perceive fewer categories separating the anchor from the stimulus being judged (i.e., those who show relatively poor ability to discriminate) may show marked assimilation tendencies.

DISCRIMINABILITY, OWN ATTITUDE, AND ANCHORING

We turn now to a study which attempted to clarify further the operation of anchoring phenomena in judgments of social stimuli. Atkins (1964) sought to experimentally deal with the three sets of variables outlined above, namely: the influence of alternating stimulus contexts, the influence of own-attitude positions of the judges, and the influence of individual differences among judges in ability to discriminate among stimuli. Drawing upon the research of Bieri, Orcutt, and Leaman (1963) discussed above, this study used an alternation of anchor design for the judgment of statements expressing attitudes toward college fraternities. Subjects who differed in their own attitudes toward fraternities were required to judge the favorableness of the "stand" toward fraternities represented in a moderate statement presented either in the context of two extremely pro-fraternity statements or two extremely anti-fraternity statements. Judgments were made in a sequence of four trials in which the judgmental context was alternated from trial to trial.

Four basic hypotheses were advanced concerning the expected anchoring effects. These hypotheses stated that:

1. Significant differences would occur in the judgment of an identical moderate statement, depending upon whether this statement was judged in the context of an extremely favorable anchor or an extremely unfavorable anchor.
2. Displacement of this moderate statement would occur in the di-

rection of *contrast* from the anchor context on the initial trial, followed by displacement in the direction of *assimilation* towards the context anchors on subsequent trials.

3. These contrast and assimilation tendencies would be enhanced under conditions where the subjects' own attitudes were congruent with the context anchor (and thus would reinforce this anchor) and would be attenuated when the subjects' own-attitude positions and the context anchors were incongruent (where the context anchor and own-attitude anchor competed).

4. Subjects who showed a more limited capacity to discriminate among statements describing attitudes toward college fraternities would show greater susceptibility to the anchoring effects found at each trial than subjects who showed a relatively greater capacity to make such discriminations.

Initially, subjects were given a Student Activities Questionnaire designed to obtain information on students' attitudes toward extracurricular activities on the college campus. Students rated items on a variety of topics, including the degree to which they felt that fraternities were desirable on the college campus. On the basis of these ratings, 96 subjects —32 pro-fraternity, 32 neutral toward fraternities, and 32 anti-fraternity—were selected and requested to attend two experimental sessions. The stimuli to be judged were statements expressing attitudes toward college fraternities. These statements had been compiled by Segall (1959) and ranged from extremely anti-fraternity items, such as "Fraternities are collections of stupid, prejudiced, childish people" to extremely pro-fraternity items, such as "Fraternities are among the finest institutions yet devised by Western man." Subjects were required to make judgments of twelve statements presented in groups of three on each of four different trials. Each group of three statements consisted of two extremely pro (or two extremely con) statements, constituting a context anchor, and one moderate, midrange statement. All three statements were judged. The anchor conditions were alternated from each trial to the next; that is, if a subject judged a moderate statement initially under a pro context anchor, on the next trial he judged a moderate statement under a con context anchor, and so forth. The order of presentation of the four moderate statements was counterbalanced, providing a 2 x 3 x 4 factorial design which allowed for variation in two conditions of initial anchor (pro or con), three conditions of own attitude (pro, neutral, and con), and four different moderate statements with identical anchors. Table 3 presents an abbreviated form of the counterbalanced design used.

Table 3. Order of Judgments of Moderate Statements for Each Experimental Group

Initial Context	Own Attitude	Trial 1	Trial 2	Trial 3	Trial 4
	Pro	PPM	CCM	PPM	CCM
Pro	Neutral	PPM	CCM	PPM	CCM
	Con	PPM	CCM	PPM	CCM
	Pro	CCM	PPM	CCM	PPM
Con	Neutral	CCM	PPM	CCM	PPM
	Con	CCM	PPM	CCM	PPM

P = Pro Statement C = Con Statement M = Moderate Statement

Discriminability Measure

A technique which would yield a measure of an individual's ability to discriminate among the stimuli to be used in the anchoring task was required. Although there seems to be consensus in the research literature concerning the importance of specifying more directly how stimulus information is discriminated, little agreement seems to exist concerning how discrimination should be measured. The efforts that have been made to describe the ways in which stimulus information is organized provide, at best, a rather general indicator of discriminability. For example, Pettigrew (1958) has devised a measure of "category width" which is designed to reveal the individual's characteristic manner of estimating the extremes (the darkest and lightest, the highest and lowest) of a wide number of situations. In estimating the extremes of such diverse categories as the length of whales and the annual rainfall in specified cities, individuals tend to be consistently broad, medium, or narrow in their category widths. Similarly, Rokeach (1951) has delineated three types of categorizers—comprehensive, narrow, and isolated—from the responses of subjects to a task in which they described the possible interrelationships of various terms, such as Buddhism, Capitalism, Democracy, and others.

Informational analysis (Attneave, 1959) offers what seems to be a potentially more systematic assessment of attitude discrimination than do the methods described above. Considering the discussion of Chapters 3 and 4, it is reasonable to suggest that discriminability of an attitudinal continuum may be empirically analyzed by use of measures derived from information theory. If channel capacity represents the limit of one's ability to transmit information concerning an array of stimuli, it would appear valid to consider such discriminability in the context of one's ability to discriminate among positions along some attitudinal continuum. More specifically, discriminability should indicate one's capacity for discriminating between the degrees of favorableness-unfavorableness represented in statements which comprise the attitudinal continuum. As we have noted, the measure of discriminability reflects both the number of *different* response categories used by the subject as well as the *reliability* with which these categories are used. This method would therefore seem to not only offer a measure of one's ability to discriminate between statements along some attitudinal continuum but also would be an indicator of one's consistent mode of response to the particular social attitude being studied.

Using this as a point of departure, subjects judged twenty-one statements ranging in content from extremely pro-fraternity to extremely anti-fraternity on a fifteen-point graphic rating scale in terms of the degree of favorableness of the attitude represented in each statement. These statements (which were different from those used in the anchoring task) were presented for judgment in random order four times, twice in each of the experimental sessions. In this way, a discriminability measure ($T_{x;y}$), reflecting both the number of categories used on the scale as well as the reliability with which these categories were used, was calculated for each subject. These discriminability scores ranged from 2.07 bits to 2.94 bits for the 96 subjects, with a median of 2.65 bits. It should be pointed out that 2.07 bits is equivalent to approximately four perfect discriminations, while 2.94 bits is equivalent to approximately eight perfect discriminations.

Results

In order to clarify the findings we shall present a series of figures which summarize the results.

1. Will an alternation of context anchors lead to anchoring effects in the judgments of social stimuli? Figure 2 presents the overall mean judgments of the moderate statements obtained under each of the context anchors at each trial. The solid line in Figure 2 represents the groups receiving the pro-con-pro-con sequence of anchor statements, while the broken line represents the groups receiving the con-pro-con-pro sequence of anchor statements. It is apparent that on Trial 1, moderate statement judgments did not differ whether they were paired with extremely favorable or extremely unfavorable anchor statements. However, subsequent judgments on Trials 2, 3, and 4 indicate that differences were obtained as a function of differential context anchoring, these effects being statistically significant for Trials 2 and 4.

In terms of the effects of own attitude, an analysis of variance carried

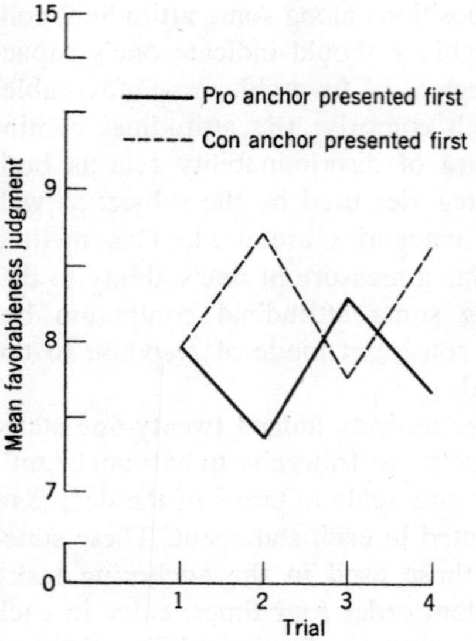

Figure 2. Mean judgments of pro- and con-anchored moderate statements (overall curves).

out at each trial (Table 4) revealed that while no context effects were found on Trial 1, significant differences due to own-attitude conditions were obtained. Although no effects attributable to own attitude were obtained on the second and fourth trials, a significant third-order interaction between context, own attitude, and moderate statements was found

Table 4. Analysis of Variance of Judgments of Moderate Statements at Each of Four Sequential Trials

Source	df	Trial 1 F	Trial 2 F	Trial 3 F	Trial 4 F
Between groups	23	2.66 [a]	3.36 [a]	3.16 [a]	3.42 [a]
A. Context	1	. . .	15.10 [a]	1.87	7.81 [a]
B. Own Attitude	2	3.29 [b]	. . .	1.09	. . .
C. Moderate statements	3	14.04 [a]	14.99 [a]	13.41 [a]	18.34 [a]
A x B	2	1.04	1.39	. . .	. . .
A x C	3	. . .	.89	. . .	2.34
B x C	6	. . .	1.13	1.19	. . .
A x B x C	6	. . .	.82	2.92 [b]	. . .
Within groups	72				
Total	95				

[a] $p < .01$ (two tails) [b] $p < .05$ (two tails)

on Trial 3. It would appear that the influence of own-attitude positions, while of major significance on the initial trial, reappears with less impact on Trial 3. Interestingly, it is on Trial 3 that judgments were made in the same context as on Trial 1.

2. Will the use of alternated anchors promote assimilation tendencies? The second and third analyses pertained to the *direction* of the displacement of the moderate statements in relation to the context anchors. To facilitate this analysis, Figure 3 represents the mean anchored judgments of the moderate statements made by each of the own-attitude groups in relation to a control group judging under full-range conditions. It can be seen that on the first trial both pro (own attitude) groups judged the moderate statements as higher or more favorable than did the control group, while both con (own attitude) groups judged these statements as lower or less favorable than did the control group. In this sense, the judgments of all four groups demonstrated *assimilation to own-attitude* positions, with context anchors showing little effect.

However, on the second trial, when the anchor statements were at the opposite end of the scale from Trial 1, five of the six groups judged the moderate statements to be *closer* to the context anchor than did the control group. Although the results for only one of these groups approached statistical significance, the consistency in *assimilation* tendencies in the

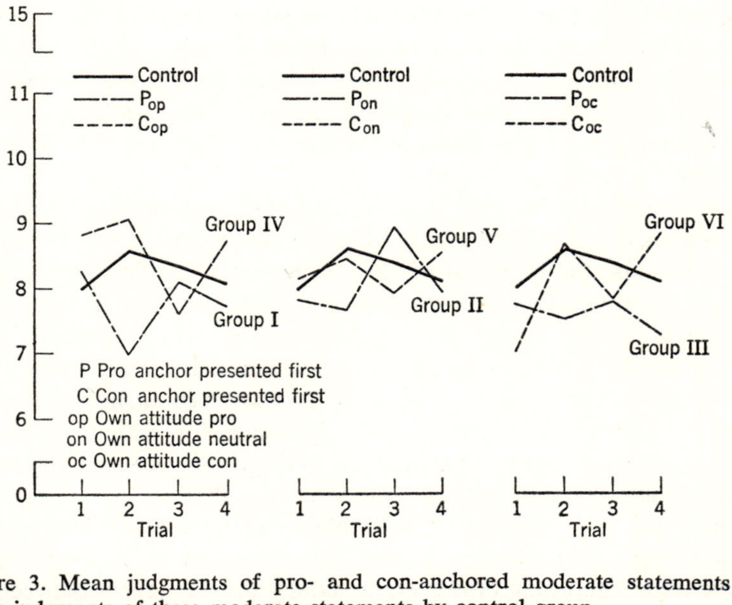

Figure 3. Mean judgments of pro- and con-anchored moderate statements and mean judgments of these moderate statements by control group.

direction of the *context anchors* was quite striking. No systematic effects of congruency of own attitude and context anchor were obtained on this trial or on subsequent trials.

On Trial 3, where the anchor was again at the same end of the scale as in Trial 1, the judgments of four of the six groups shifted again in the direction of assimilation to the context anchors, but not significantly. Generally, although the shifts of these curves were in the expected direction, the deviations from the control-group judgments were not as marked as on the previous trial.

Since judgments of the moderate statements showed lessened context effects on the third trial, one might tentatively have concluded that having experienced both extremes of the scale, the subjects were beginning to discriminate more accurately between the anchors and the moderate statements. However, the results obtained on the fourth trial did not support this conclusion. On Trial 4, all six groups showed deviations in the expected direction relative to the control group. That is, all six groups displayed assimilation tendencies on this trial. Although the analysis of variance (Table 4) indicates that the effects of the two anchor conditions on Trial 4 produced significant differences in the direction of assimilation towards the anchors, when the more stringent criterion of deviation from control-group judgments was used, these differences did not reach statistical significance.

3. Will limited ability to discriminate stimuli increase the likelihood of assimilation? On the basis of the discriminability ($T_{x;y}$) values obtained, the sample of 96 subjects was dichotomized at the median score for the total group. Figure 4 presents a comparison made at each trial between the pro-anchored and con-anchored judgments of both the low and high discriminators.

The differences between the pro-anchored and con-anchored judgments are not significant for either high or low discriminators on Trial 1. If we examine the direction of these differences, we find that although these differences are small, the low discriminators show some contrast tendencies relative to the context anchors. The mean judgments of the high discriminators show less evidence of contrast relative to their context anchors. On Trial 2, differences between pro-anchored and con-anchored judgments are statistically significant for both high and low discriminators. It can be seen that for both groups these differences are in the direction of assimilation to the context anchors.

On Trial 3, judgments of both high and low discriminators again show similar shifts in the direction of assimilation, although neither difference is significant. However, on Trial 4 the differences between pro-anchored and con-anchored judgments are statistically significant for the

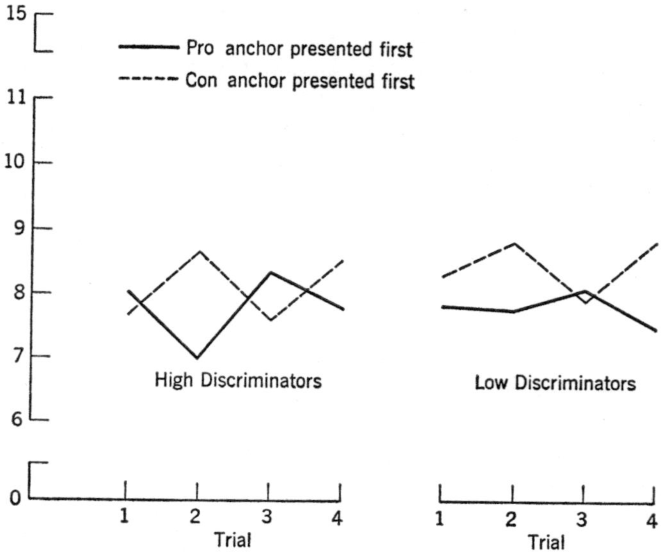

Figure 4. Mean judgments of moderate statements by high and low discriminators under pro-and con-context anchor conditions.

low discriminators but only approach significance for the high discriminators.

The results of this study are in general consistent with the findings of Bieri et al. (1963) discussed earlier and present some confirmation of the reliability of such an experimental approach for obtaining assimilation trends in clinical and social judgments. If we consider the role of own-attitude (internal) anchors in this study, in general there is support for the belief that judgments are initially influenced by own position operating as some internalized predisposition or "set." However, the influence of this internalized anchor dissipates after the initial trial and reappears with only diminished effect when the initial judgment context is repeated. Why these own-attitude anchors do not maintain a stable influence throughout the task is a matter for speculation. Later in this chapter we shall discuss the issue more fully.

The observation that only on the final trial do low discriminators show greater susceptibility to assimilation suggests that discriminability may be only indirectly related to susceptibility of judges to anchoring phenomena. Further evidence on this problem was obtained, however, in relation to judgments of physical stimuli. In conjunction with this study, Atkins (1964) developed an anchoring task for physical stimuli identical in design to the social stimulus task in order to gain further evidence concerning the generality of anchoring phenomena across stimulus realms. In particular, he sought to discover whether the predicted differences in discriminability would be obtained. Subjects judged the size of squares, in terms of the length of a side, presented in triads (two of the largest squares in the series with a moderate-size square; or two of the smallest squares in the series with the same moderate-size square) using the same four-phase alternation of anchors. Thus, half the subjects (48)

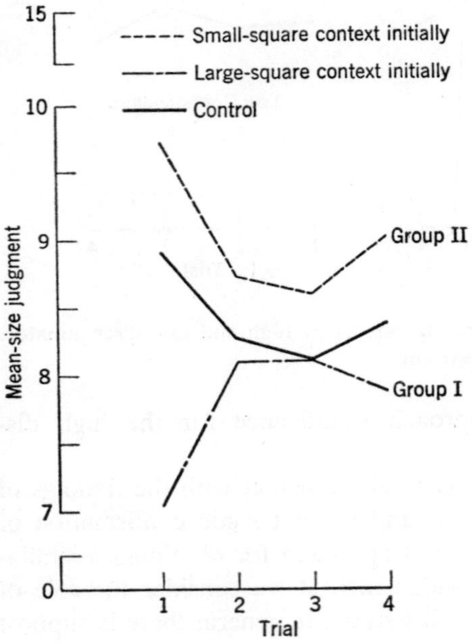

Figure 5. Mean judgment of moderate-size squares by groups anchored with large-size and small-size squares in relation to control group judgments.

judged initially under a large-square context and half (48) under a small-square context. Judgments were made on a fifteen-point scale as in the social stimulus task, with "1" representing the smallest square and "15" the largest. The smallest square was 2 inches, the largest square was 5½ inches, and the moderate-size square was 3¾ inches.

The results are presented graphically in Figure 5. With these physical stimuli, strong *contrast* effects were obtained on Trial 1 (even more marked than with clinical stimuli). Trials 2 and 3 were less clear, however. Depending on the criterion of anchoring employed, the second trial effects can be interpreted to indicate slight assimilation, although on the basis of between-trial shifts such an interpretation is questionable. On the last trial significant differences in the direction of *assimilation* can be observed.

More pertinent, however, are the findings on discriminability. A measure of discriminability of physical stimuli was used which was analogous to that designed for the social stimuli above. At four different times 96 judges were presented fifteen squares singly in random order ranging in size from 2 inches to 5½ inches. Each square differed from the next larger one by ¼ inch. Size judgments were made on a fifteen

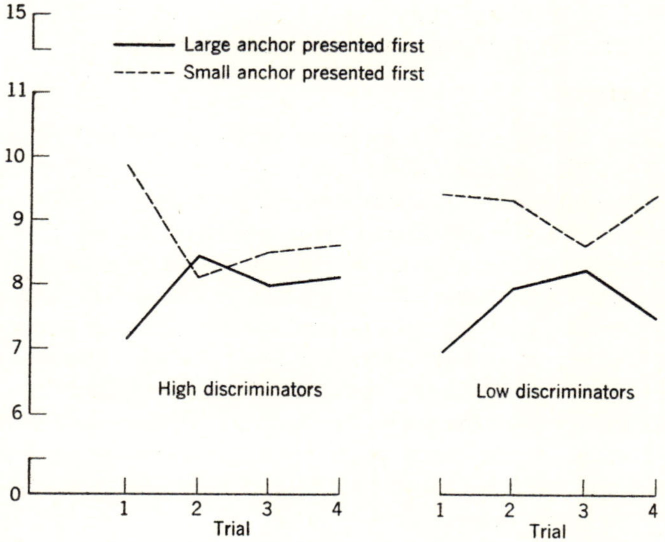

Figure 6. Mean judgments of moderate-size squares by high and low discriminators under large-context and small-context anchor conditions.

interval scale with "1" the smallest square and "15" the largest. The information measure $T_{x;y}$ was calculated for each judge as his discriminability score. These ranged from 1.69 bits to 2.80 bits, with the median at 2.34 bits.

Judges were placed into high and low discriminator groups by using a median split for these discriminability scores. Figure 6 presents a comparison of the high and low discriminators on each trial.

Both high and low discriminators show significant contrast tendencies relative to their context anchors on Trial 1. On Trial 2, the curves indicate marked differences; the low discriminators show strong and significant assimilation effects whereas the high discriminators manifest a slight, insignificant contrast effect. Then, on the next trial, no significant differences are found for either group. If we consider the mean judgments of the high discriminators over the first three trials, there is a strong suggestion that the high discriminators have begun to show greater accuracy in their judgments. The results of Trial 4 lend support to this interpretation, insofar as there appears to be very little difference, for high discriminators, between the judgments in the two anchor conditions from the third to the fourth trials. On the other hand, the differences in the judgments under both contexts for the *low* discriminators are significant and tend in the predicted direction of *assimilation* on the fourth trial. There is, then, at Trials 2 and 4, support for the hypothesis that low discriminators do show greater assimilation tendencies.

IMPLICATIONS

In tracing the research developments in the anchoring literature from relatively simple, unidimensional physical stimulus situations to more complex, multidimensional social stimulus situations, we have observed both uniformities and differences. In a variety of judgmental tasks, we have seen that the extension of the judge's subjective scale of judgment following the introduction of an anchor stimulus may take various forms, depending on (1) the nature of the stimulus being judged, (2) the method of stimulus presentation, (3) the type of response system available to the judge, and (4) cognitive abilities and motivational factors affecting the judge. Furthermore, we have noted the necessity of investigating the functional interrelations between external stimulus factors and internal own-attitude factors within the broad framework of anchoring phenomena.

As we have pointed out throughout this chapter, current theoretical formulations provide only general guidelines for the analysis and interpretation of anchoring effects. This is especially true when we note that few systematic efforts have been made to incorporate both internal and external anchors in a conceptual approach to anchoring phenomena. The use of different methodological procedures as well as different criteria by which to assess the presence of anchoring has, in addition, limited comparisons among empirical studies.

A number of questions can be raised at this point, but one major consideration concerns the role of internal own-attitude anchors. Although we have observed that these internal anchors do influence judgments, the nature of this influence needs further research attention. Why did the extreme judges display such marked assimilation trends, contrary to the findings of Sherif and Hovland, and others, that one could expect contrast under these conditions? Similarly, why did these effects dissipate after the initial trial?

In dealing with affectively charged social issues, we see perhaps most clearly the need for further analysis of the dispositional tendencies of the judge. While it has been suggested (Sherif and Hovland, 1961) that highly involved judges will show greater contrast tendencies, such an approach overlooks certain intricate relations between affective arousal and judgment. We may hypothesize that to the extent that heightened affective arousal affects a judge's *discriminability,* his tendency to assimilate may be increased. If affective arousal tends to decrease the number of subjective categories of judgment available to the judge, or to increase the width of the categories which are used, it is reasonable to expect that assimilation of moderate stimuli may occur. Although it is possible to argue from previous research that heightened arousal may reduce discriminability, research support for this relationship in the attitude realm is lacking. For example, does heightened involvement affect discriminability across the entire scale of judgment or only in specific portions of the subjective scale? Indirect evidence suggests that involvement may affect discrimination in certain areas of the scale. However, there is disagreement as to whether this reduced discrimination occurs in that portion of the scale near one's own position or distant from one's own position. If it can be demonstrated that discriminability varies in relation to heightened involvement and varies especially in the portion of the scale closest to the judge's own position, a step may be made toward an understanding of the basis for assimilation to internal own-attitude anchors. Furthermore, the persistence of these assimilation effects toward own position across a series of trials may also prove to be a function of the degree of heightened involvement. It may well be that a lower degree of involvement reduces the ultimate effect of internal anchors and increases the likelihood of susceptibility to context anchors on subsequent trials.

We should note, however, that in the study by Atkins (1964) involvement was not investigated independently of extremity of scale position. If a more extreme position on an attitude scale does indicate a more involved attitude toward the issue in question, it is possible to assume that this greater degree of own-position involvement may represent a heightened affective reaction to the stimuli being judged. However, such an assumption requires empirical testing, since the involvement variable has been shown to have complex properties. In Chapter 9 we shall return to a more detailed consideration of the type of empirical analyses needed to explicate the influence of affective variables in judgment. Such research effort should contribute to a more complete conceptual understanding of anchoring phenomena in the clinical and social realms of judgment.

chapter 7 COGNITIVE STRUCTURE AND JUDGMENT

We next turn our attention to a consideration of those aspects of the judge's personality which might influence his ability to discriminate behavioral information. Individual differences in information processing ability may be analyzed in terms of two major types of personality dispositions, the *motivational* states of the judge and the *cognitive* characteristics of the judge. That motivational dispositions influence judgmental behavior is regarded as a truism in clinical and social judgment, as well as in the more general field of perceptual behavior. Despite the feverish production of empirical studies ushered in by the so-called "New Look" research on needs and perception in the forties and fifties, few if any systematically substantiated propositions about the role of motives in perceptual processes have emerged. In fact, even if we delimit this field more narrowly to consider the relation between emotionality and discrimination behavior, theoretical and empirical analysis reveals major inconsistencies (Easterbrook, 1959). For example, the relation of the anxiety level of the judge to his ability to discriminate stimuli has generally been considered to be a positive one, although reports of research studies have not consistently yielded such a function (Eriksen and Wechsler, 1955; Brod, Kernoff, and Terwilliger, 1964).

As we turn to the more complex fields of social and clinical judgment the analysis of the influence of motivational processes upon judgment is therefore largely undeveloped in terms of empirical research and theoretical formulation. The discussion in Chapter 6 of our work and in the work of others on the influence of one's own position or attitude upon anchoring effects exemplifies one approach to the study of the effects of motivational states upon judgment. An analogous area of research in clinical judgment concerns the influence of the motivational state of the clinician upon his inferences about a client. It is commonly assumed that a therapist who has developed intense counter-transference feelings towards his client may overlook or suppress behaviors which are germane to the motives aroused by his feelings about the client. Considering the emphasis given to this problem in clinical training, the evidence for such biasing on the part of the clinician is scant indeed (Cutler, 1958).

Similarly we have only limited evidence, and even less in the way of systematic conceptualization, concerning stable motivational dispositions which may be related to accuracy or creativity in clinical inference. It may be presumed that such needs and dispositions as intraception, nurturance, affiliation, and psychological-mindedness should relate to heightened sensitivity to subtle behavioral cues, yet psychologists (in spite of their stress upon research sophistication) have not been notably more active in exploring the role of such motivational variables in clinical judgment than have psychiatrists or social workers. Indeed, the clinical dictum of "know thyself" still appears to gain greater currency for psychological practitioners in terms of instigating years of their own analysis propaedeutic to practice than in terms of stimulating research in the on-going judgmental behavior of the cognizing professional.

When we consider the cognitive characteristics of the judge we are confronted with a wide variety of variables which may impinge upon the judgment process. Such dispositions as intelligence (measured in its various general or specific forms), reasoning ability, and creative imagination may be of relevance to individual differences in clinical and social judgment. At present, aside from the area of intelligence as it is customarily assessed, we have little in the way of either method or theory to guide us empirically in studying the role of intuitive processes or creative thinking in judgment [although such approaches as that of Mednick (1963) may be of value in this regard].

In our own work, however, we have approached this cognitive domain in terms of the potential influence of *cognitive structures* upon the judgmental process. In particular, we shall be concerned with the effects of the relative complexity-simplicity of the judge's cognitive system upon his discrimination behavior. Our focus on this one structural variable should not be construed as a devaluation of other cognitive factors in judgment such as intelligence or associational fluency. Rather, our emphasis is dictated by one simple but powerful systematic consideration, the feasibility of analyzing the nature of a judgment task in the same terms that are used to describe the judge's cognitive structure. This approach permits us to relate differences in judgmental tasks directly to differences in cognitive structure. Before we elaborate our viewpoint, we shall consider the concept of cognitive structure.

THE NATURE OF COGNITIVE STRUCTURES

Basically, a cognitive structure is a hypothetical link between stimulus information and an ensuing judgment which refers to those cognitive processes which mediate the input-output sequence. The conceptualization of cognitive structures has been broached variously in psychological theories, including notions such as *schemata,* as used by Bartlett and Piaget, Tolman's concept of *cognitive maps,* and Klein's conception of *cognitive controls.* From a more purely associationistic viewpoint, Mandler (1962) defines structures as ". . . temporal and probabilistic linkages of inputs and behavior which are available in functional units." He suggests that cognitive structures are ". . . rules of behavior, maps, or schemata laid down which connect various behaviors and environmental inputs." Rapaport (1957), by contrast, has considered cognitive structure in relation to the psychoanalytic theory of autonomous ego functions and has indicated that the concept refers both to relatively enduring means and to the creation of new means for man's organization of the information that he gains from his environment.

Although there are a variety of definitions of cognitive structure that refer to different psychological processes, there are at least two common areas of agreement among cognitive theorists. First, cognitive structures refer to organized systems whose properties are dependent upon the interrelations of the various elements in a given system. Second, knowledge of cognitive structures implies that predictions can be made of the way in which the person copes with his environment.

Contemporary conceptualizations of the properties of cognitive structure have been influenced to a large extent by the analyses of Lewin (1951), especially in relation to the properties of a person's "life space." Lewin analyzes the various parts of a given life space in terms of their interdependence and organization. Thus, he refers to the *degree of differentiation* of a region as the number of distinct elements within such a region and *hierarchical organization* as a unit of behavior which subsumes different levels of hierarchical behavior. Lewin's attempt to develop a mathematics of hodological space essentially was an effort to define these theoretical concepts in an operational form (Deutsch, 1954). Although theoretical distinctions are made between the concepts of differentiation and organization, investigators have had little success in deriving independent measures of such concepts. One recent effort is that of Zajonc (1960), who employed measures of differentiation, complexity, unity, and organization. However, he too implies there is difficulty in defining such concepts so that they lead to independent measurements.

In our conceptualization of cognitive structure, we are following a point of view which is derived from Kelly's theory of personal constructs (1955) and which incorporates Lewin's concept of degree of differentiation. Our assumption is that each person has a system of dimensions which he uses in construing his social environment, and that the characteristics describing the relations among these dimensions refer to a person's cognitive structure. While little is known concerning the development of cognitive structures, it is commonly assumed that there is an increased differentiation of one's social environment and an increased variety of behavior as this development progresses (Bieri, 1964). The work of Witkin et al. (1962) on psychological differentiation and Harvey et al. (1961) on the development of conceptual systems reflects recent interest in the developmental aspects of cognitive structures.

Cognitive Complexity-Simplicity

The property of cognitive structure upon which we shall focus is that of cognitive complexity-simplicity (Bieri, 1955; 1961). In its most general meaning, cognitive complexity is a construct which is intended to indicate something about the person's structuring of his social world. More specifically, we consider cognitive complexity to be an information processing variable which helps us predict how an individual transforms *specified* behavioral information into social or clinical judgments.

We can begin to identify the nature of this structural variable by noting that cognitive complexity is intended to reflect the relative differentiation of a person's system of dimensions for construing behavior. It should be noted that although cognitive complexity is closely related to the notion of differentiation, we consider a more complex structure to be a more differentiated structure in a particular sense. That is, we are concerned with the differentiation of *dimensions* of judgment, rather than with categories, concepts, or regions. Cognitive complexity may be defined as the capacity to construe social behavior in a multidimensional way. A more cognitively complex person has available a more differentiated system of dimensions for perceiving others' behavior than does a less cognitively complex individual. As we have noted, an advantage of this approach is that it brings the analysis of the cognitive structural variable into closer systematic relation to the stimulus conditions within which judgment occurs. If we wish to predict differences on a task between judges who differ in cognitive complexity, we believe it is of value to analyze the stimulus in terms of its relative dimensionality. Exactly how one can specify the relative dimensionality of a social stimulus is not easy to resolve. However, the application of this type of analysis will be presented later in this chapter in relation to a number of empirical studies.

DIMENSIONAL THEORIES OF JUDGMENT

It is apparent from the preceding discussion that our approach to a dimensional analysis of cognitive structure was influenced by the theory of personality developed by G. A. Kelly (1955), which he calls the *psychology of personal constructs*. At this juncture, a discussion of several contemporary approaches to judgment which assume a dimensional basis to judgment will be briefly presented to indicate to the reader some of the diversities of emphasis which can be found. In addition to Kelly, we shall consider the work of Sarbin, Taft, and Bailey (1960) and that of Osgood, Suci, and Tannenbaum (1957).

Sarbin develops a theory of clinical inference which attempts to describe how a clinician cognizes other persons. Defining inference as "a process in which a particular instance is assigned characteristics of a universal class on the basis of its being a member of that class," Sarbin proceeds to explicate a six-stage model of the process of clinical inference which draws heavily on the syllogism as used in classical logic. Stated briefly, the judge is assumed to have a postulate system, comprised of interlocking cognitive dimensions, for organizing his social environment. In attempting to arrive at an inference the inferrer deduces a major premise from his postulate system and looks for occurrences that can provide inputs for the formation of the minor premise. *Instantiation* then occurs, i.e., an occurrence is converted into "an instance of a general class," and the minor premise is formed. Finally an *inferential product* or conclusion is made on the basis of the major and minor premises of the syllogism. Once the conclusion is made, the inferrer then makes a prediction.

Having described an inference model, Sarbin and his associates attempt to formulate a general theory of cognition which includes their inference model. Utilizing Brunswik's notions, they present the thesis that the ecology can be described as a system of dimensions. They make a distinction between the organization of ecological dimensions and the organization of cognitive dimensions but point out that this theoretical distinction is difficult to maintain in practice. The basic problem, they believe, resides in the fact that it is difficult to assess the ecology of the social environment independently of one's cognitive organizations of the social environment.

Sarbin, Taft, and Bailey conceive of a *module* as the "cognitive representation of the ecology," which is intended to reflect the unit of cognitive organization. Cognitive organization is considered to be made up of a hyperspace with an indeterminate number of dimensions. The coordinate values of intersecting dimensions refer to a module, and cognitive organization (or modular organization) is defined as a set of modules. Their conceptualization assumes that an Euclidean geometry can be used to describe the relations of dimensions in an n-dimensional hyperspace. The derived factors in factor analyses of an individual's pattern of responses on such devices as adjective check lists would be conceived as his modules for that situation. Modules are essentially efficient representations which characterize the properties of a person's system of dimensions.

In contrast to the six-stage model of Sarbin et al., Osgood, Suci, and Tannenbaum assume a two-stage process in judgment. In the first stage of *decoding,* the organism interprets the stimuli in his environment. In the second stage, *encoding* takes place, i.e., the organism expresses his intentions by responding in some way. A link between stimuli and responses is postulated in a *representational mediation hypothesis.* They assume that stimuli evoke previously learned responses, which in turn act as stimuli for other sets of associated responses. The reinforced association of a nonsignificate stimulus with a significate results in a "fractional portion of the total behavior elicited by the significate." This fractional behavior is referred to as a representational mediation process. The concept of a representational mediation process is used to define the meaning of a sign and is represented as a point in a multidimensional semantic space. In order to specify a semantic space comprised of an indeterminate number of dimensions, the semantic differential was developed. The underlying assumption is that a semantic space can be described by a specific number of factors, and the "meaning" of any concept can be specified on the limited number of derived scales.

A point of similarity between Sarbin's measurement of modules and Osgood's measurement of meaning is to be noted here. When the semantic differential for a single subject is factor analyzed, the resulting factorial structure can form the basis for locating either Sarbin's modules or Osgood's mediations. Thus the assessment of individual and group differences in factorial structures on a semantic differential is one way to determine differences in cognitive structures. However, Osgood and his associates intended the semantic differential to be applicable as a measuring device for many diverse situations.

Kelly's theory of personality (1955) is based on the idea that each individual has available a number of personal constructs for cognizing and perceiving events. The foundations of Kelly's theory are centered on his formulation of a fundamental postulate: "a person's processes are psychologically channelized by the ways in which he anticipates events." From this postulate a system of corollaries is evolved which emphasizes the nature of constructs and the differences among individuals in the constructs they employ for construing their environment. A construct is conceived of as a dimension for construing the way in which persons are alike and different from others. Constructs are assumed to be bipolar, an assumption which corresponds to Osgood's component of direction in the semantic differential. Kelly's Role Construct Repertory Test (Rep Test), designed to elicit an individual's system of role constructs, shall be described in detail subsequently. Although a number of modifications of the original form (Kelly, 1955) of this procedure have been used in research, the basic procedure involves judging a number of persons on a series of construct dimensions. These judgments are cast onto a grid or matrix from which analyses of the judge's dimensional space are carried out.

The notion of an *n*-dimensional hyperspace is central to the concepts of "space" employed by Sarbin, Osgood, and Kelly. All three of these theorists suggest that factor analytic procedures are appropriate for describing an efficient representation of an individual's cognitive, semantic, or psychological space. Therefore, it is apparent that the approach to the measurement of cognitive structure as derived from the factorial structure of the relations of an individual's system of dimensions is rather similar for the three investigators. However, Sarbin, unlike Osgood and Kelly, has not developed an independent technique such as the semantic differential and the Rep Test for measuring cognitive structure.

Kelly considers that the process of decision making or judgment follows a cycle of circumspection, preemption, and control (the C-P-C cycle). In a judgment situation the judge first construes his environment by *circumspection.* He does this by employing a series of propositional constructs to determine what judgment alternatives are available. In effect, the judge perceives the situation in a multidimensional way. Having considered the available alternatives, he narrows the range of alternatives by selecting what he considers the most relevant axis on which to construe his situation. This is the phase of *preemption,* where a choice point is set up for the judge. The final phase in the C-P-C cycle is the act of *control,* which is the choice of only one alternative.

Although Sarbin has specified his theory of the process of forming an inference in terms of a syllogistic analog, his ideas bear certain similarities to Kelly's formulation. Both theories assume that the judge has a system of constructs (or postulates) for perceiving his world and that he begins the judgment process by scanning the available alternatives that are relevant for the judgment situation. The range of alternatives is narrowed down by the process of instantiation for Sarbin and by preemption for Kelly. These processes result in a choice (or prediction), which is the end product in the process of judgment.

THE MEASUREMENT OF COGNITIVE COMPLEXITY

No less vexing than the precise delineation of the nature of cognitive structures is the problem of their measurement. An analysis of some of these assessment problems has been presented elsewhere (Bieri, 1964; Scott, 1963), but for the present purpose of providing an introduction to the empirical studies which follow, we shall focus on the measurement of cognitive complexity. As in so much experimental research in personality, the empirical operations for measuring a concept are likely to shift from study to study. Certainly this has been true in relation to cognitive complexity. Although these changes in method lead to certain ambiguities in the comparison of results from certain studies, more precise measurement of one's concept is likely to occur in the context of substantive research. More purely "methodological" analysis of one's measurement operations obviously cannot answer all questions of the merit of the assessment procedures until questions of predictive utility are answered in substantive research. Perhaps an exaggerated form of this "need" for method analysis to evolve into substantive concerns is found in research on response sets, in which such sets as acquiescence and social desirability have been transformed into more substantive personality dispositions (Couch and Keniston, 1960; Crowne and Marlowe, 1964).

We have previously indicated that the measurement of cognitive complexity is based on the Rep Test originated by Kelly (1955). In the group version of the Rep Test the subject is presented with a grid containing spaces for persons to be judged (columns) and rows for constructs. The list of role titles represents a sampling of individuals presumed to be of personal importance to the subject. These may include parents, friends, teachers, relatives, and so forth, including both positive or liked and negative or disliked persons. After identifying each role person at the top of each of the several columns, the subject is asked to consider three of these persons (delineated by the examiner) at a time. Constructs are formed by having the subject indicate in what way two of these persons are alike and different from the third. Following this, a second triad of persons is considered for each row of the grid, and so on. As each construct is generated, the subject checks the two cells in the matrix under the two similar persons and leaves the cell of the third person void. The construct dimension is entered next to the row and is indicated by a bipolar similarity and contrast. After constructs have been elicited for each row of the grid, the subject is asked to reconsider each dimension and check all those in addition to the two already checked to whom the similarity pole of the construct applies.

A major difference between the Rep Test as originally developed by Kelly and the semantic differential resides in whether or not the constructs are provided for the subject (as in the semantic differential) or elicited from the subject (as in the Rep Test). In some of the studies of cognitive complexity and judgment to be reported, we have developed a version of the Rep Test grid which employs constructs *provided* by the experimenter rather than the subject's *own* construct dimensions. Such a modification of the Rep Test, which brings it into closer kinship with the semantic differential, assumes that the sampling of personal constructs provided for a judge is representative of that judge's own constructs elicited in describing similarities and differences among people. We shall shortly present several sources of evidence consistent with this assumption.

Figure 1 represents the modified group version of the Rep Test employed in our more recent studies. Each judge is presented with a 10 x 10 grid. Each of the ten columns is identified by a different role type selected to be representative of the meaningful persons in the judge's social environment. The ten rows of bipolar constructs which are *provided* were selected on the basis of being representative of the dimensions elicited from college-trained subjects. After the judge has listed the name or initials of each of the ten persons who best correspond to the ten role types, he is instructed to use a six-step Likert-type scale in rating all ten persons he has listed on the first provided construct. For example, the first construct dimension is "outgoing-shy." Each judge rates each of the ten persons on a scale of +3(outgoing) to −3(shy). Following this, the judge rates all 10 persons on the second construct dimension and so on through all 10 rows. Thus each subject makes ten ratings for each of the role types, for a total of 100 ratings.

Cognitive complexity is measured by comparing each rating in a row with the rating directly below it (i.e., for the same person) in the other rows on the matrix. In comparing any two construct rows, a score of one is given for every exact agreement of ratings on any one person. This matching procedure is carried out for all possible comparisons, and the scores for each comparison are added to give one total score. Since there are 45 possible row comparisons in a 10 x 10 matrix, the highest possible score is 450. A score of 450 would indicate that the judge gave the same rating on all bipolar constructs to all of the role types. This judge would be relatively cognitively simple because he is using his construct dimensions in an identical manner to construe all the individuals

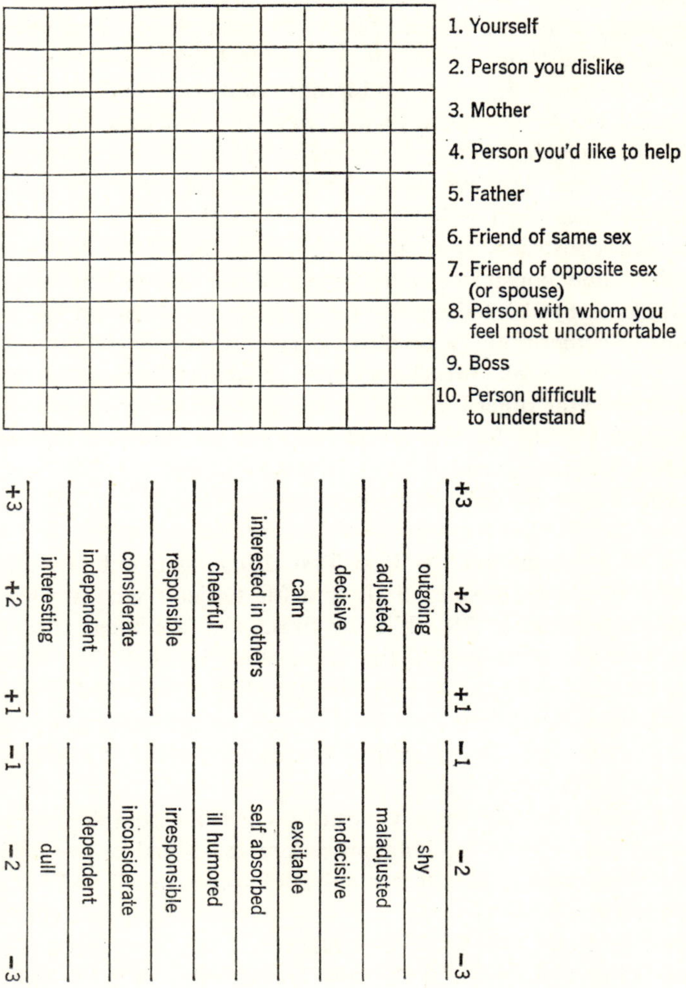

Figure 1. Modification of Rep Test for assessing cognitive complexity.

on the grid. On the other hand, a person with a score as low as 100 is presumed to be relatively cognitively complex because he uses constructs differently in discriminating among people.

We mentioned above that the comparability of own and provided constructs as a basis for measuring cognitive complexity has been studied empirically. Tripodi and Bieri (1963) have obtained evidence that supports the assumption that comparable complexity indices are derived from own and provided constructs. Sixteen graduate students in social work were asked to list five bipolar constructs that they would use in judging people who were representative of ten role types. The judges were instructed to rate those people on a six step Likert scale ranging from +3 to −3 for each of their *own* bipolar constructs. Following that, the judges rated the same people on five bipolar constructs that were provided by the experimenter. Each judge therefore filled out two matrices with ten columns and five rows. Two scores of cognitive complexity were derived for each judge, one based on the matrix in which the judge's own constructs were used, the other based on the matrix in which the same constructs were provided for all judges. Wilcoxon's signed ranks test indicated no significant difference between the two distributions. Furthermore, a significant rank order correlation (rho = .50, $p < .05$) was obtained between the two distributions of complexity scores. Several other studies are in line with these results. Kieferle and Sechrest (1961) have reported results which indicate that the way in which judges use provided constructs is functionally equivalent to the way in which they use their own constructs.

Jaspars (1964) also reports positive correlations between measures of cognitive structure on the Rep Test using own and provided constructs. Interestingly, Jaspars finds that for subjects who are least neurotic the correlation is .78 while for those who are most neurotic (on Eysenck's neuroticism scale) the correlation is only .26. These and other results reported by Jaspars suggest that for *clinical* populations, the use of own dimensions may be a more sensitive method of assessing individual differences in cognitive structure. Certainly additional research on this problem seems desirable.

A final method problem in measuring cognitive complexity concerns the metric used. The matching procedure described above which we used in our research is akin to a number of correlational and factor analytic approaches. One of these, a nonparametric factor analytic method developed by Kelly (1962), allows one to consider the amount of variance *not* explained by the first factor as an index of complexity. This measure seems preferable to using the number of factors extracted, which may be too few for a reliable measure (Pedersen, 1958). The results of Jaspars (1964), in turn, indicate that Kelly's first factor is a good approximation of the first centroid factor. In our own work we have found a correlation of .90 between our matching procedure and the factor analytic measure derived from Kelly's procedure when six-category judgments were reduced to two-category judgments.

The use of multidimensional scaling methods offers yet another approach to the measurement of cognitive complexity and has increased in recent years (Torgerson, 1958). Unfortunately, some of the judgment procedures such as paired comparisons or the method of triads used with this approach are quite tedious for the subject. For example, with the group form of the Rep Test grid in Figure 1, a total of 100 judgments are required. However, if one were to use the complete method of triads (Torgerson, 1958), a total of 360 judgments for 10 stimulus persons would be necessary $(n(n\text{-}1)(n\text{-}2)/2)$, inasmuch as each person in the triad is compared with the other two persons in that triad. Jaspars (1964) has found in a pilot study an average correlation between the interpoint distances obtained with the Rep Test and the distances found with the complete method of triads of .35, a correlation which is significant ($p = .01$). The comparability of correlational and multidimensional scaling approaches to cognitive structure remains to be explicated. Methodological studies such as that of Todd and Rappoport (1964) may provide needed answers to questions of method in this area, particularly if the various structural measures which are analyzed are in turn systematically related to meaningful variables of behavior.

COGNITIVE COMPLEXITY AND JUDGMENT

A number of empirical studies dealing with the relation of cognitive complexity to judgmental behavior have appeared in recent years. An overview of this research may provide us with some understanding of the potential value of this structural variable in a cognitive analysis of behavior. In spite of variations in method concerning the measurement of cognitive complexity, a number of studies have indicated that this variable is related to information processing in social and clinical judgment (Bieri, 1961). For example, if we assume that the more complex judge has a more versatile cognitive structure for construing others' behavior, he should then manifest greater accuracy in his judgments about others. In the first study employing the concept of cognitive complexity, Bieri (1955) found that on a task involving prediction of behavior in common social situations the relation between cognitive complexity and predictive accuracy was significant, although not of a high absolute value. However, when two independent components of the accuracy measure were isolated, cognitive complexity was significantly related to the accurate perception of *differences* between oneself and the other ($r = .35$) but was not related to the accurate perception of similarities ($r = .02$). Furthermore, cognitively more simple judges tended to perceive unwarranted similarities between themselves and others. These results suggest a difference in mode of processing information between high and low complex judges which continues to be observed in subsequent studies. Thus, Leventhal (1957) found that cognitively complex judges tended to judge another person more accurately than did less complex judges, although this relation was not significant ($p < .10$). Complex judges tended, furthermore, to be more accurate in predicting differences while simple judges were more accurate in predicting similarities, although neither trend was statistically significant. Leventhal also found that cognitively simple judges predicted significantly more similarity between others' behavior and their own than did more complex judges. Finally, we may note an unpublished study by Plotnick (1961) which involved the clinical judgments of 129 graduate social work students concerning the attitudes toward authority of three outpatients in a mental hygiene clinic. Using synopses of clinical histories and diagnostic evaluations, he found that the high complex judges, as a group, predicted the mean attitude toward authority scores of the three patients in the correct rank order, while low complex judges could not discriminate accurately between two of the three patients. Plotnick also observed that judges who were both more cognitively complex and more intelligent (as measured by tests of vocabulary and mathematics) had significantly higher mean accuracy scores for judgments of two of the three clients than did judges who were low on both complexity and intelligence indices. The interested reader will find reports of additional studies on judgmental accuracy and cognitive complexity in the review by Bieri (1961).

A second area of research has been concerned with the relation of cognitive complexity to behavior change. In the research by Leventhal (1957) mentioned previously, the effects of varying amounts of information on judgments were studied as a function of level of cognitive complexity of the judges. With an increase in the amount of information available, less complex judges tended to improve their predictions at a greater rate than did more complex judges. This improvement was observed particularly in relation to the accurate prediction of differences. Because the added information contained self-description material, Leventhal thought that this information served to correct the disposition of less complex judges not to discriminate between themselves and others. Lundy and Berkowitz (1957) predicted that more complex subjects would manifest greater attitude change than less complex subjects, reasoning that additional information must be relevant to existing constructs if it is to be conceptualized differently. Attitude scales in three different areas were administered before and after information which concerned the attitudes of others presumed to be influential was presented. Although Lundy and Berkowitz did find that least change occurred with subjects who were lowest in complexity, the most complex subjects displayed a negative change or boomerang effect in that they *in-*

creased the level of their initial attitudes. Subjects who were moderate in complexity were either more consistently susceptible to change or were more variable on the various subscales.

Perhaps more specific understanding of the relation of cognitive complexity to change in behavior can be found in studies in which there is both an increase in the *amount* of information to be judged as well as a change in the *kind* of information to be judged. Two recent studies have analyzed the relation of cognitive complexity to change in judgments following the presentation of information which is inconsistent or contradictory to previous information received. Mayo and Crockett (1964) had one group of judges (selected in terms of being either high or low on cognitive complexity) make judgments based on positive information about a person. Following this, negative information was provided and a second set of judgments was made based upon the pooled information. Another group of judges received the negative information first followed by the positive information. Consistent with their expectations, Mayo and Crockett found that on an adjective check list judgment task, high and low complex judges differed significantly in their resolution of the inconsistent information. While the initial impressions did not differ as a function of judges' complexity, the second impressions of low complex judges revealed striking recency effects whereas high complex judges retained a more ambivalent impression. Presumably, low complex judges attempted to maintain a more univalent impression of the person, and thus manifested greater changes in judgment upon receipt of the subsequent contradictory information. It should be noted that in this study the index of complexity was the number of *verbal* constructs generated rather than the rating-matching precedure.

Leventhal and Singer (1964) have also studied the relation between cognitive complexity and resolution of contradictory information in an impression change study. They presented stimulus information which varied in terms of being initially favorable, neutral, or unfavorable to judges who were either high, moderate, or low in cognitive complexity as assessed by the row-matching procedure (Bieri, 1955). Judges were asked to react to this initial information in terms of several attitude and social distance items, trait impressions, and impression organization as assessed by the method of Zajonc (1960). In addition, each judge was asked to report on such matters as the clarity of his impression and the need for additional information. Following this, inconsistent information about the same person was provided and a new set of judgments was obtained. Although all the results of this detailed study cannot be summarized briefly, it was found that simple judges reported greater clarity on the basis of initial information than did complex judges, especially for the two more emotionally toned figures. This significantly greater uncertainty on the part of complex judges will be discussed below in relation to the study by Tripodi and Bieri (1964). Following the presentation of contradictory information, the simple judges showed more change in the unclarity of their impressions, particularly for the two figures about which the greatest clarity existed initially. In terms of changes in attitudes toward the figures, simple judges became more negative than the other complexity groups in relation to the initially most positive figure, a finding consistent with some of the results reported by Mayo and Crockett (1964). Overall, Leventhal and Singer believe that their results support the expectation that cognitively simple judges manifest greater change in impressions than do more complex judges. However, they stress that their clearest findings suggest that simple judges responded more to the outer, normative quality of others' behavior while complex judges search for information concerning inner states such as maladjustment. Such an external vs. internal orientation had been noted previously in content analyses of personal constructs (Bieri, Bradburn, and Galinsky, 1958).

COGNITIVE COMPLEXITY AND THE DISCRIMINATION OF MULTIDIMENSIONAL STIMULI

Earlier in this chapter we noted that one potential advantage of a construct such as cognitive complexity was that it permitted one to analyze both the nature of the stimulus and the cognitive structure of the judge in common terms, i.e., in terms of the relative *dimensionality* of each. In the several studies reported above concerning the relation of cognitive complexity to judgmental behavior, it is evident that an analysis of the relative dimensionality of the stimuli would be difficult. One could assume, as we did in the study by Miller and Bieri (1963) reported in Chapter 4, that as new information of a qualitatively different sort is added to previous information (e.g., developmental history added to interview behavior) the stimulus becomes more "multidimensional." Indeed, it will be recalled that slight increments in information transmission did occur as the information which was judged increased from one, to two, to three sources of information.

The question we now ask is, can we specify more precisely the relative dimensionality of a behavioral stimulus? If so, can we observe differences in discriminability as a function of the cognitive complexity of the judge and the relative dimensionality of the stimulus? We shall present two empirical approaches which bear upon this problem, the first employing informational analysis in terms of information transmission and the second using a concept-attainment approach to judgment.

Discriminability of Multidimensional Stimuli and Cognitive Complexity

In this first approach (Tripodi and Bieri, 1964) a major focus was on the question of whether judges who were more cognitively complex would discriminate more among multidimensional stimuli than less cognitively complex judges. In order to study the effects of increasing stimulus dimensionality on information transmission as a function of cognitive complexity, it was considered necessary to specify both the *quantity* and the *type* of stimulus information in the input.

Three behavioral dimensions were selected (aggression, body anxiety, and social withdrawal) which pretesting had indicated to be relatively independent and which could be combined to form stimulus conditions of increased dimensionality. Each of the dimensions contained eight items which were constructed to cover a range of pathological behavior from a slight degree to an extreme degree of maladjustment. Eight body anxiety (X) items and a set of eight social withdrawal items (W) were derived largely from the MMPI. In addition, three sets of eight items each (A_1,A_2,A_3) were selected from Orcutt's scaled aggressive items (Orcutt, 1962). One set of the aggressive items (A_1) was combined with W and X items to form stimulus conditions of increased dimensionality. The other two sets of aggressive items (A_2 and A_3) were combined to form stimulus conditions of an increased quantity of information with the dimensionality, or the types of stimulus information, held constant. Thus three stimulus dimensions with eight degrees of articulation were delineated.

When the dimensionality of a stimulus is increased there is a concomitant increase in the quantity of information (not to be confused with the *amount* of information in information theory terms). The quantity of information in a given stimulus dimension may be increased with the dimensionality held constant, however, by adding only information that is from the same behavioral dimension. Furthermore, two dimensions may be combined in a *congruent* manner if items from each dimension have the same values on a third dimension (such as pathology) which underlies the two original dimensions. On the other hand, two dimensions may be combined in an *incongruent* manner if items from the two dimensions reflect opposing values of pathology.

In order to represent conditions of increased stimulus dimensionality the dimensions were combined in the following ways. Items from the dimensions of aggression and social withdrawal were combined to represent two congruently combined dimensions ($A_1 + W$) and two incongruently combined dimensions ($A_1 - W$). In addition, items from the three dimensions of aggression, social withdrawal, and body anxiety were combined to form three congruent dimensions ($A_1 + W + X$). Two sets of aggression items, A_2 and A_3, were combined in two different ways to represent two congruent ($A_2 + A_3$) and two incongruent ($A_2 - A_3$) sets of items from the same behavioral dimension.

A group of 64 graduate students in social work were systematically assigned to the following four experimental groups ($N = 16$ in each group):

Experimental Group	Increased Stimulus Dimensionality	Stimulus Dimensionality Constant
I	$A_1;W;X$ (not combined)	. . .
II	$A_1 + W$	$A_2 + A_3$
III	$A_1 - W$	$A_2 - A_3$
IV	$A_1 + W + X$	$A_2;A_3$(not combined)

Each stimulus was judged on an eight step maladjustment sale ranging from 1 as "very mild maladjustment" to 8 as "severe maladjustment." Each subject replicated his judgments in two sessions separated approximately by one week to permit calculation of information transmission for each judge. Following the second session each judge was asked to make one global judgment of confidence for each stimulus condition for which he had made ratings of maladjustment on a scale that ranged from 0 per cent confidence to 100 per cent confidence. Cognitive complexity was assessed for each judge by using the row-matching technique described earlier in the chapter.

Considering first the values of information transmission for each of the judgment conditions, the means and variances of amounts of transmitted information, $T_{x;y}$, are presented in Table 1. These individual or *within* judge scores of information transmission in Table 1 are to be distinguished from the *among* judge measures of information transmission discussed in Chapter 4 in which nonreplicated judgments are collapsed across all subjects.

The results presented in Table 1 indicate that information transmission follows a curvilinear relation as stimulus dimensionality increases. Thus, as the stimulus dimensionality is increased from one dimension (A_1) to two congruent dimensions ($A_1 + W$), information transmission tends to decrease, although not significantly. On the other hand, there is a significant *increase* in information transmission when the dimensionality of the stimulus increases from two dimensions ($A_1 + W$) to three dimensions ($A_1 + W + X$). When the quantity of infor-

Table 1. Means and Variances of Amounts of Transmitted Information within Judges (in Bits) for Judgments of Maladjustment
(Tripodi and Bieri, 1964)

	Group I		
	A_1	W	X
$\bar{x}$	1.98	2.02	2.01
s^2	0.04	0.04	0.06
	Group II		
	$A_1 + W$	$A_2 + A_3$	
$\bar{x}$	1.86	2.02	
s^2	0.05	0.05	
	Group III		
	$A_1 - W$	$A_2 - A_3$	
$\bar{x}$	1.65	1.63	
s^2	0.05	0.08	
	Group IV		
	$A_1 + W + X$	A_2	A_3
$\bar{x}$	2.06	2.06	2.04
s^2	0.03	0.03	0.08

Note: $N = 16$ in each group.
(By permission, Duke University Press)

mation is increased while the dimensionality of the stimulus is held constant (from A_2 or A_3 to $A_2 + A_3$), information transmission remains the same. It is apparent from Table 1 that the judgments of incongruent information (stimulus conditions $A_1 - W$ and $A_2 - A_3$) yielded the lowest amounts of transmitted information.

Although it is not clear why the two-dimensional condition ($A_1 + W$) produced lower information transmission than the A_1 and $A_1 + W + X$ conditions, this may have been due to the fact that the dimensions of aggression and social withdrawal were relatively more independent than the dimensions of social withdrawal and body anxiety. Thus the addition of a third dimension (X) may aid a judge in discrimination because he may be able to ignore one of the three dimensions and selectively attend to the two dimensions that he perceives as more complementary.

The relation of cognitive complexity to stimulus dimensionality is analyzed in Table 2 in terms of comparisons between stimulus condi-

Table 2. Means and Variances for Information Transmission within Judges for Cognitively Complex and Cognitively Simple Judges

	Cognitively Complex Judges ($N = 8$ in Each Group)		Cognitively Simple Judges ($N = 8$ in Each Group)	
Stimulus Dimension	Mean	Variance	Mean	Variance
A_1	2.05	0.04	1.90	0.04
$A_1 + W$	1.89	0.06	1.79	0.04
$A_1 + W + X$	2.03	0.03	2.09	0.05
A_2	2.09	0.04	2.04	0.02
A_3	2.06	0.04	2.04	0.05
W	2.06	0.05	1.97	0.02
X	1.98	0.05	2.04	0.06
$A_2 + A_3$	2.06	0.07	1.93	0.06
$A_1 - W$	1.69	0.04	1.62	0.06
$A_2 - A_3$	1.69	0.03	1.57	0.15

tions for high and low complex judges. It will be noted that for the ten stimulus conditions presented in Table 2, discriminability was higher for high complex judges than for low complex judges for all conditions except two—$(A_1 + W + X)$ and X. While the curvilinear function between the three conditions of stimulus dimensionality held for both complexity groups, the increase in information transmission from two to three dimensions was statistically significant only for the low complex judges ($t = 3.00$, $p < .01$). These findings may be compared to the results of Leventhal (1957) who found that judges low in cognitive complexity tended to improve their predictions as a function of increased stimulus information. Our results suggest that an increase in degree of differentiation in the stimulus is more likely to aid discriminability for a low complex judge than for a judge with a higher degree of cognitive differentiation in his system of personal constructs.

In Table 2 it is evident that for both complexity groups, incongruent information ($A_1 - W$ and $A_2 - A_3$) was discriminated less well than congruent information. The tendency for high complex judges to discriminate incongruent information better than low complex judges (Table 2) was also found when information transmission was measured *among* judges. For stimulus conditions $A_2 - A_3$ and $A_1 - W$, judges high in cognitive complexity transmitted significantly more information *as a group* than did low complex judges. These results, suggesting that judges high in complexity were better able to discriminate incongruent information, are similar to those of Mayo and Crockett (1964) who found that cognitively complex judges were able to integrate contradictory information better than less complex judges.

Cognitive Complexity and Confidence Judgments

Further evidence that cognitively complex judges and cognitively simple judges respond differently as a function of the nature of the stimulus conditions is obtained by studying the relations between cognitive complexity and confidence judgments. As a result of research carried out by Higgins (1961), who observed that more complex judges favored more moderate probability preferences, it was inferred that high complex judges would be less confident than low complex judges in making judgments of behavioral stimuli. Mean confidence judgments for judges high and low in cognitive complexity are presented in Table 3. It is observed

Table 3. Confidence Judgments (in Percentages) of Maladjustment Ratings by Judges High and Low in Cognitive Complexity
(Tripodi and Bieri, 1964)

	High Cognitive Complexity		Low Cognitive Complexity	
Stimulus Condition	Mean	Range	Mean	Range
A_1	59.37	75.00	76.25	20.00
W	61.88	90.00	66.88	35.00
X	62.50	75.00	75.00	25.00
$A_1 + W$	68.75	50.00	70.00	30.00
$A_2 + A_3$	60.62	50.00	73.50	48.00
$A_1 + W + X$	66.25	45.00	80.00	35.00
A_2	55.00	55.00	76.88	25.00
A_3	53.12	45.00	70.62	75.00
$A_1 - W$	73.75	35.00	53.12	75.00
$A_2 - A_3$	74.38	50.00	58.12	70.00

Note: $N = 8$ in each complexity group.
(By permission, Duke University Press)

that high cognitively complex judges were consistently *less* confident of their judgments than low cognitively complex judges for all stimulus conditions except those involving incongruent information ($A_1 - W$ and $A_2 - A_3$). For these more ambiguous stimuli, judges high in cognitive complexity tended to be *most* confident in their ratings of maladjustment while low complex judges were *least* confident.

These results are consistent with those of Leventhal and Singer (1964) who found that although simple judges reported greater clarity in their initial judgments, following receipt of contradictory information they showed significant decrements in judged clarity. Further evidence for the relation of certainty and complexity as a function of stimulus incongruity was found in a study by Tripodi and Bieri (in press). In one part of this study, 72 judges were asked to rate either of two stimuli for degree of pathology. One stimulus was congruent information comprised of four moderately aggressive items while the other stimulus consisted of incongruent information of two highly aggressive statements and two moderately aggressive statements. Each judge was asked to indicate the degree of certainty of his rating from 0 per cent to 100 per cent certainty. The results indicated that high complex judges had significantly higher mean certainty ratings for their judgments of incongruent information than for their judgments of congruent stimulus information. As in the studies reported above, high complex judges tended to be *less* certain than low complex judges in their judgments of congruent information and these high complex subjects tended to be *more* certain than low complex judges in their judgments of incongruent or inconsistent information.

One further aspect of this problem concerned the attribution of conflict in imaginative, TAT-like stories by another group of 64 subjects (Tripodi and Bieri, in press). In a series of three story-telling tasks, it was found that high complex subjects perceived significantly more conflict than did less complex subjects. Although no evidence was available concerning the degree of conflict in the subjects themselves, previous research has indicated that on comparable subjects a slight correlation ($r = -.16$) existed between a general measure of anxiety such as the Taylor Manifest Anxiety Scale and cognitive complexity scores. (That is, more complex subjects tended to be slightly more anxious.) These results suggest that a cognitive structural basis for perceived conflict in fantasy behavior may exist. This structural basis may exist either in lieu of or in addition to the "projection" of conflict stemming from the subject's own personality. Such a disposition for more complex judges to perceive greater conflict is compatible with the previously noted finding of Leventhal and Singer (1964) that in an impression formation task, high complex judges appeared to search for information related to inner states such as maladjustment whereas low complex judges responded to more surface qualities of behavior.

Social Concept Attainment and Cognitive Complexity

The second approach we have used in studying the relation between cognitive complexity and the judgment of multidimensional stimuli has been to employ the method of concept attainment as exemplified in the work of Bruner, Goodnow, and Austin (1956). As we noted in Chapter

2, a concept is an aggregate of stimulus elements or attributes which have dimensional properties. Specifically, what we have referred to as *differentiation* reflects the number of different stimulus dimensions represented by a concept and *articulation* denotes the number of intervals represented on each of these dimensions. If a judge is dealing with multidimensional stimuli, and his task is to judge which of a series of these multidimensional stimuli matches a criterion stimulus, then we may consider this to be a concept attainment task.

For example, in our initial study using a concept attainment procedure (Rigney, Bieri, and Tripodi, 1964) the differentiation of the criterion stimulus (concept) was represented by two dimensions of behavior, aggression and dependency. Within each behavioral dimension, one social concept was articulated in terms of *three* degrees of intensity, whereas a second concept was articulated in terms of only *two* degrees of intensity. In this manner two social concept attainment tasks (SCAT I and SCAT II) were constructed. For both forms of the SCAT, the criterion concept contained the behavior of an individual who was extremely high on dependency and extremely low on aggression. This criterion person was presented as a 35-year-old male whose behavioral characteristics were reflected in the following two items:

> He was always afraid that somehow he would get lost and not find his way home, so he relied on a companion to accompany him wherever he went.
>
> After being dealt five poor poker hands in a row, he blurted out, "Blast it, I've got lousy luck tonight."

The judge's task was to match each of twelve test stimuli against the criterion concept and decide whether the test stimulus was an *exemplar* or a *nonexemplar* of the criterion concept. After each judgment, the subject was informed as to whether his response was correct or incorrect. Each form of the SCAT contained six exemplars and six nonexemplars presented in a predetermined order. From such a procedure, several indices of concept attainment may be derived, including the total number of errors on all twelve trials, the number of errors on the first six trials compared with the number of errors on the last six trials, as well as the number of errors on the six exemplars and on the six nonexemplars.

In a series of studies relating social concept attainment to cognitive complexity (Hornsby, 1964), five versions of the SCAT were used which differed in terms of the number of stimulus dimensions, the content of the stimulus dimensions, and the number of articulations required. Seven subgroups of judges were used in these studies, each subgroup receiving one version of the SCAT to judge. A total of 211 judges were involved in the seven subgroups, all of whom were either undergraduates or graduates in college. If we consider the results across all seven subgroups in terms of *overall* accuracy of high and low complex judges, no consistent advantage in social concept attainment was found for either high or low complex judges. However, if errors between complexity groups on the SCAT are analyzed separately in terms of exemplars and nonexemplars, it is observed that although no consistent differences in accuracy on nonexemplars were found across the seven subgroups, consistent differences were found relative to the judgment of exemplars.

In six of the seven subgroups, low complex judges had a lower mean number of errors in judging exemplars than did high complex judges, whereas the mean number of errors was equal in the seventh subgroup for high and low complex judges. The reasons for this better performance of low complex judges in identifying exemplars may well be related to the previously noted tendency for low complex judges to benefit more from additional information in a sequential judgment task (Leventhal, 1957). It is reasonable to consider that the nonexemplars provided little relevant information concerning the nature of the concept to be attained. A number of workers have observed, in this regard, that negative instances may be less effective aids in learning a concept than are positive instances (Hovland and Weiss, 1953; Bruner et al., 1956). We might therefore expect that in our task in which exemplars and nonexemplars were presented sequentially to judges, low complex judges would manifest more improvement in their concept attainment later in the test series than high complex judges. Support for this expectation is found when the performance on the first half of the series is compared with performance on the last half of the series for the study containing the largest group of judges ($N = 72$). Here it was found that significantly more low complex judges than high complex judges improved in the concept attainment task, improvement being defined as the ratio of the number of correct judgments in the first half of the test series to the number correct in the second half of the series (Chi square $= 6.68$, $p < .01$). Furthermore, when this improvement is analyzed in terms of performance on exemplars and nonexemplars, it is observed that the greater improvement for the low complex judges is due to their greater improvement on judging *exemplars* in the second half of the task in contrast to the stable performance for high complex judges.

RECAPITULATION

The overview presented in this chapter of the empirical research which has centered on the relation between cognitive complexity and judgmental behavior suggests several avenues for further inquiry into the cognitive structural bases of individual differences in judgment. A number of these studies suggest that high and low complex judges differ in how they deal with information which varies in terms of its relative dimensionality. At least within the range of stimulus dimensionality sampled in these studies, low complex judges appear to manifest more of an increase in discriminability as the dimensionality of the stimulus increases, when these additional dimensions are *congruent* with previous information available to the judge. On the other hand, high complex judges appear to be more certain of their judgments of *incongruent* information and as a group tend to discriminate among incongruent stimuli better than low complex judges. It is therefore likely that in addition to the parameter of the relative dimensionality of the input, at least two additional aspects of the stimulus need to be specified in analyzing differences in information processing between high and low complex judges.

These aspects are first the internal structure of the multidimensional information, and second the sequential characteristics of the mode of stimulus presentation. Turning to the problem of the internal structure of the stimulus, we have in mind particularly the need to specify whether the several stimulus dimensions are combined in a congruent manner or in an incongruent manner. The studies we have reviewed suggest that high complex judges are "set" to seek diversity in terms of their judgments of the social environment, particularly diversity which is conflictual or contradictory in nature. It is as if the high complex judge has a need or *preference* for complexity in his behavioral stimuli akin to the preferential disposition for artistic complexity posited by Barron (1953). Low complex judges, on the other hand, are perhaps "set" to perceive regularity in the social environment, and prefer to emphasize consistencies and recurring uniformity in their processing of social stimuli. It would appear fruitful, therefore, to hypothesize that differences in complexity of judges relate not merely to differences in the relative differentiation of the stimulus but also to the mode of internal relations among multidimensional stimuli. Certainly the work to date represents only a beginning in this regard.

We must further complicate the picture, however, by taking into account a second aspect of the stimulus which appears to be central in judgmental differences between high and low complex judges. This feature concerns the *sequential* nature of the stimulus information. As we have seen in the discussion of anchoring effects in sequential judgments (Chapters 5 and 6), the analysis of serial judgments provides increased understanding of the cognitive operations involved in tendencies to assimilate new information to prior judgments. If the new information is congruent with previous information, we may expect that low complex judges can integrate this subsequent information effectively into their new discriminations. High complex judges, however, may regard such sequential consistency as "too pat" and in this sense be intolerant of such clarity. Such considerations suggest, for example, that in a sequential judgment task in which the new information is relatively ambiguous in terms of its relational consistency with prior information (as in the sequential anchoring studies reviewed in Chapter 6), we might expect systematic differences between high and low complex judges, with the former exhibiting more contrast effects and the latter more assimilation effects. Indeed, trends consistent with these expectations have been observed in recent analyses of individual differences in anchoring effects (Atkins, Meyers, and Kujala, 1965).

chapter 8 SITUATIONAL FACTORS IN JUDGMENT

In a paper on decision rules in medical diagnosis, Scheff (1963a) argues persuasively that physicians tend to favor Type II over Type I errors in making their diagnostic judgments whereas jurists, in arriving at legal judgments of guilt or innocence, prefer making Type I rather than Type II errors. How might one explain this striking difference in error preferences between physicians and jurists?

A typical approach to this problem within the traditions of judgment theory might consist of an attempt to relate these differences in error preference to differences between physicians and jurists along certain personality and cognitive dimensions. Worthwhile as such an approach might be, Scheff's analysis suggests that more relevant and possibly more fruitful explanations can be found through an analysis of certain *situational* conditions under which physicians and jurists make their professional judgments. Specifically, as Scheff indicates, the situational risks or costs associated with each type of error differ substantially in medicine as compared to jurisprudence. In medical practice the physician is more likely to be subject to condemnation and even legal action for a failure to diagnose illness when it is in fact present (Type I error) than he is for diagnosing illness when the patient is healthy (Type II error). In response to the relative risks associated with the two types of error, physicians, Scheff suggests, follow a decision rule which stipulates "when in doubt, diagnose illness." * In law, on the other hand, the weight

* One would expect, of course, that the decision rule would vary as a function of the social and legal consequences associated with the two types of error. Thus,

of moral and legal sanctions is directed against the conviction of innocent men (Type II error) at the cost of acquitting some guilty defendants (Type I error). In law, therefore, a decision rule stipulates, "when in doubt, acquit."

The above example serves to illustrate three assumptions underlying the material to be discussed in this chapter. The first assumption, almost a truism, is that situational factors such as socio-legal constraints on response preferences in the example given can influence social and clinical judgments. Next, these effects are not trivial. And third, the study of situational factors provides a promising direction for research on judgment.

We noted in our discussion in Chapter 1 that there has been a tendency to ignore situational influences in research on judgment. At best, situational influences typically have been viewed as sources of error and thus as factors to be controlled or, if possible, eliminated. With some exceptions it is only quite recently that investigators have begun to regard situational influences as constituting an important substantive and theoretical problem.

To a considerable extent, the inattention to situational factors in judgment research probably reflects the lack of theories which systematically take these factors into account. Although some judgment theories acknowledge the existence and importance of situational influences, as in Helson's conception of "background" stimuli (Helson, 1964), these influences for the most part are treated rather loosely, usually as qualifying conditions. An example is provided by the following statement:

> As a result, the stimulus conditions affecting the formation of a reference scale have to include the social setting: established norms, the properties of the interaction between the individuals involved, the general setting of their interaction, and prevailing pattern of relationships among them, and so on (Sherif and Hovland, 1961, p. 13).

It is clear that Sherif and Hovland attach considerable importance to "the social setting" of judgment. Yet they have not systematically incorporated this class of influences in their theoretical formulations even though they have given more attention to situational factors than many other theorists.

One objective of the present chapter is to propose some directions for research on situational influences in judgment. We make no claims that the material which follows provides a theory of situational factors in judgment. Rather, our more modest aim is to suggest a framework

---

in the Soviet Union, where a primary task of the physician is the detection of malingering, it is possible that Type I errors may be taken more seriously than in our society.

which hopefully will help to organize existing research and provide an orientation for future studies in this area. As we mentioned in the initial chapter, distinguishing among the cognitive processes involved in judgment and in decision making is not an easy matter. When we move into the realm of situational influences on judgment, the merging of judgment and decision making is especially apparent. One of our aims in the present chapter is to elaborate the nature of this merger and to discuss some research strategies that may be useful in pursuing this important issue. In particular, we shall see that decision making becomes salient in relation to those judgment situations in which the *evaluation* of response alternatives is highlighted.

It is important to begin with what will be meant here by situational factors in judgment. The concept is a rather difficult one to define, not so much because it is vague—it refers in fact to some very specific phenomena—but because it is broad and inclusive. It is the sort of concept that one is tempted to define by listing a series of examples followed by an *et cetera,* because the term suggests a plethora of specific referents. In one sense, the term situational influences refers to all factors that can affect subjects' responses other than the nature of the stimulus, the available response alternatives, and the intervening psychological and biological processes. On the other hand, if one assumes that the latter three categories subsume all relevant response determinants, situational factors can be classified either as stimulus, response, or mediating variables. The latter issue need not concern us here, however. As we have said earlier in this book, the lack of attention given situational factors in judgment theory and research makes it desirable that these factors be considered separately at this stage in the study of judgment, regardless of where the principle of parsimony ultimately will locate these variables.

In the study of judgment it is useful to distinguish three classes of situational influences. The first class consists of those influences arising from the specific social *setting* in which the judgment is made. As used here, setting refers to the relatively stable characteristics of the social structure within which the subject makes his judgment. For example, as a setting for clinical judgment, private practice differs markedly from the community mental hygiene clinic and both of these settings contrast sharply with the correctional agency. The clinician making a prognostic judgment in a correctional setting is expected to temper his judgments by a concern for the protection of the community, a responsibility which falls much more lightly on the clinic practitioner and usually is of even less immediate importance to the clinician in the setting of private practice.

A second class of situational factors concerns the nature of the relationship between the judge and the person judged, or what we will call the *interpersonal situation.* This set of factors can be subdivided further into (1) the *role, purpose,* or *inferential set* of the judge vis-à-vis the person judged, (2) the *involvement* of the judge in the stimulus person and in the judgment task, and (3) the *similarity* between the judge and the stimulus person. In certain respects, of course, the interpersonal situation is determined by the *social setting,* but of greater interest here are those aspects of the interpersonal situation which are relatively independent of the setting. For example, clinicians in *all* types of settings will, to use the Jones and Thibaut typology (Jones and Thibaut, 1958), make clinical judgments sometimes under an evaluative set and at other times within a causal-genetic set. Similarly, the degree of the clinician's ego-involvement in his relationship with the stimulus object can vary independently of the setting; both the psychoanalyst in private practice and the probation worker may become deeply involved participants in their relationships with some clients.

The third set of situational factors are *situational contingencies,* consisting primarily of situational events usually categorized as "accidental." For example, a clinician's judgment of patient B whom he interviewed at 10:00 may have been influenced by his interview with patient A in the immediately preceding hour; such "ordering effects" are well known. The fact that patient B was interviewed at 10:00, the fact that the clinician saw patient A rather than another type of patient before his interview with patient B, the fact that patient A behaved in a certain way toward the clinician (e.g., so as to antagonize him)—all these are contingencies with reference to the clinician's judgments about patient B. Because some of these variables, such as ordering effects, were discussed in the chapters on anchoring, this third set of situational influences shall receive little attention in this chapter.

Even though situational factors have tended to receive little attention in research on judgment, these influences have by no means been completely ignored. Most experimental studies of judgment incorporate features designed, at least implicitly, to control the influence of situational factors. For example, standardized instructions are usually given to judges in an experiment partly in an attempt to control aspects of the judgment task which otherwise could be construed variously by different judges as a function of, among other things, their social setting. Another example is the attempt to control ordering effects by systematically varying presentation of the stimulus persons.

With few exceptions, the designs typically employed in studies of judgment have succeeded in controlling at most only situational contingencies and not possible effects of the other two classes of situational influences described above. Thus investigators have not hesitated to combine, in the same sample, clinicians practicing in different settings. In view of evidence indicating that judgments can vary as a function of the setting in which the clinician practices (Briar, 1963; Siegal, Kahn, Pollack, and Fink, 1962), a potentially important source of variance has been overlooked. Similarly, most studies seem to be predicated on an assumption that standardization of the stimulus person serves to control what we have called interpersonal situation influences, even though there are good reasons to doubt the validity of this assumption. Strupp (1960), for example, has shown that clinicians vary in their sentiments (i.e., like-dislike) toward standardized stimulus persons and that judgments about the stimulus person vary in relation to the clinician's sentiments.

EFFECTS OF SETTING

Detailed analysis of the structure and organizational dynamics of the agency settings in which clinicians practice is beyond the scope of this chapter. For purposes of the present discussion these settings can be thought of as situational contexts which influence the meaning, application, and probability of occurrence of clinical judgments. In particular, we shall consider these influences as constraints on stimuli and responses in the judgment process, in ways discussed below.

Constraints on Stimuli

One important dimension along which clinical settings differ consists in the *range* in types of clients served. These differences are most obvious in the case of conspicuously dissimilar settings, as is illustrated by the contrast between the client groups served in a counseling center on a university campus and those processed in the diagnostic and classification center of a state prison system. But marked differences in ranges of clientele can also be found between settings of similar type, as seen, for example, in the differences between the patient populations served in state and private psychiatric hospitals. The range and distribution of client "types" seen in a particular setting provides the empirical base for a set of more or less explicitly stated probabilities concerning the occurrence of certain classes of clinically relevant stimuli. It is on the basis of these *stimulus probabilities* that clinicians in a particular setting make statements about "typical" and "rare" cases or clinical phenomena. Thus what is assumed to be "typical" in one setting may be considered "rare" in another. Moreover, clinicians often tend to extend those probabilities beyond the client population served in their particular setting to a more general population. For example, the clinician in a university counseling center who says, "we seem to be seeing more and more persons with identity confusion—persons who do not know who they are," is usually commenting not simply on a state of affairs in his clinic but on what he assumes to be a trend in a much larger segment of the population than the sample which finds its way to his setting.

The stimulus probabilities which prevail in the setting where the clinician practices serve, we suggest, to constrain the clinician's selection and processing of stimuli in the judgment process. If senile psychosis has a low probability of occurrence, as it may for the clinician in a community mental health clinic, one is less likely to search for and attend to the signs of it than one would in a setting where the probability of senile psychosis is much higher—as it typically is, for example, in state hospitals. Furthermore, it could be expected that, confronted with the task of discriminating between cases of senile psychoses and other types of disturbance, the community clinic practitioner would be more likely to commit Type I errors whereas the state hospital clinician would be more prone to Type II errors. In other words, the clinician's selective orientation to the stimuli presented to him in the judgment process will be influenced by the stimulus probabilities which prevail in his practice setting.

It is important to re-emphasize that "setting" refers to more than the individual clinician's personal experiences with clientele in a particular setting. The stimulus probabilities acquired by a clinician in a particular setting are only partly based on his own experiences. To an equal or greater extent they are based on the pooled or shared experiences of his colleagues.

In fact, it is entirely possible that in response to colleague consensus a clinician could assimilate stimulus probabilities that depart markedly from the actual distribution of these stimuli in his own firsthand experience. For similar reasons the clinician may exchange one set of probabilities for another when he changes jobs. Much of the orientation of a new staff worker in clinical settings consists of conveying to him, informally and formally, the typical and atypical attributes of the agency's clientele. For example, the new staff member describes to his colleagues an experience with a client and learns whether the experience is of the order "Oh yes, we see that all the time here" or "No, that doesn't happen here very often."

In much the same manner as has just been decribed, within each clinical setting *typical cases* are identified which serve essentially as referents or anchors for judgment. Such typical cases often are used explicitly in the socialization of new staff members. Many illustrations of this phenomenon could be mentioned; in the child placement field of social work, for example, an important decision made by clinicians is the choice between foster family and institutional care for the child who needs to be placed outside his own home. One way this decision seems to be made is by reference to certain typical cases which exemplify the types of children for whom each form of care is thought to be most appropriate. These typical cases and their location along certain underlying dimensions may vary markedly from one child placement agency to another (Chesnut, et al., 1961). For instance, one dimension usually considered to be relevant to this decision is the degree of emotional disturbance or psychopathology of the child. Presumably, somewhere along this dimension is a point at which the appropriate form of foster care shifts from one type (foster family placement) to the other (institutional care). The location of this point seems to vary from one placement agency to another. These variations are attributable to a variety of factors, one of the most important of which appears to be the relative availability of the two types of placement resources. That is, in an agency with limited resources for institutional care, the decision point is likely to be located near one end of the dimension so that relatively few of the children seen in the agency are perceived as in need of institutional care. This is illustrated in Figure 1. In the situation illustrated by this diagram different placement decisions would be made about the

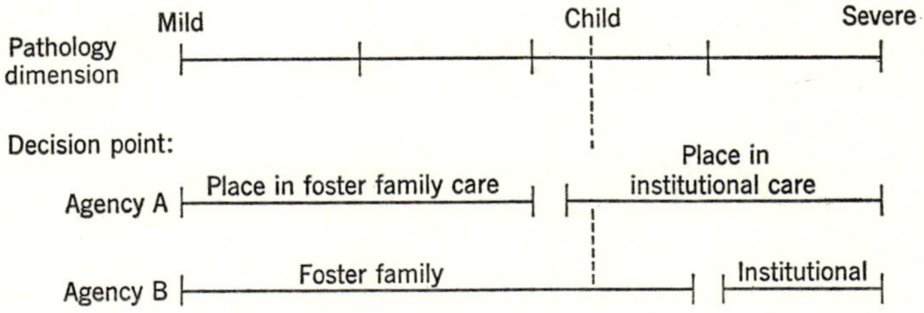

Figure 1

same child in Agency A as compared to Agency B, even though the clinicians in these agencies may have had similar training and experience. Rather, the differences can be attributed to different assumptions in each setting about the types of children for whom one or the other form of care would be deemed appropriate. Thus the decision point in Agency A would fall within the foster family decision region in Agency B.

This state of affairs may be further complicated by variations between settings in the location of a particular child on the pathology dimension per se. Thus in Figure 2 the same child would be perceived as more severely disturbed in Agency A than in Agency B because of differences in the range and frequency of cases in the two agencies. Similar examples could be cited from other clinical fields.

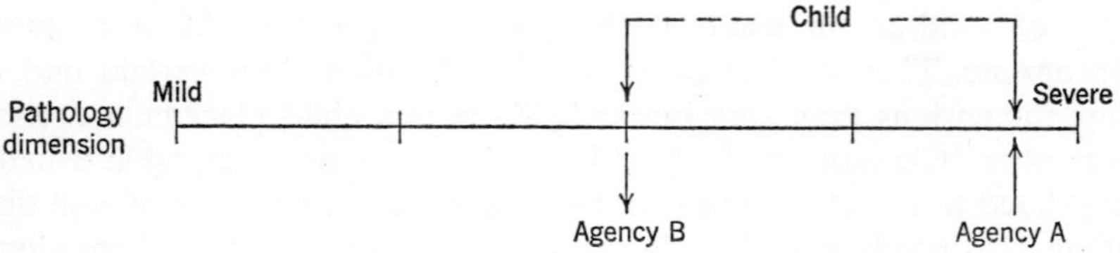

Figure 2

The constraints imposed upon judgments by the range and distribution of cases within a setting may be conceptualized in various ways. In general terms, what is being suggested here is that the norms of the practice setting serve as what Sherif and Hovland (1961) have called external reference scales which constrain the clinician's selection and categorization of stimuli. More specifically, the systematic analysis by Parducci (1963) of adaptation-level effects in terms of the range-frequency compromise discussed in Chapter 5 would appear to be a useful framework for the empirical analysis of these setting characteristics upon judgment. In this connection, one important question concerns the extensiveness of these influences on judgment. In other words, although the clinician may be influenced by these stimulus constraints when he makes judgments within his setting, to what extent will these influences operate when he makes judgments about clients outside this situational context? This question has considerable practical as well as theoretical significance for research on judgment. At present, evidence bearing on this question is very limited. However, one study by Briar (1963) indicates that setting influences may persist even when clinicians are instructed to ignore the norms of their practice setting when making judgments in experimental situations. However, much additional research must be done before any firm answers to these questions can be given. For the present, the available evidence suggests that at least under some conditions setting influences are significant and persistent across different response situations.

Constraints on Responses

The setting places constraints on responses as well as stimuli. There are two general ways in which the setting may constrain responses:

(1) by affecting the *availability* of response alternatives and (2) by influencing the *evaluation* of available responses.

Availability of Response Alternatives. The most evident variation here is simply the number of response alternatives presented in a setting in relation to a specific judgment task. For example, at the point of intake in clinical settings the clinician is often expected to make a disposition decision and is presented with two discrete alternatives: (1) to accept the patient for treatment in the clinic, or (2) to decline to accept the applicant as a clinic patient. For other judgment tasks a larger but still specified number of discrete response alternatives may be provided. Thus, in a study of disposition decisions regarding juvenile offenders made by police officers, Piliavin and Briar (1964) reported that the police officers in the community studied had available to them five discrete dispositions, ranging from outright release to arrest and incarceration. Finally, there are judgment tasks for which the number of available response alternatives is large and unknown, though not infinite. An example is the judgment task posed by the question "what is the appropriate interpretation of this dream?" The number of response alternatives available for such a clinical inference is indefinite and possibly quite large. However, the number is not unlimited; for example, clinicians with a classical psychoanalytic orientation presumably would exclude interpretations which do not include reference to a wish component in the dream.

The number of available response alternatives has important consequences for the probability of occurrence of a specific response in a sample of clinicians. Some of these consequences are obvious yet merit a few comments as a prelude to the discussion which will follow. Using the examples given in the preceding paragraph, it is clear that in the judgment task for which two discrete response alternatives are provided the probability of occurrence for *one* of these alternatives must be $\geq .50$. In the police example, in which five alternative dispositions were available, the probability of occurrence for at least one of these alternatives must of course be $\geq .20$. In the case of the third example, where the exact number of alternative responses was unknown, no such general assertions can be made about the exact probabilities of occurrence for any of the responses. One can, however, recognize the possibility that the probabilities can become extremely small if the number of available responses is sufficiently large (thus, if 100 discrete responses are available, the probability of occurrence for any one of these responses does not have to be greater than .01, and so on). An instance of this which is by now well-known is the vignette reported by Reik

(1948) and used by Meehl (1954) and Sarbin et al. (1960) in their discussions of the clinical versus statistical prediction issue, in which the patient commented "There's a book standing on its head," and Reik responded "But why did you not tell me that you had had an abortion?" (1948, p. 263). Although the number of response alternatives available to a clinician in this situation is unknown, the probability for occurrence of the particular alternative selected by Reik obviously is extremely small, as indicated by the surprise it is expected to evoke in the reader. The above examples simply represent, of course, the application of conventional probability theory to the relation between the number of alternative responses and the expected probability of specific responses.

If we apply a general stochastic model (Estes, 1957; Restle, 1958) to the task of predicting judges' responses in the examples given above, our best strategy might be to assume that the response alternatives have an equal likelihood of occurrence and then to calculate expected probabilities accordingly. Thus, in a judgment task with two response alternatives, the expected probability for each alternative is .5; in the judgment task confronting police, each of the five available alternatives would have an expected probability of .2, and so on. Theoretically, we can improve our predictions if we have information about the judges' previous behavior in relation to this set of response alternatives. That is, in a binary decision situation (e.g., whether or not to accept an applicant as a patient), if the distribution of previous responses by clinicians to this judgment task is .3 (accept) and .7 (not accept), then by using these probabilities rather than the assumed probabilities of .5 and .5 we should be able to improve our predictions of their future judgments in response to this task. The validity of this model, especially when applied to judgments and decisions of the complexity considered here, has not yet been established, although some support for it in less complex cases has been reported (Edwards, 1961; Suppes and Atkinson, 1960).

Assuming that a clinician's responses to judgment or decision tasks are partly a function of the relative frequency of his previous responses to these tasks, we suggest, for reasons discussed earlier, that in some instances the response frequencies in the setting may actually be substituted for the clinician's *direct* personal experience. Consider as an example a setting in which the acceptance-rejection rates for new applicants for treatment is .8 for acceptance and .2 for rejection. A clinician joins the staff of this agency and of the first ten applicants he observes that eight are rejected and only two are accepted. In such situations the relevant response frequencies for predicting the clinician's future responses may be those in the *setting* and not in the clinician's personal experience, because he may learn in a variety of ways that his experiences up to that point were markedly atypical (e.g., he may hear comments such as, "we've had a run on the kinds of cases we don't accept here—we don't often see those cases"). Obviously, some period of time in the setting is required for such socialization to occur, and we would therefore expect that the longer a clinician has practiced in a specifiic setting the more his judgments and decisions will conform to the actual response probabilities in the setting. There is some preliminary evidence consistent with this hypothesis (Chesnut et al., 1961; Piven, 1961).

Apart from general attestations to the importance of situational influences in the judgment process, little evidence has been reported which bears on the relationship between actual response frequencies in a setting and judgments by clinicians practicing in that setting. One study cited earlier (Briar, 1963) reports some findings which relate to this question. In that study, which focused on a dichotomous foster placement decision (i.e., foster family versus institutional placement) made by social workers, it was found that the workers' placement decisions varied directly in relation to the response frequencies on this dichotomy in the settings where they were employed. Subsequent research addressed to this question should, as part of the design, present a series of stimulus objects to the judge, since the response probabilities in the setting can be expected to be predictive only of the *distribution* of the clinician's responses and not of his response in any single instance. Moreover, for reasons discussed earlier in this chapter, the stimulus series should represent the range of objects which the clinicians in the study sample could be expected to encounter in their practice.

Additional complexities and subtleties in this area appear when one considers constraints on response alternatives emanating from the setting as a possible source of error in studies of judgment focused on other variables. As we have indicated, most studies of clinical judgment have not taken these factors into account, neither in the selection of judges nor in the analysis of data. We want to examine particularly the variations arising from differences between settings in (1) the number of response alternatives, and (2) the response probabilities for the same set of alternatives.

Let us consider an experimental situation in which a sample of clinicians drawn from two settings, A and B, are given the task of recommending the appropriate treatment from among five alternative treatments for a series of patients. In setting A these five treatments are available and are used selectively for patients treated in that setting. In setting B, on the other hand, only two of these five alternatives are available. What differences might be expected between the responses of clinicians from these two settings? For the clinicians from setting A, we might predict that their responses to a series of patients would correspond to the actual response frequencies in their setting. Assuming for the sake of simplicity that the response frequencies in setting A are equal for all five alternatives, the responses by this group of clinicians would yield the proportionate distribution shown in Table 1.*

Table 1. Proportionate Distribution of Clinicians' Choices of Treatment

Group	Treatment Alternatives 1	2	3	4	5
Clinicians from Setting A	.20	.20	.20	.20	.20
Clinicians from Setting B	.40	.40	.08	.06	.06
Combined sample	.30	.30	.14	.13	.13

The hypothetical response proportions for clinicians from setting B are predicated on the assumption that clinicians from this setting will make infrequent use of the response alternatives not available in their setting (alternatives 3, 4, and 5), and that their use of alternatives 1 and 2 will approach but not equal the actual response probabilities in setting B (assumed here to be equal for the two treatments available). Moreover, although not shown in Table 1, clinicians from setting B might be expected to use alternatives 3, 4, and 5 less reliably than clinicians from setting A. In Table 1 we also have calculated the response proportions obtained by combining the two groups of clinicians to illustrate how the differences between them would be obscured.

Similar variations might be expected if clinicians are drawn from different settings in which the same number of response alternatives are available but the response probabilities differ. Suppose, for example, that in the hypothetical experiment described above we also ask the clinicians to judge a series of patients on a five-point pathology scale. Let us assume that this scale is consistent with response dimensions used to judge pathology in both settings A and B, but that the actual response distributions in these settings are skewed toward the mild end of the scale in setting A and toward the severe end of the scale in setting B. In

* Although this example is hypothetical, it is not difficult to find actual settings which correspond to the example given. For instance, if treatment alternative number 1 represented individual psychotherapy, alternative number 2 group psychotherapy, and treatments 3, 4, and 5 various somatic therapies, and if setting A represented a large state hospital and setting B a mental hygiene clinic, the use of these treatment methods might approximate—and perhaps even exaggerate—those shown in Table 1.

the experiment we might expect (assuming that the responses in the experiment are related to actual response probabilities in the setting) that the response distributions for clinicians from settings A and B also will be skewed in a direction consistent with that which exists in the two settings. Some evidence consistent with such an hypothesis has been reported in one study (Berfield et al., 1963). In this research it was hypothesized that social workers employed in family service settings would judge a client to be more severely disturbed than would social workers in probation agencies. This hypothesis was based in part on the notion under discussion here, namely that response probabilities for judgments of pathology in these two types of settings vary in the direction predicated by the hypothesis. Although findings were consistent with the hypothesis, more systematic research is needed before a relationship can be clearly established between the response probabilities in specific settings and clinicians' responses in experimental situations.

Evaluation of Response Alternatives. Clinicians are usually not indifferent or neutral about the judgment alternatives available to them; on the contrary, the alternatives may vary greatly in their attractiveness or value for the judge. In discussing these variations and the effects of setting on them, it may be useful to employ certain concepts from decision theory (Edwards, 1961; Galanter, 1962). These concepts conceive of judgments as choices between alternatives with outcomes represented by a pay-off matrix specifying the expected values or utilities associated with each alternative. The usefulness of such a model for research in choice behavior has been demonstrated in a variety of studies (e.g., Becker, 1958; Chernoff and Moses, 1959; Friedman and Savage, 1948), and the importance of situational conditions in decision theory has been emphasized by a number of investigators in this area (e.g., Feather, 1959).

There are theoretical and operational problems which make it difficult at present to empirically apply formal models of decision-making to more than a limited range of clinical and social judgment tasks. Consequently, the use of decision theory in the present discussion will be essentially heuristic and will be focused primarily on three conditions presumed to affect decision-making: (1) *value,* the attractiveness of the alternatives; (2) *risk,* the costs of error; * and (3) *feedback,* the

* This is a somewhat different definition of risk than is ordinarily used in decision theory. In the latter, decision-making under risk usually refers to decision-making in situations where the objective probabilities are known as opposed to decision-making under uncertainty where the objective probabilities are not known (Edwards, 1961). Decision theory incorporates costs in the pay-off matrix, e.g., as negative utility (thus utility subsumes value and cost), but at present this is more difficult to do in the case of social and clinical judgments where outcome often cannot be expressed in precise quantitative terms.

availability of information about outcome after a decision is made.*

The central questions in this discussion are: (1) do variations in these conditions affect judgments? and (2) in what ways do these conditions vary systematically by setting? To consider the first question, we noted earlier that a substantial body of research has shown the usefulness of these factors in understanding decision-making (Edwards, 1961), and some studies have indicated their relevance to certain aspects of psychophysical judgment (Galanter, 1962).

A few beginning attempts have been made to study the effects of these conditions on social judgments. One example is the study by Swinehart (1962) in which he varied magnitude of reward and subjective probability of obtaining a given reward. The stimulus objects were descriptions of girls whom subjects were asked to assume they had dated several times. However, Swinehart's method of varying subjective probability actually seemed to consist more of another manipulation of reward rather than of subjective probability. His dependent variables were (a) vigilance (cue searching) and (b) selectivity and distortion. Swinehart's major findings were that perceptual vigilance is greatest under conditions of moderate reward, and that "the greater the expectancy (i.e., subjective probability), the more frequently were favorable traits seen as possibly present and unfavorable traits as possibly absent" (p. 5). Another example is Jessor and Readio's (1957) study of the relation between the value of an event and the expectancy of its occurrence. Their findings indicate that value can influence expectancy, although there appear to be interaction effects between these two factors. The latter finding has been reported in a number of decision-making studies (Crandall, Solomon, and Kelleway, 1956; Irwin, 1953; Marks, 1951; and Morlock and Hertz, 1964). In addition, decision theory concepts have been used in some studies of moral judgment (e.g., Rettig and Rawson, 1963). As a final example, mention might be made of Scheff's (1963a) analysis of medical and legal decisions discussed earlier in this chapter.

Although little research on clinical and social judgment has made explicit use of decision theory concepts, it is not difficult to find examples of judgment situations to which these concepts might usefully be applied. For instance, judgments usually considered most critical and difficult by clinicians, such as those involved in determining whether a pa-

* Most decision theories do not treat feedback as a variable, although the operation of feedback is implicit in the design of most decison-making experiments (i.e., subjects receive information about the outcomes of their decisions). Also, decision theories usually include another factor, "expected (objective or subjective) probability of occurrence," which is analogous to the concept of "response probability" discussed earlier in this chapter.

tient will act on his suicidal thoughts or whether a child molester has improved sufficiently to be released from the psychiatric hospital, appear to be characteristically high risk, high feedback judgment situations. Here the (presumably) most desirable alternative is also the one to which the greatest risk is attached (i.e., the patient will not act on his suicidal thoughts; the child molester is "cured"). Conversely, it is partly the no feedback, low risk, and low value character of many judgment experiments which has led some critics to question the validity of comparing them to judgments in real life situations, on the grounds that the clinician experiences little sense of responsibility for his responses under such conditions. Such examples suggest that variations in these conditions may influence, among other things, subjects' *involvement* in the judgment task. The role of such affective variables in judgment shall be considered in greater detail in the next chapter.

Although attempts have been made to analyze the role of the setting or the social structural context in decision-making (Simon, 1956), we are not aware of any comparable efforts where clinical judgments are concerned.* Probably more empirical research in this area is needed before a more systematic formulation of these relationships can be developed. Some studies cited earlier in this chapter obtained data which could be interpreted as indicating that value, risk, feedback, and expected probability of outcome do vary as a function of the setting. Thus, the subjects in Briar's (1963) study of foster care placement decisions reported that in actual practice their placement decisions were determined largely by the expected availability of placement resources rather than by the stimulus properties of the child about whom they were making the decision. For example, practitioners employed in settings which had a residential treatment center stated that their decisions regarding foster family versus institutional care varied in relation to the number of openings available in the residential center. To cite another example, in their study of decision-making by police officers, Piliavin and Briar (1964) found a leniency effect in officers' decisions, indicated by their inclination to invoke milder rather than more severe dispositions for youthful offenders. This effect appeared to be attributable in part to (1) officers' valuations of the disposition alternatives, and (2) officers' estimates of the probable outcomes associated with alternative dispositions. That is, officers expected that severe dispositions would more likely be nullified by the court, an outcome which involved several risks, including possible public criticism of the police and loss of officers' authority in the eyes of offenders. And, in a study of social

* Sarbin et al. (1960) do discuss ecological influences on clinical judgment, but their treatment of this subject is general and not particularly systematic.

components in decisions about mental illness, Scheff (1963b) found patterned differences in release planning decisions between two types of psychiatric hospitals, patterns which were associated with the orientations of these hospitals.

Examples such as these do not, of course, provide firm support for the hypothesis that the evaluation of judgment alternatives is influenced by setting, nor do they provide an adequate basis for a systematic account of such influences. They do indicate, however, that in real life situations, or what Edwards (1961) has called "dynamic decision making," situational contingencies play an important role and appear to vary by setting. Decision theory concepts explicitly subsume these situational contingencies, and for this reason these concepts seem to offer promising tools for research on situational and social structural influences on judgment.

THE INTERPERSONAL SITUATION: EFFECTS ON JUDGMENT

In real life clinical and social judgment situations, the judge and the person judged stand in some definable relationship to each other, and our aim in this section is to discuss the influence of this relationship on judgment. The nature of the relationship between judge and judged can be characterized and differentiated in a variety of ways, among which a familiar example is the use of role terminology, e.g. doctor-patient, teacher-student. The present discussion will focus on three dimensions or attributes of the judge-object relationship:

1. *Intentionality* or the judge's goal and set vis-à-vis the person judged.
2. The nature and degree of the judge's *involvement* in the relationship.
3. *Similarity-dissimilarity* between the judge and object.

These, of course, do not exhaust all the possible dimensions along which the judge-object relationship could be analyzed, but we do suggest that the above three dimensions provide a useful way of ordering some important aspects of this relationship.

Intentionality: Interaction Goals and Sets

Jones and Thibaut (1958) have proposed three classes of interactive behavior distinguished by the individuals' personal goals in the interaction, each of which gives rise to a different inferential set:

	Interaction Goal	*Inferential Set*
1.	facilitation of own personal goal attainment	value-maintenance
2.	deterministic analysis of some other's personality	causal-genetic
3.	application of social sanctions	situation-matching

Jones and deCharms have reported evidence (1957, 1958) that these sets can be aroused with appropriate instructions and that, when aroused, they affect judgments in hypothesized directions. Thus, the work of Jones and his associates not only attests to the importance of interaction goal in judgment but also represents an important beginning effort to conceptualize this aspect of the judgment process. Their work therefore provides a good starting point for our discussion of interaction goals and sets in judgment.

Jones and deCharms (1958), in discussing the three interaction sets just listed, point out that actually both the value-maintenance *and* the situation-matching sets are *evaluative* sets which differ essentially in the criteria used: in the former the criterion is the judge's personal goal(s), whereas in the latter it is some situational norm. Only the causal-genetic set, they suggest, is value-free or at least more nearly so, and it is this set which most often characterizes the clinician's orientation to his client. These assumptions are open to question on several grounds. Questions have been raised (e.g., London, 1964; Szasz, 1961) about the alleged evaluative neutrality of the psychotherapist, even when he is engaged in purely diagnostic activities. It has been suggested, on the contrary, that clinicians are inescapably involved in making evaluative judgments—i.e. normative moral judgments—although the evaluative character of their judgments is partially masked by the use of "scientific" terminology. The importance of this issue, the merits of which cannot be discussed at length here, is that the position taken by Jones et al. suggests (or at least it could be so construed) that the clinical judgment process, as the prime example of the causal-genetic act, differs *qualitatively* from the judgment process in other interaction contexts because it lacks the evaluative component present in the latter. However, this interpretation probably would be a misreading of Jones' position. That is, Jones and Thibaut (1958) note that their three interaction sets rarely, if ever, can be found in pure form, and that the difference between them is essentially one of *degree.* (They also point out that the judge may be pursuing different interaction goals simultaneously and they give examples of situations in which clinicians' personal goals entered into their perceptions and actions.) The notion that these sets differ in degree suggests that they may represent points along some underlying dimension or dimensions. If so, it would be useful if these could be explicated.

One dimension which seems clearly to be present in this scheme is the degree of *normative evaluation* involved in the relationship between judge and person judged. At one extreme, the relationship is such that the judge is clearly expected to make a good-bad judgment about the person: a clear example of this is the relationship between the judge and the accused. The other end of this dimension is more difficult to specify, since it is difficult to conceive of human interaction situations in which the evaluative dimension is entirely absent (Osgood, Suci, and Tannenbaum, 1957). However, as Jones et al. suggest, interaction situations do vary in the degree to which evaluative considerations are central or peripheral, depending in part on the extent to which (1) the actor's role (his judgment task) invokes evaluative considerations, and (2) his judgments have normative consequences. In the courtroom, for example, the evaluative component is central to the expectation of the judge's role and his judgments clearly have normative consequences. At the other extreme, the task of predicting the responses of an anonymous stimulus person to a check list in a person perception experiment represents a role in which the evaluative component is minimal, both with regard to the expectations of the judge and the consequences of his judgments.

A second dimension in the classification scheme developed by Jones et al. appears to be the *personal-impersonal* character of the evaluative criteria invoked by the judge. This dimension ranges from the intrapersonal, subjective criteria used by the judge in the value-maintenance set, to the extra-personal, consensual, normative standards applied in the situation-matching set and the impersonal, objective, "scientific" criteria employed in the causal-genetic class of interactions.

The diagram shows the location of Jones' three sets in relation to the *evaluative* and *personal-impersonal criteria* dimensions. Also included in the diagram is the above-mentioned example of the predictive behavior experiment. Although no examples are given in quadrant III, it presumably would include, among others, those situations in which, although personal criteria are involved, the specific judgment task has a low evaluative component (e.g., the student attempting to predict the questions his professor will give on an examination). One advantage of this scheme is that it allows for *independent* manipulation of these two dimensions.

An important set of questions raised by this scheme has to do with the determinants of set arousal, i.e., placement along these dimensions. In our view, placement on the *evaluative* dimension is determined largely by the judge's role and the specific judgment task confronting him. Thus the evaluative component of the jurist's role in the courtroom remains constant whether he is applying impersonal criteria from codified law or basing his judgment on personal standards aroused by his indignation over the defendant's behavior.* (In the latter instance, of

* An illustration of this point is provided by a *New Yorker* cartoon depicting two robed judges engaged in conversation. One judge says to the other, "Don't

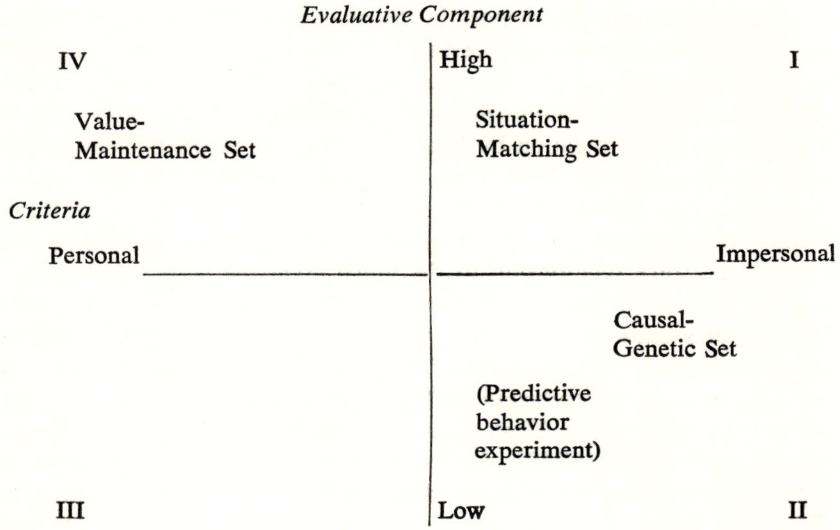

course, the evaluative consequences of the jurist's judgments may be nullified subsequently *because* he departed from impersonal criteria.) Although it appears that a variety of factors may enter into the determination of placement along the *personal-impersonal* dimension, one factor which clearly seems to be operating is the degree of the judge's personal *involvement* in the relationship with the stimulus person. This factor will be discussed more fully in the next section.

Unfortunately, in spite of the important and suggestive work by Jones et al. the role of interaction goals and sets in judgment has not received the systematic attention it would seem to deserve.

Involvement: The Arousal of Personal Motives

A person's involvement in an interaction situation can vary in at least two principal ways. First, involvement can vary in *intensity,* from the situation in which the person is an active participant seeking highly valued personal goals to that in which the person is only a bystander observing an interaction which has little personal relevance. Second, involvement can vary in its *attributive properties,* i.e., in the sentiments, dispositions, and traits by which it can be characterized. Both types of variation have been investigated in studies of judgment, although attributive properties have been given substantially more attention than has intensity.

---

worry about it. One day you're feeling down and you dish out twenty years to some poor devil. The next day you feel great and everybody gets a suspended sentence. It all evens out in the end."

In his review of convergences in the analysis of interpersonal behavior, Foa (1961) concluded that the empirical results in this area could be described adequately by a circumplex structure around two orthogonal axes, *dominance-submission* and *love-hostility*. These axes, which echo an earlier formulation by Leary (1957), are also sufficient to describe the research which has been done on the attributive properties of the relationship between the judge and the person judged. Some of these studies have focused on the effects of the attributive properties of the stimulus person's relationship to the judge upon the latter's judgments. For example, studies of the effect on judgments of variations in the stimulus person's attitude along the love-hostility axis (variously referred to in these studies as "like-dislike," "friendly-hostile," "approval-disapproval") have been conducted by Masling (1960), Harvey, Kelley, and Shapiro (1957), Jones, Hester, Farina, and Davis (1959), and Jones, Gergen, and Davis (1962). Moreover, some investigations have been reported concerning the effects of differences in client attitude along this dimension upon clinicians' subjective reactions (Russell, 1961) and their overt behavior in clinical interviews (Heller, 1962). These studies have shown that variations in the attitude of the stimulus person (O) on this dimension (1) can produce variations in the anxiety level of the judge (J); (2) tend to evoke reciprocal behavior from J; (3) influence J's evaluation-devaluation of O; and (4) affect the favorability of J's clinical appraisal of O. More generally, O's attitudes on the love-hostility axis tend to evoke comparable attitudes from J (i.e., love evokes love, and hostility evokes hostility), and the sign of J's judgments about O tend to vary directly with the sign of O's attitude to J on the love-hostility dimension. This generalization is also supported by the results of studies focused primarily on J's attitudes toward O on the love-hostility axis, e.g., Pastore (1960), Schiffman and Wynne (1962), and Vroom (1959).

Far fewer studies have been conducted concerning the interactive effects on judgment of J's and O's attitudes on the dominance-submission dimension, but some of the findings which have been reported suggest that there may be important differences between the effects of variations on this axis and those found in relation to the love-hostility dimension. An especially clear example of this point is provided by Heller's study (1962) which found that dominant or submissive behavior on the part of O evoked not comparable responses (as in the case of love-hostility behaviors) but inverse responses from J. That is, when O was submissive, J's behavior was dominant, and vice versa. Although Heller was studying clinicians' interview behavior and not their judgment, these results suggest that the possible effects of such factors on judgment should be examined. Jones, Jones, and Gergen (1963) found radical variations in judgments of O's conformity to the views of another person as a function of O's attributed dependency (submissiveness) on the other person. In general, O's conformity was devalued as his submissiveness increased.

It might appear that studies of the effects of status differentials between J and O would be relevant to a discussion of dominance-submission, but status differentials derive from the social-structural characteristics of the judge-other relationship and are not necessarily related to the attitudinal and dispositional properties of J's and O's involvement in the interaction situation. Partly for this reason, we shall discuss status differences in a separate section below.

As we noted earlier, *intensity* of involvement has received relatively little attention in research on judgment. This is unfortunate and even surprising in view of the emphasis in psychotherapeutic theory on the possible distorting effects of intense involvement by the clinician in the therapeutic relationship. Moreover, research by Jones et al. (1959), for example, found that involved participants and bystanders made quite different judgments about a stimulus person, differences related to the stimulus person's attitude toward the participant judge. Also relevant here is research on judgment differences as a function of the degree of the judge's motivation (e.g., Sistrunk and McDavid, 1962).

It is perhaps in relation to the influence of involvement upon judgment that we see most clearly the relative neglect of systematic research in situational factors in judgment. This lack is particularly evident in terms of the impact of involvement or affective arousal upon discriminability. The studies reviewed in Chapter 4 concerning those factors which impinge upon the judge's ability to discriminate among stimuli clearly have not incorporated involvement as an important parameter of the judgment task. As we have seen, such an omission misrepresents the true nature of interpersonal factors in many clinical and social judgment situations. In the next chapter we shall discuss this problem in greater detail. However, we can say here as an initial generalization that the overall effect of heightened involvement or affective arousal upon judgment may be expected to be a *lowering* of the discriminability of stimuli to be judged. As we shall see, this general statement needs to be qualified and modified in terms of the little evidence we have to date on this issue (e.g., Easterbrook, 1959; Eriksen and Wechsler, 1955). However, considering such factors as the effects of feedback upon judgments and the intensity and nature of the affective disposition aroused, significant directions for subsequent research in clinical and social judgment may be discerned.

Similarity-Dissimilarity

Similarity, and especially assumed similarity, has been a persistent focus of attention in research on social perception (Bieri, 1953). A central concern of this research has been with the relation between assumed similarity and accuracy. Although the findings generally have supported the hypothesis of a positive relationship between similarity and accuracy, some exceptions have been reported (e.g., Spanner, 1961), and there are well-known methodological problems which make it difficult to obtain independent measures of accuracy and assumed similarity (Cronbach, 1958).

Thus far, there have been few attempts to investigate the relationship between similarity and judgment variables other than accuracy, although findings from related areas of inquiry suggest that such studies might be fruitful. For example, several writers (e.g., Pepinsky and Karst, 1964; Rosenfeld, 1964) have called attention to the mounting body of evidence which indicates that similarity between therapist and patient (called "convergence" by Pepinsky and Karst and "strangeness" by Rosenfeld) appears to be related to continuance and outcome in treatment. Another example is afforded by the studies of the relationship between similarity and interpersonal attraction (e.g., Newcomb, 1961).

In the future it might be useful to distinguish between three types of similarity-dissimilarity which have not always been clearly differentiated. One type, which might be called *belief congruence,* consists of the degree of similarity (assumed or actual) between the attitudes and personality traits of A and B. A second type is what has been termed *social distance* or A's degree of acceptance of B. And the third type, which we will call *status differential,* is the difference in social status, e.g., social class, between A and B. Although in some instances these three types of similarity-dissimilarity may be related, this is not always true; for example, A and B may have high belief congruence even though A is upper class and B is lower class. Moreover, it should be noted that similarity-dissimilarity in each of the above types is not necessarily a unidimensional construct, as Triandis (1964) has shown in the case of social distance.

CONCLUSION

As we noted in the introductory section, our aim in this chapter has been essentially heuristic. That is, we have attempted to call attention to a set of factors which have received insufficient attention in judgment research and to indicate the probable, and in some instances demonstrable, importance of situational factors in the judgment process. As such, this chapter echoes somewhat similar pleas made earlier by, among others, Hunt and Jones (1962), and Sarbin et al., (1960), and it reflects the parallel growth of interest in situational factors in other fields of psychology.*

Moreover, we have outlined a number of directions for future research in this area and have presented a general framework for ordering studies of situational influences on judgment. Although we have not been able to offer a systematic account of the operation of these influences in the judgment process, we identified some points where the study of situational factors might be articulated to more rigorous formulations in other areas of psychology, as in the case of decision theory.

In part, the neglect of situational factors has been made possible by the assumption that such factors can be controlled or excluded without great difficulty in the experimental situation. However, research (e.g., Orne, 1962; Winkel and Sarason, 1964) casts serious doubt on this assumption and suggests, instead, that we may pay increasing attention to the operation of situational factors, even in the experimental laboratory. In Chapter 9 we shall further explicate our view that conceptualization of the judgment process will be incomplete if it does not systematically take into account factors stemming from the nature of the situation.

* See, for example, the work of Orne (1962), Rosenthal (1964), Sarason and Minard (1963), and Winkel and Sarason (1964).

chapter 9 STRUCTURE AND AFFECT IN JUDGMENT

DISCRIMINATION AND JUDGMENT

Our concern throughout this book has been to analyze those factors in the judgment situation which may influence the discriminability of clinical and social stimuli. We shall now recapitulate our analysis in order to gain as clear a grasp as possible of this approach and its range of applicability. First, we should note that our primary emphasis has been upon those judgment situations in which *maximum* discriminability is implicitly called for. That is, a judge is presented with a variety of stimuli and a variety of responses and is required to assign output categories to the several inputs. As such, our approach has stressed those factors which influence the relative versatility of the clinician or judge in maximizing his discriminations among a group of stimuli.

Our studies to date suggest that the capacity of a judge to discriminate among an array of social or clinical stimuli is *not* large. Certainly in terms of discriminability *among* a group of judges, as in the Miller and Bieri study of Chapter 4, the number of reliable discriminations is not much in excess of 1 to 1.5 bits, or two to three discriminations. Within any given judge, discriminability is apt to be greater, and probably approximates that for *simple* physical stimuli in a comparable judgment task. For example, in the study of Atkins (Table 5, Chapter 4), judges were able to make about six reliable discriminations among a group of items concerning fraternities, or, in informational terms, acheived a mean $T_{x;y}$ of about 2.65. These same judges discriminated sizes of squares with somewhat less facility (mean $T_{x;y} = 2.34$). Bieri and Atkins (1965) found that a group of judges had comparable capacity in the discriminability of aggressive stimuli (mean $T_{x;y} = 2.12$) and of sizes of squares (mean $T_{x;y} = 2.01$).

Thus, although we might consider social stimuli to have inherently greater dimensionality, they are not necessarily more easily discriminated than physical stimuli *when relatively simple response systems are used.* We stress this last point because it is certainly possible that social stimuli attain maximal discriminability when more complex response systems are invoked than those we have used. For one thing, we have *provided* response categories for our judges and have not allowed them to invoke their own more idiosyncratic categories. Furthermore, we have used rather simple response systems of an ordinal sort, such as *degree* of pathology, *amount* of hostility, or *relative* positiveness toward fraternities. Even in the Miller and Bieri study (Chapter 4) in which clinical response categories (e.g., diagnostic classifications) were used, it is possible that a judge would make finer discriminations with a response system of his own "natural" selection.

On the other hand, we have observed that at least with behavioral dimensions which are integrated in a fashion consistent with a dimension of pathology, discriminability among stimuli is not greatly enhanced, and in fact under certain conditions may *decrease* (Tripodi and Bieri, Chapter 7). Thus we may tentatively conclude that within any given dimension of social judgment, such as pathology or attitudes toward fraternities, the judge's discriminability is not great and is not markedly facilitated by increasing the dimensionality of the stimulus. If this is indeed the case, are we then dealing with a limiting function or channel capacity in clinical and social judgment? Our tentative answer, contingent upon more research bearing upon this problem, is "yes." That is, it seems likely that the addition of more dimensionality to the input will operate not to allow a more complex response, but rather to allow the judge to *identify* information relevant to the judgment at hand. Thus, assuming no bias in the selection of material, a ten-page case history is more *likely* to contain the relevant dimension or few dimensions for making a particular judgment than is a brief one-paragraph history. If such is the case, then certainly a prime concern for research should be the determination of *what* input dimensions are *relevant* for *what* type of judgment system. Studies of the clinical inference process may be of value here in pinpointing those stimulus elements which receive greatest weight when combined in inferring a particular response (Hammond, Hursch, and Todd, 1964).

It must be noted, however, that the response categories may again be too simple in nature to capture all the subtlety of clinical and social judgment. In the typical inference study, for example, a judgment of intelligence level may be required on the basis of MMPI scores, Rorschach, and behavioral data. So once more we are left with a need to define, *if possible,* the nature of these more involved systems of response which may be complex enough to capture the nuances contained in the stimulus. We must again rely on clinicians to make more explicit what these more complex judgments are. As we observed in Chapter 2, we are not entirely convinced that this is a matter of relative sophistication in response complexity. Rather, we need to explore the possibility that any *constraint* imposed by a fixed number of alternative responses may set limits upon the ability of a judge to discriminate social and clinical stimuli. Two factors would seem to be relevant here. The first is the ability of the judge to *go beyond* the information given in terms of the relative *remoteness* of his judgmental association to the stimulus. If a judge can associate a stimulus with other, possibly more remote, response alternatives, he may be constrained by the categories imposed by the experimenter. Presumably, such a tendency to generate more "creative" responses could be studied empirically, as we shall note below. Second, judges may differ in the *number* of associations they can generate from any given stimulus. Such response variability contributes to unreliability in judgment and causes a lowered discriminability or information transmission. In this sense, the most "sophisticated" judge is likely to be the judge who discriminates most poorly among an array of stimuli. As we observed in Chapter 7, it may be the judge with the least cognitive complexity who benefits most from additional information in terms of adding to his ability to discriminate among stimuli.

STRUCTURAL FACTORS IN JUDGMENT: CONVERGENT, CONSERVING, AND DIVERGENT TASKS

Our emphasis upon analyzing information transmission in situations in which maximal discriminability among stimuli is stressed is, of course, upon only one of several types of judgment situations. That is, if we compare the relative amount of information in the input and in the output in judgment tasks, a typology can be evolved to characterize such tasks. Posner (1964) has recently reviewed a number of such typologies, including three major models of information processing tasks. The usual information transmission model which emphasizes maximal retrieval of input, he calls *conversation* tasks. Our work on information transmission in clinical and social judgments (Chapter 4) has been primarily of this nature, which we can schematize as follows:

Conserving Judgment Task: $H_x = H_y$

If, as in much of our work, we focus on discriminability in judgment, then we wish to know how much of the information presented to the judge can be *conserved* in his judgments when the amount of information input (H_x) is equal to the amount of information in the response alternatives (H_y). By providing at least as many response alternatives as we do stimulus alternatives, assessment of relative information transmission or discriminability can be obtained. Now it is cerainly evident that such a conserving judgment task is characteristic only of some judgment situations and not of others. In those clinical situations in which, e.g., differential diagnosis among a group of cases is called for, such an emphasis on discriminability analysis would appear justified. Similarly, in studies of social perception, we may inquire as to how reliably the judge can discriminate among a series of other persons using a number of social dimensions of judgment.

Alternatively, we may require the judge to generate as many different responses as possible to a given stimulus and assess in this manner his *divergent* abilities in judging this stimulus. Such a model of judgment, which Posner (1964) refers to as a *creation* model, may be represented as follows:

Divergent Judgment Task: $Hx < Hy$

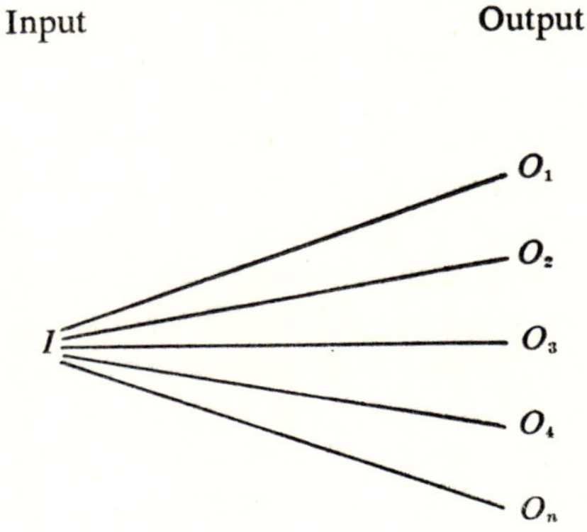

This type of judgment task has not been featured in the work we have discussed in this book, although a number of applications to the field of clinical judgment can be mentioned. On the one hand, we may consider that any one stimulus in the conserving judgment task which upon replication elicits more than one response is an example of the divergent model of judgment. That is, divergent responding is *unreliable* when construed within the framework of discriminability of stimuli. On the other hand, one could argue that much of clinical judgment partakes of this type of *alternative,* divergent judgment, which we may construe as *creative hypothecation.* The clinician certainly must entertain alternative hypotheses concerning any given input which he is to judge, and one might argue that such "cognitive complexity" on the part of the clinician is an essential attribute to diagnostic versatility. It is conceivable that such divergent judgments can be construed as representing the *mediating* process of judgment in a conserving or discriminability judgment task. That is, each stimulus in the array elicits a finite number of possible output associations, any one of which may be selected as most representative of the input on some matching basis, as in Restle's analysis of judgment discussed in Chapter 2. Or, any two or more of the divergent associations may be integrated into a common framework which in turn forms the judgment which is associated with the input. Thus, a patient's verbalization about his mother may create for the clinician a variety of inferences including the judgment that the mother rejected the patient and the judgment that this particular verbalization was both conceptually disorganized and spoken with flat affect. Such judgments might then be subsumed within a rubric of "schizophrenic."

It seems reasonable that such a sequential alternation process between divergent and convergent cognition is characteristic of many judgment tasks and needs more direct study than has been developed to date. In this regard, the development of measures of individual differences in creative or divergent judgment among clinicians should be feasible, perhaps within the general empirical approach developed by Mednick (1963) in his Remote Associations Test. As one approach to the problem of clinical intuition, such a venture would seem opportune. Alternatively, one might expect that performance in such a divergent judgment task would be sensitive to differences in the cognitive structure of the judge, and that high complex judges could generate more response alternatives than low complex judges. The empirical findings (Chapter 7) that high complex judges do not necessarily transmit more information in their judgments than low complex judges could be due to this "overdivergency" which renders a more reliable association between one input and one output less likely for these judges.

Finally, if we provide a number of stimuli but limit the judge's response system, we have a *convergent* judgment task in which the judge must match attributes in the stimuli with a particular proscribed response category. Posner (1964) has referred to this class of information processing task as one of information *reduction.*

Convergent Judgment Task: $Hx > Hy$

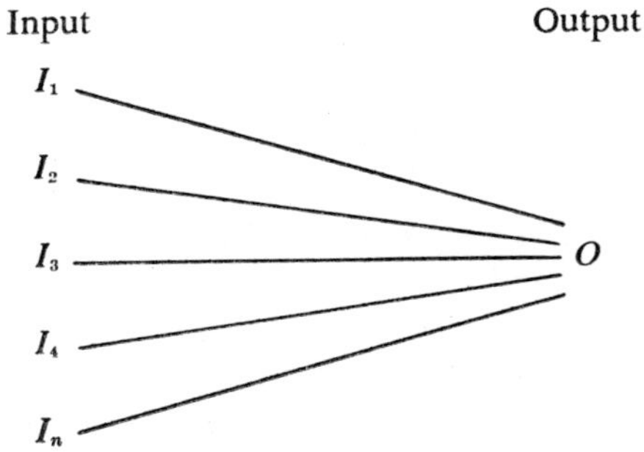

Such convergent processes in judgment are represented in our work on social concept attainment (Chapter 7), in which a multiple input is matched against an "ideal" or criterion response. Although we focused on how performance in concept attainment might vary as a function of the judge's ability to differentiate between dimensions and to articulate within dimensions of behavior, it is certainly possible that other aspects of the judgment process may be analyzed in such convergent tasks. For example, it is important to study not only the discriminability aspects of the task but also the ways in which the judge selectively *organizes* his discriminations in the process of matching the stimulus to the response category or concept.

Such organizational strategies in the judgment of multiple cues have been of concern to researchers in both social and clinical judgment. The "historical" background is provided by the work of Asch (1952) on the role of central and peripheral traits in impression formation. Asch emphasizes the "structural" relations among multiple cues in forming impressions of others, and the influence of a *central* trait or stimulus in organizing the various more "peripheral" cues. More recently, others have attempted to show that knowledge of the correlation between each cue *separately* in the array and the criterion judgment will predict how the final judgment is determined (Bruner, Shapiro, and Tagiuri, 1958; Wishner, 1960). Mahrer and Young (1961) have applied a similar analysis to clinical judgments. The results of such studies indicate that a judge may summate various stimulus components in arriving at a final judgment and that no more involved organizational principle may be operating. Evidence for this simple summation of stimuli in social judgments of inconsistent information is also reported by Bieri (1962). More recently, Fishbein and Hunter (1964) have contrasted "summation" and "balance" models in attitude organization and impression formation.

A related concern in the clinical judgment realm revolves around the issue of the linearity or nonlinearity of the mode of organizing multiple cues. As we noted earlier, such studies characteristically provide the judge with a variety of inputs, such as test scores and demographic data, from which the judge is asked to make a global prediction. This is a convergent judgment task *par excellence*. Such work as that of Hammond et al. (1964) and Oskamp (1962) is representative of this approach. Oskamp analyzed the judgments of 44 clinical psychologists about a dichotomous criterion (psychiatrically hospitalized or not). Each judge had 15 variables upon which to base his convergent judgment, including 13 MMPI scale scores, education, and age. Oskamp concluded that ". . . despite the vaunted possibilities of configural decisions from the Multiphasic, every judge in this study was imposing an overly simple structure on underlying complexity and using the test in an essentially linear manner." Furthermore, Oskamp found that only about five cues were being used to any extent by each judge, and one of these (the *Sc* scale) was by far the most predominant.

Hammond's group considers that this multiple-regression approach to clinical inference strongly supports the linear view of response systems, at least with relatively simple judgments such as IQ level. They note:

> We are confident that linear response systems will appear in future studies of this type, and that such studies will find small differences between the cognitive processes of the clinician, or any human subject, and the multiple-regression equation. (Hammond, Hursch, and Todd, 1964, p. 452)

Meehl (1959), on the other hand, has been particularly emphatic in stressing the potential superiority of the *nonlinear* or *configural* quality of the judge's cognitive processes in convergent tasks. He states:

> By the term "configurated" I do not mean merely non-linear. I mean the specific *kind* of non-linearity which is produced by the existence of significant interaction effects among pairs, triads, tetrads, etc. of the predictor variables. Most simply put, it means that the influence of one predictor is not invariant with respect to values of the others. (p. 103)

In a study comparing the efficiency of *clinical* predictions with one linear and three configural *statistical* methods of prediction, the configural methods proved to be most effective (Meehl, 1959). The clinical judgments proved somewhat better than the linear method of actuarial prediction (discriminant function). This study tells us little directly concerning the use of configural processes in the clinical judgments themselves. Obviously, this issue awaits further clarification empirically, particularly in relation to the necessity for sampling more diverse types of stimulus materials and more complex forms of response.

Finally, we may note that convergent and divergent judgment tasks can be conceptualized in terms of conjunctive and disjunctive concept attainment, as discussed by Bruner, Goodnow, and Austin (1956). A conjunctive category is one in which the various attributes constituting the concept are *invariably* present. Any stimulus to be identified as a member of this category must have all of its defining attributes. These common attributes converge, as it were, upon the criterion category or concept involved in the particular task. Such an approach is analogous to the categorical-matching analysis of judgment advanced by Restle which we discussed in Chapter 2. In contrast, the disjunctive concept is one in which the number or combination of defining attributes can be *variably* present. For example, in the clinical realm, the concept of "sociopath" would be considered disjunctive if it were defined in terms of a person being either overly ingratiating *or* low in social anxiety *or* self-punishing, or any combination of these three attributes. Such an either-or, contingent quality of disjunctive concepts renders them more difficult to deal with than conjunctive concepts, which share a fixed set of attributes. Because of this variable and shifting quality of attributes in disjunctive concepts, it is not surprising that, as Bruner et al. note, there is a tendency to an "abhorrence of disjunctiveness" in judgment tasks.

Furthermore, it is reasonable to assume that the judge can process cues more efficiently if they can be subsumed along a common dimension. The first stage in organizing cues in such a dimensional direction would be to aggregate the inputs in terms of a conjunctive concept, so that, e.g., a sociopath would be identified *only* if he is ingratiating *and* low in social anxiety *and* self-punishing. Note, however, that, as with the disjunctive concept, the judge must still discriminate these three attributes in order to attain the conjunctive concept. What he has gained over the disjunctive concept is a set of correlated inputs, so that if he knows Mr. X is low in social anxiety, he can also test to determine if he is self-punishing and ingratiating. Such invariable associations among cues represent an important gain in ease of concept attainment. A second stage would result when a common dimension was invoked to subsume each of the attributes defining the concept. Such a dimensional "condensation" of attributes is by no means easily attained in relation to many clinical and social categories of judgment. In part, this difficulty explains why certain diagnostic categories such as sociopath are regarded as "catch-alls," since no unifying rubric can be easily invoked to subsume the disparate defining attributes. Such conceptual condensation of attributes, it may be noted parenthetically, is characteristic of many theories of personality in which a "master" motive or drive is postulated as the unifying basis for a number of disparate motives in personality development. As we noted in our discussion of schizophrenia in Chapter 2, one way to achieve relations among attributes is to redefine them in terms of a common dimension, such as the degree of pathology. Thus an individual may be considered schizophrenic if his various behavioral attributes can be articulated in terms of a high degree of pathology. In the example of the attributes of sociopathy above, one might invoke a common dimension of guilt and relate all the attributes in terms of their possessing in common a low amount of guilt.

We may consider, then, that in any judgment task which is structured so that a disparity exists between the amount of information in the input and the output relationship, the judge would seek to reduce this disparity by some appropriate condensation of alternatives or reduction in uncertainty which would bring the input-output relation closer to a point of equilibrium. In the convergent task, in which the amount of information in the input is greater than the amount of information in the output, search for a common conceptual dimension or attribute would be characteristic, especially if the judge was constrained by the nature of the task to use all of the cues in the input. If this latter requirement is not present, as in clinical inference studies from multiple cues, then a selective weighting of a few of the cues would accomplish the condensation of alternative stimuli. In either case, however, those cues which are used in the judgment have been placed along a common dimension defined by the response alternative.

In the case of the divergent judgment task, in which greater uncertainty resides in the output than in the input, the judge could attempt to reduce this greater response uncertainty by some appropriate selection process. He could place all response alternatives along a common dimension of judgment, such as the pathology dimension in clinical judgment, and then "simply" articulate some value along this common response dimension. Or the judge could reduce the output uncertainty by opting for that alternative which met some additional criterion in the judgment task. This output selection could be determined by the correspondence of one alternative with a prior judgment made by the clinician, as when an interpretation "fits" because of its correspondence with some earlier interpretation. Or the output uncertainty may be reduced by considering only those alternatives which meet some further criterion of use or value, in a problem-solving sense. As we noted in Chapter 8, many situational constraints operate to reduce this output uncertainty in terms of essentially "extrajudgmental" expediencies or pressures.

From the foregoing discussion, we can appreciate the potential importance of the structural constraints imposed by the nature of input-output relations upon the judgment process itself. We may conclude that in the conservation type of task, which we have focused upon primarily in our work, both divergent and convergent judgmental processes may *mediate* the information transmission. It seems likely that some ultimate representation of the judgment process in these terms must subsume intervening cognitive processes of both the convergent and divergent sort. At the same time, we think that subsequent conceptual and empirical efforts must consider, in addition to these structural properties, the influence of *affective* variables in clinical and social judgment, a topic to which we shall now turn.

AFFECTIVE PROCESSES IN DIMENSIONAL JUDGMENTS

Throughout this book we have had occasion to refer to the potential impact of affective processes upon judgment. In particular, we have discussed the role of own attitude upon anchoring phenomena (Chapter 6), congruent with the notion that such affective involvement in an issue may operate as an internal anchor and systematically bias judgments accordingly. In Chapter 8 we discussed a number of situational variables which involve affective factors impinging upon the judgment process. When we consider that judgments of others' behavior occur in interpersonal contexts in which affect and emotion can be pronounced, as in the therapy situation, it is indeed puzzling and striking that so little effort has been expended in analyzing the influence of these affective forces upon judgment. We consider this to be an important next step in research on judgment, and would like to consider here just how these affective processes might be expected to influence stimulus discriminability.

Affect and Discriminability

Perhaps the most concentrated efforts to conceptualize affective variables in judgment were the "New Look" studies of need and perception. However, a major concern of much of this research was the effect of need arousal upon subthreshold phenomena in perception, as exemplified in the work on subception. A somewhat related emphasis is found in the current work on motivational and feedback phenomena in signal detectibility (Atkinson, 1963; Atkinson, Carterette, and Kinchla, 1964). The relative lack of systematic analyses of affective factors influencing the discrimination of *suprathreshold* stimuli is noteworthy in view of the fact that most events which the individual is called upon to discriminate in social and clinical situations involve such above threshold stimuli. Thus it is not surprising that the kind of systematic statements that can be made concerning the impact of affective variables upon judgment are rather general in nature, and that the evidence for these generalizations is at best equivocal, if not contradictory. For example, a review of areas of research related to this issue can yield the following rather disparate cluster of generalizations: (1) affective arousal serves to limit the range of cue utilization (Easterbrook, 1959); (2) heightened drive decreases the width of cognitive maps (Tolman, 1948); (3) objects which are valued by the perceiver or which have been associated with positive *or* negative reinforcement may be judged to be larger than neutral objects (Allport, 1955; Postman, 1953); and (4) increased stress or anxiety may increase stimulus generalization (Mednick and Freedman, 1960) or may increase response stereotypy (Eriksen and Wechsler, 1955). This last generalization reflects an important issue in any attempt to relate affective variables to judgmental behavior, and that is to what extent it is possible to isolate these effects in terms of sensory processes of judgment and to what extent it is possible to isolate them as response effects. It is certainly possible to concentrate exclusively on response factors, and consider, for example, that affective arousal serves primarily to change the threshold for the evocation of competing responses. However, it is possible to formulate a number of orienting assumptions which could guide research on the relations between affective arousal and discriminability of stimuli and which include an emphasis on input variables as well as output or response characteristics.

Orienting Assumptions

A first assumption in this regard would relate to our consideration of the concept of channel capacity as it was presented in Chapter 3. That is, we assume that in discriminating among stimuli which are continuously variable along an intensity dimension, a judge has available a finite number of categories within his subjective scale of judgment. It is assumed that the number and nature of these categories determine in part the ability of the judge to discriminate among stimuli along a given continuum. A second assumption is that affective arousal tends to *decrease* the number of subjective categories of judgment available to the judge. Or, stated differently, affective arousal tends to increase the width of those categories which are used. A third guiding assumption is related to the second; not only is it assumed that affective arousal limits discrimination *within* a dimension, but it is also assumed that arousal decreases the ability of the judge to differentiate *among* dimensions.

It is evident that in order to transform these general assumptions into hypotheses concerning the effects of affective arousal upon dicrimination, it is necessary to specify both the nature of various types of affective arousal and the nature of other variables in the judgment task with which affective arousal might interact to influence discriminability. These task variables include: (1) the type of disposition aroused, (2) the level of arousal, (3) the nature of the stimuli to be judged, (4) the role of response factors, and (5) the personality of the judge, particularly as it relates to individual differences in the strength of affective arousal. We shall consider each of these variables briefly and then, as a specific example, discuss how future studies of anchoring might incorporate these affective variables in relation to stimulus discriminability.

Type of Disposition Aroused

Some theorists consider affective arousal as a general state of affairs which will influence behavior irrespective of the particular disposition system involved. For example, the tendency to view certain types (if not all) of human motivation as manifestations of affective arousal results in a generalizing notion concerning the influence of arousal (McClelland et al., 1953; Duffy, 1957). Even here, however, one can distinguish between negative affect associated with aversive drives (such as anxiety) and positive affect which is associated with appetitive drives such as sex. Such a distinction leads to the question whether increased arousal of negative affect has the same effect upon discrimination as the increased arousal of positive affect. In the realm of social judgment, some evidence on this point does exist. For example, Miller and Bieri (1965) have found that judges discriminate significantly better among persons who are both more negative in connotation and more socially distant than among figures who are regarded more positively by the judge. Berkowitz and Goranson (1964) report less contrast effect in judging liked persons than in judging less-liked persons. In the *attitude* realm we see perhaps most clearly the interrelation between affective processes and cognitive discrimination. That is, as we discriminate different substantive positions associated with an issue, the affective regard of the person towards these positions changes from positive to negative. Although it is customary to consider the effects of positive or of negative affect to be similar regardless of the disposition with which the affect is associated, little is known concerning this generality across such dispositions as needs, motives, attitudes, and beliefs.

Level of Arousal

In addition to the type of disposition aroused, and its association with positive or negative affect, the effects upon discrimination of the *level* of arousal must be considered. It is possible to isolate two somewhat different problems concerning the relation between level of arousal and discrimination. The first of these concerns whether deviation in level of affect away from some adaptation level of arousal is associated with positive affect, so that too much stimulation, whether positive or negative, is associated with negative affect (Berlyne, 1960; McClleland et al., 1953). This view is perhaps congenial to the notion that what is important in discrimination is amount of change in affect rather than its positive or negative tone. A second problem concerns the effects upon discrimination accuracy as increases beyond some basal level of arousal are experienced. Here the question as to the linear or curvilinear relation between level of arousal and discrimination is raised (Easterbrook, 1959). Extremely low levels of affective arousal, as in monotonous tasks or sensory deprivation situations, may be associated with poor discrimination as might extremely high levels of affective arousal, as in traumative experiences or crises of various sorts. In this sense, level of affective arousal and discrimination effectiveness may assume a curvilinear relation consistent with such traditional formulations as that of Yerkes and Dodson. That is, for more difficult discrimination tasks, a lower level of motivational arousal may lead to better performance whereas for high levels of arousal better performance is found with simple discriminations (e.g., Broadhurst, 1957). Such interaction effects between drive level and performance as a function of stimulus complexity have been observed in discrimination tasks with animals, and in studies of animal learning (Bruner, Matter, and Papanek, 1955) and human learning (Spence, Taylor, and Ketchel, 1956). However, systematic variation of arousal level and difficulty of the discrimination task has not been reported frequently in the research literature.

In the study most relevant to the problem of discriminability and affective arousal, Eriksen and Wechsler (1955) varied level of affective arousal (using electric shock) within a task which involved discriminations of sizes of squares. Using informational analysis, they observed that affective arousal did not lower discriminability appreciably, as measured by $T_{x;y}$, but did reduce response variability, as measured by H_y. Such effects on response variability we shall consider below.

Nature of the Stimulus

The influence of affective arousal upon discriminability of stimuli involves the consideration of three important characteristics of the stimulus material. These are (1) the relevance of the stimulus domain being judged to the conditions of affective arousal, (2) the range of variation in the stimuli to be judged, and (3) the relative dimensionality of the stimulus.

Considering *relevance* first, it is frequently assumed that the effect of increased arousal upon perceptual judgments involves only those stimuli which are substantively relevant to the disposition being aroused. Such relevance may be assumed in terms of differences among judges in previous experiential histories, as in the Bruner and Goodman (1947) study of size estimation of coins by poor and well-to-do children. Or, relevance may be manipulated directly in the experimental situation, as in the study of Ashley, Harper, and Runyon (1951). While both these approaches appeared to favor the hypothesis that need increases the accentuation of size, other studies have questioned such a generalization. Gilchrist and Nesberg (1952) studied illuminance judgments under conditions of hunger drive and observed that aroused needs may have accentuation effects irrespective of the specific relevance of the stimulus content to the need. As Postman (1953) and Allport (1955) have pointed out, such accentuation effects may be observed with stimuli which are associated with both positive *and* negative reinforcement, suggesting that these affective states (whether needs or reinforcement value) serve to "emphasize" stimuli with which they are associated. In this regard, Dukes and Bevan (1952) used the method of constant stimuli to study children's weight estimations of personally relevant stimuli (candy) and irrelevant stimuli. Their results suggested that while relevance was related to enhanced sensitivity, the range of responsiveness was reduced. In a study of subthreshold perception which varied strength of need (affiliation), degree of arousal, and stimulus relevance, Atkinson and Walker (1956) observed that need strength did relate to recognition accuracy although no interaction with arousal was found. At a more general level, research with schizophrenics has explored the hypothesis that social stimuli should be less well discriminated than nonsocial stimuli because of the former's greater relevance to the anxiety or social learning experiences of the schizophrenic. Evidence which is both consistent and inconsistent with this supposition has been reported in research by Rodnick and Garmezy (1957), Whiteman (1954), and Kates and Kates (1964).

Considering all the various types of studies of the importance of stimulus relevance to discrimination processes, this variable would appear to have significance in subsequent research on dimensional judgments. As we shall note below, it would appear that a more precise evaluation of the influence of stimulus relevance can be obtained by experimental manipulation of level of arousal in subjects selected on the basis of *individual differences* in strength of the affective disposition being studied.

Range of variation of the stimuli to be judged is a second stimulus variable which appears to be crucial because of its relation to the difficulty of stimulus discriminability. If we wish to analyze the interaction between level of affective arousal and difficulty of discrimination, we must consider the manipulation of the range of stimuli to be judged. If, as we assumed earlier, the width of subjective categories of judgment does increase as a function of arousal, this effect should be most noticeable when the stimuli are least discriminable, i.e., under decreased range. In the judgment of physical stimuli, it has generally been found that an increase in the range of stimuli to be judged is associated with a *slight* increase in discrimination (Garner, 1962). For example, Eriksen and Hake (1955a) report such effects in relation to size estimation. However, variation in range can further increase difficulty of discrimination if the narrowing of the interstimulus interval is severe enough (Garner, 1962) and if the more limited range does not include salient (end) stimuli found in the broader range. If the number of stimuli is constant and the intervals between stimuli are equal within a range, a decrease in the range of stimuli will result in smaller interstimulus intervals, making discrimination more difficult. In addition, if we use a continuum with salient end stimuli, the loss of these end stimuli under conditions of reduced range will further decrease discriminability of the stimuli. Thus, Johnson and King (1964) found striking decrements in discrimination accuracy in ranges of stimuli which excluded strong end stimuli (dots varying from all blue to all green). As we observed in Chapter 4, Miller and Bieri (1963) found that the end stimuli were discriminated most reliably by clinicians in their judgments, suggesting evidence of the strong natural end anchor effects created by these extreme stimuli. In a subsequent study, Miller and Bieri (1964) observed that when stimulus ranges did not include these salient end stimuli, discriminability was reduced. Similar results were found by Hunt, Schwartz, and Walker (1965) in experienced clinicians' judgments of degree of confusion in responses to test items by schizophrenics.

It is possible that the range effects upon discriminability of social and clinical stimuli will prove to be at least as crucial, if not more so, as with physical stimuli because of the apparent greater saliency of natural end stimuli in social dimensions. Although physical continua such as size, loudness, and weight are not characterized by "natural" endpoints, most social and clinical dimensions are. Certain atrocious acts seem to define the limit of human aggression, for example, whereas in the clinical realm a severely regressed schizophrenic is close to an extreme of pathology. In this regard, Miller and Bieri (1965b) observed with social dimensions the same striking end anchor effects upon discrimination as did Johnson and King (1964), whose physical continua, as we noted above, were constructed to have natural end stimuli.

A final stimulus consideration is the *dimensionality* of the stimuli to be judged. Although differences in stimulus range permit an analysis of the influence of affective arousal upon discrimination as a function of variation *within* a stimulus dimension, variation in the relative dimensionality of sets of stimuli should also produce differences in discrimination. A number of studies, which we reviewed in Chapter 4, indicate that discrimination of stimuli increases as the number of dimensions they contain also increases. Thus Eriksen and Hake (1955b) found increasing discrimination as three sensory dimensions were combined in a correlated manner. We have noted in earlier chapters that there is some evidence for increasing discrimination with increasing dimensionality of behavioral stimuli (Miller and Bieri, 1963, 1964; Tripodi and Bieri, 1964). However, little empirical work has been reported concerning the relation of affective arousal upon the ability to discriminate stimuli of increasing dimensionality.

In this regard, it may be possible to combine two stimulus dimensions so that under certain conditions of combination high arousal would lead to better discriminability whereas under a different mode of combination high arousal would lead to poorer discriminability. For example, if we consider physical stimuli, we could combine two dimensions (e.g., size and hue) in a correlated manner, so that each size and hue combination would be a unique pairing. A second mode of combining these two dimensions would be random, in the sense that the same hue would occur with more than one size. Here, hue would be a "noisy," irrelevant attribute. If we assume that high affective arousal leads to decreased cue utilization, then high arousal judges would attend better to only the relevant dimension in this latter random mode of combination, leading to better discriminability, whereas in the correlated combination condition this higher arousal should lead to poorer discriminability. Thus it is possible that under varying forms of stimulus multidimensionality, the effects of increased arousal upon discriminability will differ.

Response Factors

The importance of response factors in studying affective arousal and discriminability can be approached in several ways. First, the effect of affective arousal on systematic biasing of response tendencies in a judgment task can be assessed. For example, Eriksen and Wechsler (1955), using informational analysis, found that the frequency of dominant responses was exaggerated under conditions of increased arousal, a phenomenon certainly consistent with assumptions in learning theory concerning the multiplicative relation of drive and habit strength. Such response biasing has also been found in a number of studies of response variability in sequential responding. Kuethe and Eriksen (1957) and Brody (1964) both found significant interactions between induced muscular tension and response variability, including sequential redundancy, in a serial guessing ("ESP") task. To the extent that the nature of the stimuli or of the response scale fosters excessive use of certain categories of responding, the possibility exists that affective arousal will tend to increase such response disparities.

Another approach to the understanding of response factors in judgment is to systematically vary conditions of response bias in relation to varying conditions of stimulus range. Such a strategy permits an analysis of the interaction between stimulus characteristics and response factors as they impinge upon discrimination. For example, one could determine whether experimentally produced biasing in responding to stimuli under two different stimulus ranges will produce differences in subsequent discrimination. Such response biasing in judgments could be produced by providing feedback to the judge, after each judgment, concerning the "accuracy" of his judgment. (A similar strategy emphasizing the influence of feedback upon perception is currently being developed in relation to signal detection theory, as in the work of Atkinson, Carterette, and Kinchla, 1964.) In actuality the feedback provided would correspond to one of two predetermined schedules which are designed to produce more frequent responding either in the *middle* of the scale or at one *end* of the scale. In this sense, judges are being trained to respond differentially to portions of the scale, i.e., to use more frequently the middle categories or to use more frequently categories at one end of the scale. It is assumed that a major factor mediating response bias differences in these two range conditions is the relative saliency of the *end* stimuli, such that under one range condition strong salient end stimuli would be present and under a shortened range condition they would not be present. An example of such a stimulus continuum would be clusters of dots varying from all blue dots at one end of the dimension to all green dots at the other, with varying proportions in between (Johnson and King, 1964). Although a number of variables could be studied in such an experiment, the basic point would be that the effects of response biasing upon subsequent discriminations would be less under full range conditions, in which the presence of more salient end stimuli would aid more accurate discrimination, than under the condition of shortened stimulus range. Such feedback effects might be expected to be greatest for the middle-range biasing condition under the truncated stimulus range, in which large central tendency effects could be expected. It would seem fruitful to pursue such a problem in future research so as to understand more fully the possible interactions between response and stimulus properties in discrimination behavior.

Personality of the Judge

It is apparent that studies of the influence of affective arousal upon discriminability of stimuli must take into account individual differences among judges in arousal. Although the importance of assessing the interaction between arousal and dispositional level has been amply documented in a number of studies in related areas, few if any such studies are directly concerned with discrimination of dimensional stimuli. For example, a number of studies report significant interactions between level of induced anxiety or tension and anxiety scores of subjects in relation to response variabiity. In a study of perceptual efficiency involving a target resolution task, Shore (1958) obtained significant interactions between scores on the Taylor Manifest Anxiety Scale and induced muscular tension. Berkowitz (1960) noted that incentive conditions interacted with authoritarianism in producing differences in an anchoring task. Other investigators have studied the effects of dispositional level without considering level of affective arousal. In this latter category, Brod, Kernoff, and Terwilliger (1964) found significant positive correlations between Manifest Anxiety Scale scores and response variability (H_y) on the semantic differential. In a similar vein, Zax, Gardiner, and Lowy (1964) reported that maladjusted subjects used the extreme categories of a numerical response scale whereas normal subjects preferred intermediate categories. Although such studies are suggestive of individual differences in response bias, they are not definitive in relation to the problem of how such tendencies impinge upon stimulus discriminability.

Finally, we may note that in social judgments, we have considered (Chapter 6) how one's own position on an attitude dimension might influence anchoring tendencies. In the judgments of behavioral dimensions such as aggression, little is empirically known about the influence of own dispositional level on discriminability, although recently we have observed a low but significant correlation between aggression scores on the Buss-Durkee scale of aggression and discriminability ($T_{x;y}$) of aggressive stimuli ($r = .23, p < .05$).

OWN-ATTITUDE INVOLVEMENT, DISCRIMINABILITY, AND ANCHORING

As a final projection of future research which would tie together several of the main themes we have been considering throughout this book, let us consider how affective arousal, in the context of engagement of one's own attitude on an issue, might influence anchoring and discriminability. The linkage between discrimination of stimuli and anchoring phenomena was discussed in Chapter 6 in relation to both clinical and social judgments. For example, the research of Atkins (1964) indicated that *extremity* of own position appears to produce greater assimilation of ambiguous stimuli to one's own attitude than does a more neutral position. The way in which a more extreme position on an attitude dimension affects discrimination may be assumed to be analogous to the disposition effects discussed above in relation to anxiety, for example. If a more extreme position on an attitude scale indicates a more involved attitude toward the issue at hand, it is possible to assume that this greater degree of own-position involvement may represent a heightened affective reaction to the stimuli being judged. Experimentally, such an assumption could be bolstered by actually manipulating involvement in the issue, as through role playing or engaging in social behavior in which the issue is discussed or defended.

If we argue from our assumptions concerning the general influence of affective arousal upon judgment, we would assume that heightened arousal of an attitude reduces discrimination within that attitude dimension. However, specifically in relation to social attitudes, we may ask whether this reduced discriminability is general across the entire scale of judgment or is manifested only in a portion of the scale. Such a question appears significant in relation to social attitudes for several reasons. We have noted earlier (Chapter 5) that attitude dimensions have a *bipolar* quality ranging from strongly positive through a point of neutrality to strongly negative. In contrast, behavioral dimensions such as aggression or dependency do not have this strong bipolar characteristic but range from a low intensity to a high intensity. Thus, although affective arousal may influence discriminability most in that portion of a dimension nearest one's own position, whether it be a need disposition such as aggression or an attitude, attitude continua appear to offer the clearest opportunity to analyze such within-dimension effects of arousal upon discriminability.

Indirect evidence for the specific effects within a portion of a dimension can be inferred from a few studies which suggest involvement may affect discrimination only in certain portions of the scale (Sherif and

Hovland, 1961). However, there is some question as to whether this reduced discrimination is in that portion of the scale near one's own position or is in that part of the scale distant from own position (Zavalloni and Cook, 1965). Consistent with the assumptions concerning affective arousal and the widening of categories of judgment, we would expect poorer discrimination in that portion of the scale closest to one's own position. Such a gradient would be reflected in reduced discriminability among those categories of judgment adjacent to one's position, particularly for extreme own position judges. With these considerations in mind, we can approach the question of the stimulus discriminability and anchoring, which we discussed in Chapter 6, from this more complex vantage point. That is, if we can demonstrate in one study that discrimination *within* an attitude dimension varies (1) as a function of whether one's own position is within the range being judged, and (2) as a function of one's degree of arousal or involvement concerning the issue, *and,* in a second study demonstrate that these two factors are predictive of differential anchoring tendencies, then strong presumptive evidence would exist for the relation between discriminability and anchoring phenomena.

REFERENCES

Allport, F. H. *Theories of perception and the concept of structure.* New York: Wiley, 1955.

Allport, G. W. *Pattern and growth in personality.* New York: Holt, Rinehart, & Winston, 1961.

Alluisi, E. A., & Muller, P. F., Jr. Verbal and motor responses to seven symbolic codes: A study in S-R compatibility. *J. exp. Psychol.,* 1958, **55,** 247–254.

Alluisi, E. A., & Sidorsky, R. C. The empirical validity of equal discriminability scaling. *J. exp. Psychol.,* 1958, **55,** 86–95.

American Psychiatric Association, Committee on Nomenclature and Statistics. Diagnostic and statistical manual: Mental disorders. Washington, D.C., 1952.

Archer, E. J., Bourne, L. E., Jr., & Brown, F. G. Concept identification as a function of irrelevant information and instructions. *J. exp. Psychol.,* 1955, **49,** 153–164.

Asch, S. E. Studies in the principles of judgments and attitudes: II. Determination of judgments by group and by ego standards. *J. soc. Psychol.,* 1940, **12,** 433–465.

Asch, S. E. *Social psychology.* New York: Prentice Hall, 1952.

Asch, S. E., Block, H., & Hertzman, M. Studies in the principles of judgments and attitudes: I. Two basic principles of judgment. *J. Psychol.,* 1938, **5,** 219–251.

Ashley, W. R., Harper, R. C., & Runyon, D. L. The perceived size of coins in normal and hypnotically induced economic states. *Amer. J. Psychol.,* 1951, **64,** 564–572.

Atkins, A. L. Own attitude and discriminability in relation to anchoring effects in judgments of social stimuli. Unpublished doctoral dissertation, Columbia University, 1964.

Atkins, A. L., Kujala, K., & Bieri, J. Latitude of acceptance and attitude change: empirical evidence for a reformulation. *Amer. Psychologist,* 1965, **20,** 540. (Abstract)

Atkins, A. L., Meyers, B. A., & Kujala, K. Anchoring tendencies as cognitive styles. Paper presented at meetings of the Eastern Psychological Association, Atlantic City, April 22–24, 1965.

Atkinson, J. W., & Walker, E. L. The affiliation motive and perceptual sensitivity to faces. *J. abnorm. soc. Psychol.,* 1956, **53,** 38–41.

Atkinson, R. C. A variable sensitivity theory of signal detection. *Psychol. Rev.,* 1963, **70,** 91–106.

Atkinson, R. C., Carterette E. C., & Kinchla, R. A. The effect of information feedback upon psychological judgments. *Psychon. Sci.,* 1964, **1,** 83–84.

Attneave, F. *Applications of information theory to psychology.* New York: Holt, 1959.

Attneave, F. Perception and related areas. In S. Koch (Ed.), *Psychology: A study of a science.* Study II, Vol. 4. New York: McGraw-Hill, 1962, pp. 619–659.

Barron, F. Complexity-simplicity as a personality dimension. *J. abnorm. soc. Psychol.,* 1953, **48,** 163–172.

Bartlett, F. C. *Remembering.* Cambridge: Cambridge University Press, 1932.

Becker, G. M. Sequential decision making: Wald's model and estimates of parameters. *J. exp. Psychol.,* 1958, **55,** 628–636.

Beebe-Center, J. G., Rogers, M. S., & O'Connell, D. M. Transmission of information about sucrose and saline solutions through the sense of taste. *J. Psychol.,* 1955, **39,** 157–160.

Bendig, A. W. Transmitted information and the length of rating scales. *J. exp. Psychol.,* 1954, **47,** 303–308.

Bendig, A. W., & Hughes, J. B., II. Effect of amount of verbal anchoring and number of rating-scale categories upon transmitted information. *J. exp. Psychol.,* 1953, **46,** 87–90.

Berfield, S., *et al.* Social and clinical judgments about delinquent youth: six studies. Unpublished master's thesis, University of California, Berkeley, 1963.

Berkowitz, L. The judgmental process in personality functioning. *Psychol. Rev.,* 1960, **67,** 130–142.

Berkowitz, L., & Goranson, R. E. Motivational and judgmental determinants of social perception. *J. abnorm. soc. Psychol.,* 1964, **69,** 296–302.

Berlyne, D. E. *Conflict, arousal, and curiosity,* New York: McGraw-Hill, 1960.

Berlyne, D. E. Uncertainty and conflict: A point of contact between information-theory and behavior-theory concepts. *Psychol. Rev.,* 1957, **64,** 329–339.

Bieri, J. Changes in interpersonal perceptions following social interaction. *J. abnorm. soc. Psychol.,* 1953, **48,** 61–66.

Bieri, J. Cognitive complexity-simplicity and predictive behavior. *J. abnorm. soc. Psychol.,* 1955, **51,** 263–268.

Bieri, J. Complexity-simplicity as a personality variable in cognitive and preferential behavior. In D. W. Fiske & S. R. Maddi (Eds.), *Functions of varied experience.* Homewood, Ill.: Dorsey, 1961.

Bieri, J. Analyzing stimulus information in social judgments. In S. Messick & J. Ross (Eds.), *Measurement in personality and cognition.* New York: Wiley, 1962.

Bieri, J. Cognitive complexity and personality development. Unpublished manuscript, 1964.

Bieri, J., & Atkins, A. L. Discriminability of stimuli and anchoring effects in social and physical stimulus domains. Unpublished manuscript, 1965.

Bieri, J., Atkins, A. L., Kujala, K., & Meyers, B. A. Effects of single and grouped stimulus presentation on anchoring in judgments of physical and social stimuli. Research report MH-08334-02, 1965.

Bieri, J., Bradburn, W. M., & Galinsky, M. D. Sex differences in perceptual behavior. *J. Pers.,* 1958, **26,** 1–12.

Bieri, J., Orcutt, B. A., & Leaman, R. Anchoring effects in sequential clinical judgments. *J. abnorm. soc. Psychol.,* 1963, **67,** 616–623.

Block, W. E. A conceptual framework for the clinical test situation. *Psychol. Bull.,* 1964, **61,** 168–175.

Bourne, L. E., Jr., & Haygood, R. C. The role of stimulus redundancy in concept identification. *J. exp. Psychol.,* 1959, **58,** 232–238.

Briar, S. Clinical judgment in foster care placement. *Child Welfare,* 1963, **42,** 161–169.

Broadhurst, P. L. Emotionality and the Yerkes-Dodson law. *J. exp. Psychol.,* 1957, **54,** 345–352.

Brod, D., Kernoff, P., & Terwilliger, R. F. Anxiety and semantic differential responses. *J. abnorm. soc. Psychol.,* 1964, **68,** 570–574.

Brody, N. Anxiety, induced muscular tension, and the statistical structure of binary response sequences. *J. abnorm. soc. Psychol.,* 1964, **68,** 540–543.

Brown, D. R. Stimulus similarity and the anchoring of subjective scales. *Amer. J. Psychol.,* 1953, **66,** 199–214.

Bruner, J. S. On perceptual readiness. *Psychol. Rev.,* 1957, **64,** 123–152.

Bruner, J. S., & Goodman, C. D. Value and need as organizing factors in perception. *J. abnorm. soc. Psychol.,* 1947, **42,** 33–44.

Bruner, J. S., Goodnow, J. J., & Austin, G. A. *A study of thinking.* New York: Wiley, 1956.

Bruner, J. S., Matter, J., & Papanek, M. L. Breadth of learning as a function of drive level and mechanization. *Psychol. Rev.,* 1955, **62,** 1–10.

Bruner, J. S., & Minturn, L. Perceptual identification and perceptual organization. *J. gen. Psychol.,* 1955, **53,** 21–28.

Bruner, J. S., Shapiro, D., & Tagiuri, R. The meaning of traits in isolation and in combination. In R. Tagiuri and L. Petrullo (Eds.), *Person perception and interpersonal behavior.* Stanford: Stanford University Press, 1958.

Campbell, D. T., Hunt, W. A., & Lewis, N. A. The effects of assimilation and contrast in judgments of clinical materials. *Amer. J. Psychol.,* 1957, **70,** 347–360.

Campbell, D. T., Lewis, N. A., & Hunt, W. A. Context effects with judgmental language that is absolute, extensive, and extra-experimentally anchored. *J. exp. Psychol.,* 1958, **55,** 220–228.

Chapanis, A., & Halsey, R. M. Absolute judgments of spectrum colors. *J. Psychol.,* 1956, **42,** 99–103.

Chapman, D. W., & Volkmann, J. A social determinant of the level of aspiration. *J. abnorm. soc. Psychol.,* 1939, **34,** 225–238.

Chernoff, H., & Moses, L. E. *Elementary decision theory.* New York: Wiley, 1959.

Chesnut, G., *et al.* Selected factors in judgments about foster care placement. Unpublished master's thesis, University of California, Berkeley, 1961.

Conover, D. W. The amount of information in the absolute judgment of Munsell hues. *USAF WADC Tech. Note,* 1959, No. 58–262.

Couch, A., & Keniston, K. Yeasayers and naysayers: agreeing response set as a personality variable. *J. abnorm. soc. Psychol.,* 1960, **60,** 151–174.

Cowan, T. A. Decision theory in law, science, and technology. *Science,* 1963, **140,** 1065–1075.

Crandall, V., Solomon, D., & Kelleway, R. Expectancy statements and decision times as a function of objective probabilities and reinforcement values. *J. Pers.,* 1956, **24,** 192–203.

Cronbach, L. J. On the nonrational application of information measures in psychology. In H. Quastler (Ed.), *Information theory in psychology.* Glencoe, Ill.: Free Press, 1955.

Cronbach, L. J. Proposals leading to analytic treatment of social perception scores. In R. Tagiuri & L. Petrullo (Eds.), *Person perception and interpersonal behavior*. Stanford: Stanford University Press, 1958, pp. 353–379.

Crowne, D. P., & Marlowe, D. *The approval motive*. New York: Wiley, 1964.

Cutler, R. L. Countertransference effects in psychotherapy. *J. consult. Psychol.,* 1958, **22,** 349–356.

Deutsch, M. Field theory in social psychology. In G. Lindzey (Ed.), *Handbook of social psychology*. Vol. I. Cambridge, Mass.: Addison-Wesley, 1954.

Duffy, E. The psychological significance of the concept of "arousal" or "activation." *Psychol. Rev.,* 1957, **64,** 265–275.

Dukes, W. F., & Bevan, W. Accentuation and response variability in the perception of personally relevant objects. *J. Pers.,* 1952, **20,** 457–465.

Duncker, K. On problem solving. *Psychol. Monogr.,* 1954, **58,** 1–112.

Easterbrook, J. A. The effect of emotion on cue utilization and the organization of behavior. *Psychol. Rev.,* 1959, **66,** 183–201.

Edwards, W. Behavioral decision theory. *Ann. Rev. Psychol.,* 1961, **12,** 473–498.

Engen, T., & Pfaffmann, C. Absolute judgments of odor intensity. *J. exp. Psychol.,* 1959, **58,** 23–26.

Engen, T., & Pfaffmann, C. Absolute judgments of odor quality. *J. exp. Psychol.,* 1960, **59,** 214–219.

Eriksen, C. W., & Hake, H. W. Absolute judgments as a function of stimulus range and number of stimulus and response categories. *J. exp. Psychol.,* 1955a, **49,** 323–332.

Eriksen, C. W., & Hake, H. W. Multidimensional stimulus differences and accuracy of discrimination. *J. exp. Psychol.,* 1955b, **50,** 153–160.

Eriksen, C. W., & Hake, H. W. Anchor effects in absolute judgments. *J. exp. Psychol.,* 1957, **53,** 132–138.

Eriksen, C. W., & Wechsler, H. Some effects of experimentally induced anxiety upon discrimination behavior. *J. abnorm. soc. Psychol.,* 1955, **51,** 458–463.

Erikson, E. H. The nature of clinical evidence. In D. Lerner, (Ed.), *Evidence and inference*. Glencoe, Ill.: Free Press, 1959, pp. 73–95.

Estes, W. K. Of models and men. *Amer. Psychologist,* 1957, **12,** 609–617.

Feather, N. T. Success probability and choice behavior. *J. exp. Psychol.,* 1959, **58,** 257–266.

Fenichel, O. *The psychoanalytic theory of neurosis*. New York: Norton, 1945.

Festinger, L. A theory of social comparison processes. *Human Relations,* 1954, **7,** 117–140.

Fillenbaum, S. The effect of a remote anchor upon judgment with a salient within-series stimulus-object and with a free choice of scale. *Amer. J. Psychol.,* 1961, **74,** 602–606.

Fillenbaum, S. Contextual effects in judgment as a function of restrictions in response language. *Amer. J. Psychol.,* 1963, **76,** 103–109.

Fishbein, M., & Hunter, R. Summation versus balance in attitude organization and change. *J. abnorm. soc. Psychol.,* 1964, **69,** 505–510.

Foa, U. G. Convergences in the analysis of the structure of interpersonal behavior. *Psychol. Rev.,* 1961, **68,** 341–353.

Friedman, M., and Savage, L. J. The utility analysis of choices involving risk. *J. Political Economy,* 1948, **56,** 279–304.

Galanter, E. Contemporary psychophysics. In R. Brown, E. Galanter, E. H. Hess,

& G. Mandler, *New directions in psychology*. New York: Holt, Rinehart, & Winston, 1962, pp. 87–156.

Garner, W. R. An informational analysis of absolute judgments of loudness. *J. exp. Psychol.,* 1953, **46,** 373–380.

Garner, W. R. Rating scales, discriminability, and information transmission. *Psychol. Rev.,* 1960, **67,** 343–352.

Garner, W. R. *Uncertainty and structure as psychological concepts*. New York: Wiley, 1962.

Garner, W. R., & Hake, H. W. The amount of information in absolute judgments. *Psychol. Rev.,* 1951, **58,** 446–459.

Gibson, E. J., Perceptual learning. *Ann. Rev. Psychol.,* 1963, **14,** 29–56.

Gibson, J. J., & Gibson, E. J. Perceptual learning: differentiation or enrichment? *Psychol. Rev.,* 1955, **62,** 32–41.

Gilchrist, J. C., & Nesberg, L. S. Need and perceptual change in need-related objects. *J. exp. Psychol.,* 1952, **44,** 369–376.

Gough, H. G. Clinical versus statistical prediction in psychology. In L. Postman (Ed.), *Psychology in the making*. New York: Knopf, 1963.

Hake, H. W., & Garner, W. R. The effect of presenting various numbers of discrete steps on scale reading accuracy. *J. exp. Psychol.,* 1951, **42,** 358–366.

Hammond, K. R., Hursch, C. J., & Todd, F. J. Analyzing the components of clinical inference. *Psychol. Rev.,* 1964, **71,** 438–456.

Hartley, R. V. L. Transmission of information. *Bell Syst. tech. J.,* 1928, **7,** 535–563.

Hartman, E. B. The influence of practice and pitch-distance between tones on the absolute identification of pitch. *Amer. J. Psychol.,* 1954, **67,** 1–14.

Harvey, O. J., Hunt, D. E., & Schroder, H. M. *Conceptual systems and personality organization*. New York: Wiley, 1961.

Harvey, O. J., Kelley, H. H., & Shapiro, M. M. Reactions to unfavorable evaluations of the self made by other persons. *J. Pers.,* 1957, **25,** 393–411.

Heller, K., Myers, R. A., & Kline, L. V. Interviewer behavior as a function of standardized client roles. *Amer. Psychologist,* 1962, **17,** 334. (Abstract)

Helson, H. Adaptation-level as frame of reference for prediction of psychophysical data. *Amer. J. Psychol.,* 1947, **60,** 1–29.

Helson, H. Adaptation-level theory. In S. Koch (Ed.), *Psychology: a study of a science,* Vol. 1. New York: McGraw-Hill, 1959, pp. 565–621.

Helson, H. *Adaptation-level theory*. New York: Harper, 1964.

Helson, H. Current trends and issues in adaptation-level theory. *Amer. Psychologist,* 1964, **19,** 26–38.

Herron, W. G. The process-reactive classification of schizophrenia. *Psychol. Bull.,* 1962, **59,** 329–343.

Higgins, J. C. Cognitive complexity and probability preferences. *Student Res. Psychol. U. Chicago,* 1961, **2**(2), 1–28.

Hinckley, E. D. The influence of individual opinion on construction of an attitude scale. *J. soc. Psychol.,* 1932, **3,** 283–296.

Hinckley, E. D. A follow-up on the influence of individual opinion on the construction of an attitude scale. *J. abnorm. soc. Psychol.,* 1963, **67,** 290–292.

Holzman, P. The relation of assimilation tendencies in visual, auditory, and kinesthetic time-error to cognitive attitudes of leveling and sharpening. *J. Pers.,* 1953, **22,** 375–394.

Holzman, P., & Klein, G. Cognitive system-principles of leveling and sharpening: Individual differences in assimilation effects in visual time-error. *J. Psychol.*, 1954, **37,** 105–122.

Hornsby, J. R. Social concept attainment and cognitive complexity. Progress Report, Public Health Grant MH-08334-02, 1964.

Hovland, C. I., Harvey, O. J., & Sherif, M. Assimilation and contrast effects in reactions to communication and attitude change. *J. abnorm. soc. Psychol.*, 1957, **55,** 244–252.

Hovland, C. I., & Sherif, M. Judgmental phenomena and scales of attitude measurement: Item displacement in Thurstone scales. *J. abnorm. soc. Psychol.*, 1952, **47,** 822–832.

Hovland, C. I., & Weiss, W. I. Transmission of information concerning concepts through positive and negative instances. *J. exp. Psychol.*, 1953, **45,** 175–182.

Hunt, E. B. *Concept learning: An information processing problem.* New York: Wiley, 1962.

Hunt, W. A. Anchoring effects in judgment. *Amer. J. Psychol.*, 1941, **54,** 395–403.

Hunt, W. A., & Jones, N. F. The experimental investigation of clinical judgment. In A. J. Bachrach (Ed.), *Experimental foundations of clinical psychology.* New York: Basic Books, 1962, pp. 26–51.

Hunt, W. A., Schwartz, M. L., & Walker, R. E. Reliability of clinical judgments as a function of range of pathology. *J. abnorm. Psychol.*, 1965, **70,** 32–33.

Hunt, W. A., & Volkmann, J. The anchoring of an affective scale. *Amer. J. Psychol.*, 1937, **49,** 88–92.

Hyman, H. H. The psychology of status. *Arch. Psychol.*, 1942, **38** (Whole No. 269).

Irwin, F. W. Stated expectations as functions of probability and desirability of outcomes. *J. Pers.*, 1953, **21,** 329–335.

Jaspars, J. M. F. Individual cognitive structures. *Proceedings of the seventeenth international congress of psychology.* Amsterdam: North-Holland, 1964.

Jessor, R., & Readio, J. The influence of the value of an event upon the expectancy of its occurrence. *J. gen. Psychol.*, 1957, **56,** 219–228.

Johnson, D. M. *The psychology of thought and judgment.* New York: Harper, 1955.

Johnson, D. M., & King, C. R. Systematic study of end anchoring and central tendency of judgment. *J. exp. Psychol.*, 1964, **67,** 501–506.

Jones, E. E., & deCharms, R. Changes in social perception as a function of the personal relevance of behavior. *Sociometry,* 1957, **50,** 75–85.

Jones, E. E., & deCharms, R. The organizing function of interaction roles in person perception. *J. abnorm. soc. Psychol.*, 1958, **57,** 155–164.

Jones, E. E., Gergen, K. J., & Davis, K. E. Some determinants of reactions to being approved or disapproved as a person. *Psychol. Monogr.* 1962, **76,** No. 2.

Jones, E. E., Hester, S. L., Farina, A., & Davis, K. Reactions to unfavorable evaluations as a function of the evaluator's perceived adjustment. *J. abnorm. soc. Psychol.*, 1959, **59,** 363–370.

Jones, E. E., Jones, R. G., & Gergen, K. J. Some conditions affecting the evaluation of a conformist. *J. Pers.*, 1963, **31,** 270–288.

Jones, E. E., & Thibaut, J. W. Interaction goals as bases of inference in interpersonal perception. In R. Tagiuri & L. Petrullo (Eds.), *Person perception and interpersonal behavior*. Stanford: Stanford University Press, 1958, pp. 151–178.

Kates, W. W., & Kates, S. L. Conceptual behavior in psychotic and normal adolescents. *J. abnorm. soc. Psychol.*, 1964, **69**, 659–663.

Kelly, G. A. *The psychology of personal constructs*. Vol. I. New York: Norton, 1955.

Kelly, G. A. A further explanation of factor analysis. Unpublished manuscript, The Ohio State University, 1962.

Khinchin, A. I. *Mathematical foundations of information theory*. New York: Dover Publications, 1957.

Kieferle, D. A., & Sechrest, L. Effects in alterations in personal constructs. *J. psychol. Studies*, 1961, **12**, 173–178.

Klemmer, E. T., & Frick, F. C. Assimilation of information from dot and matrix patterns. *J. exp. Psychol.*, 1953, **45**, 15–19.

Kohler, W. *Dynamics in psychology*. New York: Liveright, 1940.

Krantz, D. L., & Campbell, D. T. Separating perceptual and linguistic effects of context shifts upon absolute judgments. *J. exp. Psychol.*, 1961, **62**, 35–42.

Kuethe, J. L., & Eriksen, C. W. Personality, anxiety, and muscle tension as determinants of response stereotypy. *J. abnorm. soc. Psychol.*, 1957, **54**, 400–404.

Leary, T. *Interpersonal diagnosis of personality*. New York: Ronald, 1957.

Leventhal, H. Cognitive processes and interpersonal predictions. *J. abnorm. soc. Psychol.*, 1957, **55**, 176–180.

Leventhal, H., & Singer, D. L. Cognitive complexity, impression formation, and impression change. *J. Pers.*, 1964, **32**, 210–226.

Levy, L. Adaptation, anchoring, and dissipation in social perception. *J. Pers.*, 1961, **29**, 94–104.

Lewin, K. *Field theory in social science*. New York: Harper, 1951.

Lewis, H. B. Studies in the principles of judgments and attitudes: IV. The operation of "prestige suggestion." *J. soc. Psychol.*, 1941, **14**, 229–256.

London, P. *The modes and morals of psychotherapy*. New York: Holt, Rinehart, & Winston, 1964.

Luce, R. D. *Individual choice behavior*. New York: Wiley, 1959.

Luce, R. D. *Developments in mathematical psychology*. Glencoe, Ill.: Free Press, 1961.

Lundy, R. M., & Berkowitz, L. Cognitive complexity and assimilative projection in attitude change. *J. abnorm. soc. Psychol.*, 1957, **55**, 34–37.

McClelland, D. C., Atkinson, J. W., Clark, R. A., & Lowell, E. L. *The achievement motive*. New York: Appleton-Century-Crofts, 1953.

McGarvey, H. R. Anchoring effects in the absolute judgment of verbal materials. *Arch. Psychol.*, 1943, **39** (Whole No. 281).

McGill, W. J. Multivariate information transmission. *Psychometrika*, 1954, **19**, 97–116.

McGill, W. J. Isomorphism in statistical analysis. In H. Quastler (Ed.), *Information theory in psychology*. Glencoe, Ill.: Free Press, 1955.

MacKay, D. M. Quantal aspects of scientific information. *Phil. Mag.*, 1950, **41**, 289–311.

Mahrer, A. R., & Young, H. H. The combination of psychodiagnostic cues. *J. Pers.*, 1961, **29**, 428–448.

Mandler, G. From association to structure. *Psychol. Rev.*, 1962, **69**, 415–427.

Manis, M. The interpretation of opinion statements as a function of message ambiguity and recipient attitude. *J. abnorm. soc. Psychol.*, 1961, **63**, 76–81.

Marks, R. W. The effect of probability, desirability, and privilege on the stated expectations of children. *J. Pers.*, 1951, **19**, 332–351.

Masling, J. M. The influence of situational and interpersonal variables in projective testing. *Psychol. Bull.*, 1960, **57**, 65–85.

Mayo, C. W., & Crockett, W. H. Cognitive complexity and primacy-recency effects in impression formation. *J. abnorm. soc. Psychol.*, 1964, **68**, 335–338.

Mednick, S. A. The associative basis of the creative process. In M. T. Mednick & S. A. Mednick (Eds.), *Research in personality*. New York: Holt, Rinehart, & Winston, 1963.

Mednick, S. A., & Freedman, J. L. Stimulus generalization. *Psychol. Bull.*, 1960, **57**, 169–200.

Meehl, P. E. *Clinical versus statistical prediction*. Minneapolis: University of Minnesota Press, 1954.

Meehl, P. E. Wanted—a good cookbook. *Amer. Psychologist*, 1956, **11**, 263–272.

Meehl, P. E. A comparison of clinicians with five statistical methods of identifying psychotic MMPI profiles. *J. counsel. Psychol.*, 1959, **6**, 102–109.

Menninger, K. With M. Mayman & P. Pruyser. *The vital balance: the life process in mental health and illness*. New York: Viking Press, 1963.

Miller, Caryl-Ann, & Engen, T. Supplementary report: Context effects on absolute judgments of length. *J. exp. Psychol.*, 1960, **59**, 276–277.

Miller, G. A. What is information measurement? *Amer. Psychologist*, 1953, **8**, 3–11.

Miller, G. A. Note on the bias of information estimates. In H. Quastler (Ed.), *Information theory in psychology: problems and methods*. Glencoe, Ill.: Free Press, 1955.

Miller, G. A. The magical number seven, plus or minus two: Some limits on our capacity for processing information. *Psychol. Rev.*, 1956, **63**, 81–97.

Miller, G. A., & Madow, W. G. On the maximum likelihood estimate of the Shannon-Wiener measure of information. Air Force Cambridge Research Center, *Tech. Report*, 1954, 54–75.

Miller, H., & Bieri, J. An informational analysis of clinical judgment. *J. abnorm. soc. Psychol.*, 1963, **67**, 317–325.

Miller, H., & Bieri, J. The judge's capacity to discriminate among behavioral stimuli as a function of range, dimensionality of the stimulus, and complexity of the response. *Amer. Psychologist*, 1964, **19**, 482. (Abstract)

Miller, H., & Bieri, J. Cognitive complexity as a function of the significance of the stimulus objects being judged. *Psychol. Repts.*, 1965a, **16**, 1203–1204.

Miller, H., & Bieri, J. End anchor effects in the discriminability of physical and social stimuli. *Psychon. Sci.*, 1965b, **3**, 339–340.

Morlock, H. C., & Hertz, K. J. Effect of the desirability of outcomes on decision making. *Psychol. Repts.*, 1964, **14**, 11–17.

Muller, P. F., Jr., Sidorsky, R. C., Slivinske, A. U., Alluisi, E. A., & Fitts, P. M. The symbolic coding of information on cathode ray tubes and similar displays. *USAF WADC Tech. Rep.*, 1955, No. 55–375.

Newcomb, T. M. *The acquaintance process*. New York: Holt, Rinehart, & Winston, 1961.

Orcutt, B. A. Anchoring effects in the clinical judgments of social work students and experienced caseworkers. Unpublished doctoral dissertation, Columbia University, 1962.

Orne, M. T. On the social psychology of the psychological experiment: with particular reference to demand characteristics and their implications. *Amer. Psychologist,* 1962, **17,** 776–783.

Osborne, J. W., Quastler, H., & Tweedell, K. S. Flash recognition-scale reading. *Control Systems Lab.,* University of Illinois, No. R-78, October, 1955.

Osgood, C. E. The nature and measurement of meaning. *Psychol. Bull.,* 1952, **49,** 197–237.

Osgood, C. E., Suci, G. J., & Tannenbaum, B. H. *The measurement of meaning.* Urbana, Ill.: University of Illinois Press, 1957.

Oskamp, S. How clinicians make decisions from the MMPI: An empirical study. *Amer. Psychologist,* 1962, **17,** 316. (Abstract)

Parducci, A. Range-frequency compromise in judgment. *Psychol. Monogr.,* 1963, **77** (Whole No. 565).

Parducci, A., & Marshall, L. M. Assimilation vs. contrast in the anchoring of perceptual judgments of weight. *J. exp. Psychol.,* 1962, **63,** 426–437.

Pastore, N. Attributed characteristics of liked and disliked persons. *J. soc. Psychol.,* 1960, **52,** 157–163.

Peak, Helen. Psychological structure and psychological activity. *Psychol. Rev.,* 1958, **65,** 325–347.

Pedersen, F. A. A consistency study of the R.C.R.T. Unpublished master's thesis, Ohio State University, 1958.

Pepinsky, H. B., & Karst, T. O. Convergence: a phenomenon in counseling and psychotherapy. *Amer. Psychologist,* 1964, **19,** 333–337.

Pettigrew, T. F. The measurement and correlates of category width as a cognitive variable. *J. Pers.,* 1958, **26,** 532–544.

Piliavin, I., & Briar, S. Police encounters with juveniles. *Amer. J. Sociol.,* 1964, **70,** 206–214.

Piven, H. Professionalism and organizational structure: training and agency variables in relation to practitioner orientation and practice. Unpublished doctoral dissertation, Columbia University, 1961.

Plotnick, H. L. The relation between selected personality characteristics of social work students and accuracy in predicting the behavior of clients. Unpublished doctoral dissertation, Columbia University, 1961.

Pollack, I. The information of elementary auditory displays. *J. acoust. Soc. Amer.,* 1952, **24,** 745–749.

Pollack, I. The information of elementary auditory displays, II. *J. acoust. Soc. Amer.,* 1953, **25,** 765–769.

Pollack, I., & Ficks, L. Information of elementary multidimensional auditory displays. *J. acoust. Soc. Amer.,* 1954, **26,** 155–158.

Posner, M. I. Information reduction in the analysis of sequential tasks. *Psychol. Rev.,* 1964, **71,** 491–504.

Postman, L. The experimental analysis of motivational factors in perception. In *Current theory and research in motivation.* Lincoln, Nebr.: University of Nebraska Press, 1953.

Postman, L., & Miller, G. A. Anchoring of temporal judgments. *Amer. J. Psychol.,* 1945, **58,** 43–53.

Prothro, E. T. The effect of strong negative attitudes on the placement of items in a Thurstone scale. *J. soc. Psychol.,* 1955, **41,** 11–17.

Prothro, E. T. Personal involvement and item displacement of Thurstone scales. *J. soc. Psycho.*, 1957, **45,** 191–196.

Quastler, H. (Ed.). *Information theory in psychology: problems and methods.* Glencoe, Ill.: Free Press, 1955.

Rambo, W. W. Effect of order of presentation of stimuli upon absolute judgments. *Psychol. Repts.*, 1961, **8,** 219–224.

Rapaport, D. Cognitive structures. In *Contemporary approaches to cognition.* Cambridge, Mass.: Harvard University Press, 1957.

Reik, T. *Listening with the third ear.* New York: Farrar, Straus, 1948.

Restle, F. Toward a quantitative description of learning set data. *Psychol. Rev.*, 1958, **65,** 77–91.

Restle, F. *Psychology of judgment and choice: a theoretical essay.* New York: Wiley, 1961.

Rettig, S., & Rawson, H. E. The risk hypothesis in predictive judgments of unethical behavior. *J. abnorm. soc. Psychol.*, 1963, **66,** 243–248.

Rigney, J., Bieri, J., & Tripodi, T. Social concept attainment and cognitive complexity. *Psychol. Repts.*, 1964, **15,** 503–509.

Rodnick, E. H., & Garmezy, N. An experimental approach to the study of motivation in schizophrenia. In M. R. Jones (Ed.), *Nebraska symposium on motivation:* 1957. Vol. V. Lincoln: University of Nebraska Press, 1957, pp. 109–184.

Rogers, S. The anchoring of absolute judgments. *Arch. Psychol.*, 1941, **37** (Whole No. 261).

Rogers, S., Volkmann, J., Reese, T. W., & Kaufman, E. L. Accuracy and variability of direct estimates of bearing from large display screens. So. Hadley, Mass., Mt. Holyoke College, 1947.

Rokeach, M. A method for studying individual differences in "narrow-mindedness." *J. Pers.*, 1951, **20,** 219–233.

Rosenfeld, J. M. Strangeness between helper and client: a possible explanation for non-use of available professional help. *Social Service Rev.*, 1964, **38,** 17–25.

Rosenthal, R. Experimenter outcome-orientation and the results of the psychological experiment. *Psychol. Bull.*, 1964, **61,** 405–412.

Russell, P. D. Counselor anxiety in relation to clinical experience and hostile or friendly clients. Unpublished doctoral dissertation, Pennsylvania State University, 1961.

Sarbin, T. R. A contribution to the study of actuarial and individual methods of prediction. *Amer. J. Sociology,* 1942, **48,** 593–602.

Sarbin, T. R., Taft, R., & Bailey, D. E. *Clinical inference and cognitive theory.* New York: Holt, Rinehart, & Winston, 1960.

Sarason, I. G., & Minard, J. N. Interrelationships among subject, experimenter, and situational variables. *J. abnorm. soc. Psychol.*, 1963, **67,** 87–91.

Scheff, T. J. Decision rules, types of error, and their consequences in medical diagnosis. *Behavioral Science,* 1963a, **8,** 97–107.

Scheff, T. J. Social components in decisions about mental illness: two field studies. Paper read at the American Association for the Advancement of Science meetings, 1963b.

Schiffman, J., & Wynne, R. Cause and affect. Paper presented at the American Psychological Association meetings, 1962.

Scott, W. A. Conceptualizing and measuring structural properties of cognition. In O. J. Harvey (Ed.), *Motivation and social interaction*. New York: Ronald, 1963, pp. 266–288.

Segall, M. The effect of attitude and experience on judgments of controversial statements. *J. abnorm. soc. Psychol.*, 1959, **58**, 61–68.

Shannon, C. E. A mathematical theory of communication. *Bell Syst. tech J.*, 1948, **27**, 379–423, 623–656.

Sherif, M. *The psychology of social norms*. New York: Harper, 1936.

Sherif, M., & Cantril, H. The psychology of attitudes, Part I. *Psychol. Rev.*, 1945, **52**, 295–319.

Sherif, M., & Hovland, C. I. *Social judgment: assimilation and contrast effects in communication and attitude change*. New Haven: Yale University Press, 1961.

Sherif, M., Taub, D., & Hovland, C. I. Assimilation and contrast effects of anchoring stimuli on judgments. *J. exp. Psychol.*, 1958, **55**, 150–155.

Shore, M. F. Perceptual efficiency as related to induced muscular effort and manifest anxiety. *J. exp. Psychol.*, 1958, **55**, 179–183.

Siegel, N., Kahn, R. L., Pollack, M., & Fink, M. Social class, diagnosis, and treatment in three hospitals. *Social Problems*, 1962, **10**, 191–196.

Simon, H. A. Rational choice and the structure of the environment. *Psychol. Rev.*, 1956, **63**, 129–138.

Sistrunk, F., & McDavid, J. W. Achievement motivation, affiliation motivation, and task difficulty as determinants of social conformity. Unpublished manuscript, University of Miami, 1962.

Spanner, M. Attribution of traits and emotional health as factors associated with the prediction of personality characteristics of others. *J. consult. Psychol.*, 1961, **25**, 210–215.

Spence, K. W., Taylor, J. A., & Ketchel, R. Anxiety (drive) level and degree of competition in paired-associates learning. *J. exp. Psychol.*, 1956, **52**, 306–310.

Stevens, S. S. On the psychophysical law. *Psychol. Rev.*, 1957, **64**, 153–179.

Strupp, H. H. *Psychotherapists in action*. New York: Grune & Stratton, 1960.

Sullivan, H. S. Tentative criteria of malignancy in schizophrenia. *Amer. J. Psychiat.*, 1927–1928, **7**, 759–787.

Suppes, P., & Atkinson, R. C. *Markov learning models for multiperson interactions*. Stanford: Stanford University Press, 1960.

Swinehart, J. W. Effects of magnitude and expectancy of reward in person perception. Paper presented at the annual meeting of the American Psychological Association, 1962.

Szasz, T. S. *The myth of mental illness: foundations of a theory of personal conduct*. New York: Hoeber-Harper, 1961.

Taft, R. Some characteristics of good judges of others. *Brit. J. Psychol.*, 1956, **47**, 19–29.

Tallent, N. On individualizing the psychologist's clinical evaluation. *J. clin. Psychol.*, 1958, **14**, 243–244.

Terwilliger, R. F. Social desirability of self-reference statements as a function of free association patterns. *J. abnorm. soc. Psychol.*, 1962, **65**, 162–169.

Thurstone, L. L., & Chave, E. J. *The measurement of attitude*. Chicago: University of Chicago Press, 1929.

Todd, F. J., & Rappoport, L. A cognitive structure approach to person perception: a comparison of two models. *J. abnorm. soc. Psychol.*, 1964, **68**, 469–478.

Tolman, E. C. Cognitive maps in rats and men. *Psychol. Rev.*, 1948, **55**, 189–208.

Torgerson, W. S. *Theory and methods of scaling*. New York: Wiley, 1958.

Triandis, H. C. Exploratory factor analyses of the behavioral component of social attitudes. *J. abnorm. soc. Psychol.*, 1964, **68**, 420–430.

Tripodi, T., & Bieri, J. Cognitive complexity as a function of own and provided constructs. *Psychol. Repts.*, 1963, **13**, 26.

Tripodi, T., & Bieri, J. Information transmission in clinical judgments as a function of stimulus dimensionality and cognitive complexity. *J. Pers.*, 1964, **32**, 119–137.

Tripodi, T., & Bieri, J. Cognitive complexity, perceived conflict, and certainty. *J. Pers.*, in press.

Upshaw, H. S. Own attitude as an anchor in equal-appearing intervals. *J. abnorm. soc. Psychol.*, 1962, **64**, 85–96.

Volkmann, J. The method of single stimuli. *Amer. J. Psychol.*, 1932, **44**, 808 f.

Volkmann, J. The anchoring of absolute scales. *Psychol. Bull.*, 1936, **33**, 742 f. (Abstract)

Volkmann, J. Scales of judgment. In J. H. Rohrer & M. Sherif (Eds.), *Social psychology at the crossroads*. New York: Harper, 1951, pp. 273–294.

Vroom, V. H. Projection, negation, and the self concept. *Human Relations*, 1959, **12**, 335–344.

Walker, C. W., & Bourne, L. E., Jr. The identification of concepts as a function of amounts of relevant and irrelevant information. *Amer. J. Psychol.*, 1961, **74**, 410–417.

Wallach, M. A. On psychological similarity. *Psychol. Rev.*, 1958, **65**, 103–116.

Weiss, W. Effects of an extreme anchor on scale judgments and attitude. *Psychol. Repts.*, 1961, **8**, 377–382.

Wever, E. G., & Zener, K. E. The method of absolute judgment in psychophysics. *Psychol. Rev.*, 1928, **35**, 466–493.

Whiteman, M. The performance of schizophrenics in social concepts. *J. abnorm. soc. Psychol.*, 1954, **49**, 266–271.

Wiener, N. *Cybernetics*. New York: Wiley, 1948.

Winkel, G. H., & Sarason, I. G. Subject, experimenter, and situational variables in research on anxiety. *J. abnorm. soc. Psychol.*, 1964, **68**, 601–608.

Wishner, J. Reanalysis of "impressions of personality." *Psychol. Rev.*, 1960, **67**, 96–112.

Witkin, H. A., Dyk, R. B., Faterson, H. F., Goodenough, D. R., & Karp, S. A. *Psychological differentiation*. New York: Wiley, 1962.

Wolfe, R. The role of conceptual systems in cognitive functioning at varying levels of age and intelligence. *J. Pers.*, 1963, **31**, 108–123.

Zajonc, R. B. The process of cognitive tuning in communication. *J. abnorm. soc. Psychol.*, 1960, **61**, 159–167.

Zavalloni, M., & Cook, S. W. Influence of judges' attitudes on ratings of favorableness of statements about a social group. *J. Pers. soc. Psychol.*, 1965, **1**, 43–54.

Zax, M., Gardiner, D. H., & Lowy, D. G. Extreme response tendency as a function of emotional adjustment. *J. abnorm. soc. Psychol.*, 1964, **64**, 654–657.

AUTHOR INDEX

SUBJECT INDEX